New England
and Foreign Relations

# New England
# and Foreign Relations
## 1789-1850

Paul A. Varg

 University Press of New England

Hanover and London, 1983

University Press of New England

Brandeis University
Brown University
Clark University
Dartmouth College
University of New Hampshire
University of Rhode Island
Tufts University
University of Vermont

Copyright © 1983 Trustees of Dartmouth College

Printed in the United States of America

*The publisher gratefully acknowledges the support of the Earhart Foundation in the publication of this book.*

LIBRARY OF CONGRESS CATALOGING IN PUBLICATION DATA

Varg, Paul A.
  New England and foreign relations, 1789–1850.

  Bibliography: p.
  Includes index.
    1. United States—Foreign relations—1783–1865.   2. New England—
Politics and government—1783–1865.   I. Title.
E310.7.V33   1982      327.73      82-40338
ISBN 0-87451-224-7

# Contents

# Preface

Historians of American foreign relations concentrate their attention on decision making in the nation's capital and give only slight attention to the role of regions in asserting their foreign policy interests. This is the first study to examine American foreign policy from the point of view of a specific region, namely New England.

It begins with 1789, as the new government under the recently framed Constitution took office, and closes with 1850. In the latter year, shortly after the close of the Mexican War, and as Congress struggled with the question of slavery in the newly acquired territories, the slavery issue became prominent, and foreign policy issues receded into the background. Sectional alignments became polarized on a north-south axis, and New England as a region, with its own political program, became largely submerged in the national crisis.

New England was never a political monolith. Important differences existed within the region, and its two political parties bitterly contested most elections. Prior to the War of 1812, the region was dominated by the Federalists; however, with the birth of the Whig party in 1834, that party took control. One-party dominance came closer to being achieved in New England than in any other region of the country.

Although this was in part a result of the importance of economic interests, it was also a result of certain regional cultural patterns. Boston was the economic and political center of the region. New England's largely homogeneous population was overwhelmingly of British ancestry. It was also a region where the Congregational church dominated religious life. A powerful British heritage and the strong hold of a conservative church colored its approach to all questions, particularly, foreign relations.

Prior to the War of 1812 the major economic interests in New

England were foreign trade and shipping. After the war manufacturing gradually replaced shipping as the major industry, and by 1828 the leading spokesmen for New England in Congress advocated a protective tariff. The need for protectionism shortly became a sacred cause about which there could be no compromise. No other issue rivaled it in importance.

The importance of the tariff issue does not, however, wholly account for the region's stands on various foreign policy questions. New England was a church centered community in which the clergy exerted a great influence on public opinion. This was most obvious before and during the War of 1812 when the clergy denounced both the war and the Republican administration, aroused by fears that French infidelity was about to triumph and that participation in the war would entail an alliance with Napoleon. The church during this time viewed itself as the protector of Christian virtues, morality, and teachings; it exalted law and order and gave its blessings to the highly stratified society. Reverence for British traditions and the long history of rule by law strengthened those values. Nothing was to be feared more than an eruption of the angry passions of the mob. Reason must rule and the church felt itself to be best qualified to determine the teachings of reason.

New England's loss of national importance as the nation leaped westward aroused fears that the more recently settled areas would impose their will and undermine respect for learning, for law, and for the restraints necessary to a civilized society. The addition of new states irretrievably reduced the number of New England representatives in the House of Representatives and added to the number of senators throughout the country. This underlying fear made itself felt in popular discussion and congressional debates whenever the issue of expansion was brought up.

I wish to acknowledge with thanks an All University Research Grant from Michigan State University, which facilitated an extended visit to various New England repositories. I am deeply indebted to the staffs of several libraries who helped me find relevant material. The research began in the library of Michigan State University where I enjoyed the generous assistance of Henry Koch and Eleanor Boyles. Visits to the

Library of Congress and the National Archives were very rewarding. I am likewise greatly indebted to the American Antiquarian Society in Worcester with its incomparable collection of early newspapers, to the Massachusetts Historical Society with its rich collection of private papers, to the Maine Historical Society in Portland, the New Hampshire State Library in Concord, the Essex Historical Institute in Salem, and the libraries of Dartmouth College and the University of Vermont. Again I wish to thank my wife, Helen, who has assisted throughout this project with note taking, the many revisions in the typing of the manuscript, proofreading, and all the tasks involved in the preparation of a manuscript.

New England
and Foreign Relations

# Windows on the Sea

New England was as tied to the sea as the western pioneer was tied to the soil. Her ships ventured to the far corners of the world. Voyages to Mauritius, Batavia, Calcutta, Canton, western Europe, and the Mediterranean offered danger and adventure to the men sailing the ships. Those in the countinghouses at home alternately experienced anxiety and satisfaction depending upon the correctness of their calculations. Theirs was a life of scrupulous attention to minutiae and daring speculation.

China, India, and the East Indies offered fine teas, cotton goods, spices and silks—goods in demand not only at home but in Europe. In 1789 Elias Haskett Derby of Salem sent a ship to Canton where he sold a load of ginseng. That same year the Perkins brothers of Boston also sent a ship to Canton loaded with ginseng and an assortment of beeswax, butter, rum, and sundries. While in port Perkin's men observed two Boston ships selling sea otter skins. The eagerness of the Chinese for the skins led the firm of Magee and Perkins to open the famous route around South America to Oregon. There they sold a variety of goods to the Indians and bought sea otter pelts. They then sailed to Canton, the only Chinese port open to trade, and traded the skins for tea. In 1790 two of Derby's ships returned with 600,000 pounds of tea. By 1805 imports at Canton in American vessels totaled over five million dollars.[1]

In 1794 the New Englanders found another profitable route. William Gray opened trade with Calcutta and the East Indies. In India the Americans bought cotton goods and in the islands they bought spices. Salem, led by the Grays, Derbys, Princes, and Crowninshields, built up an immense trade in spices with ports all over Europe. By 1805 Salem exported 7,559,244 pounds of pepper and became known as the pepper capital of the world.[2] In the years after 1800 Gray alone employed over three hundred seamen.

Trade with the West Indies flourished. Exports of fish, beef, pork, and dairy products reached respectable proportions. Between 1801 and 1810, by one careful calculation, annual exports averaged 960 tons of butter, 486 tons of cheese, 850 tons of lard, 9½ tons of bacon and ham, 75,000 barrels of pork and beef, and more than 22,000 head of livestock.[3]

The fisheries, too, brought wealth and employment. Marblehead led but every port contributed a share. From 1801 to 1807 the fisheries employed a yearly average of seven thousand seamen. In 1805 exports totaled 36,241 quintals of smoked and dried fish and 31,216 barrels of pickled fish.[4]

Closely associated with this trade was the distilling of rum. Boston alone had thirty distilleries. Newport was also a distilling center. The rum became an important export to Africa. Molasses from the West Indies was used to make rum while domestically grown rye was processed into whiskey.

New England's shipping trade not only exported domestic produce, it transported goods between foreign ports as well. The area did not produce many of the goods that found a sale in other parts of the world, and what was imported often had to be paid for in foreign specie.

Joseph Lee, one of the leading merchants who carried on an extensive trade with the East Indies, paid for his goods in the Indies with Spanish dollars.[5] Some ships carried sugar, spices, and dyestuffs to Russia and, in turn, purchased iron, hemp, and linen duck. Others carried furs from the Oregon coast to China and on the return voyage carried silks, many of which were then sold in Europe.

This carrying trade was highly speculative. Success depended upon buying cheap and selling dear, but that simple rule did not lend itself to easy observance. Prices fluctuated widely from time to time. When a number of ships arrived in Canton carrying opium or furs the prices fell and super cargos sometimes either had to wait until the prices recovered or hope for a better market elsewhere. The merchants at home were forced to calculate on the basis of limited information what prices might be six months or a year hence in some distant port. The merchant instructed the super cargo who handled the sales and purchases abroad at what prices he might sell the cargo and what he might pay for goods in return. Given the uncertainty of future conditions it was necessary to give the super cargo considerable freedom to make decisions on the spot.

William Gray of Salem was engaged in trade on a large scale around the globe. His instructions to John R. Dalling, captain of his ship *Ulysses*, prior to departure for Asia in September 1805, offer insight into the nature of trade. Dalling was ordered to proceed to Bombay. There he was to "sell the cargo now on board for the most it will fetch or such part of it as you suppose most for my interest." If he sold the whole there, Captain Dalling was to "proceed for Muscat upon the coast of Arabia, there purchase coffee, drugs, and medicines and saltpetre" and then return. However, if he could not dispose of all of his cargo at Bombay he was to proceed to Pondicherry, Madras, and Calcutta. He was also to try, if necessary, to dispose of his cargo at Malacca, then go to Canton and there invest his proceeds in nankeens, tea, "and such other goods as you suppose will produce most profit."[6]

The risks were as great as the profits were alluring. William Gray embarked on trade in 1790. By 1799 he is reported to have acquired an estate of $900,000.[7] Thomas Handsyd Perkins, probably the most successful of the merchants, left an estate of $1,600,000.[8] Elias Hasket Derby, who did more than any other to lay the foundations of trade with Asia and the Baltic, was a millionaire at the time of his death in 1799. Some voyages yielded spectacular profits. Joseph Lee realized almost 100 percent profit on one of his voyages to the East Indies.[9] Some merchants became rich but others failed: the son of Elias Derby lost most of the family fortune in trade. Most voyages averaged an estimated 6 percent profit.

The ports of Massachusetts had a larger total tonnage of ships than any other state. Salem alone had forty ships employed in the Pacific Ocean and East Indies trade. The ingenuity of merchant-shipmasters in calculating how profits were to be made by carrying goods among the ports of the world, and their enterprise in developing a flourishing trade in cotton goods from Bombay and Calcutta, spices from the East Indies, tea from Canton, hides from Brazil, and wines from France, elevated them to the status of merchant princes. And accompanying the rise of trade was the growth of a sizable shipbuilding industry.

The window to the sea gave to New England seaports a closer acquaintance with the outside world. Not all merchants traveled. Elias Derby and William Gray never went to sea, but the objects their ships brought home from China decorated the homes of the wealthy; the less privileged prized Chinese nankeens and tea. Others learned first-hand of faraway places. Thomas Perkins, at age twenty-five, visited Batavia and left detailed descriptions of the scenery and the customs of the natives, and tales of the Malayan, Chinese, and Dutch inhabitants.[10] Perkins resided in France from December 1794 to October 1795 and observed the tragic political events of that time. His diary provides a vivid account of France under the Directory.[11]

Americans' fascination with China began in those early years. In China they encountered an ancient civilization, a proud people, shrewd merchants, and customs challenging the equanimity of Bostonians. Perkins was busy disposing of his 75,000 pounds of ginseng, but he found time to visit Macao and Canton where he met other New Englanders on board four of Derby's ships. Before leaving the Americans were entertained at a feast given by the Chinese merchants.[12]

As a result of this fascination with China the importance of trade with her was exaggerated. Most voyages to Canton included stops at Isle de France, India, and the East Indies, and the trade at these ports surpassed that with the Chinese.[13] Despite this worldwide commerce, the trade with Europe was still most important.

Merchants and lawyers, who constituted the advance brigade in politics, fought for New England interests in Congress. The great majority of New England representatives in Congress were lawyers. This was perhaps inevitable and certainly in accord with the interests of merchants and, later, the manufacturers. The legal profession grew rapidly after the Revolution, and the presence of shipping and the rapid growth of industry after 1820 dictated its importance. In 1740 there had been only one lawyer for every 10,108 inhabitants in Massachusetts. By 1840 the ratio had risen to one for every 1,153 persons.[14] The lawyers, trained in presenting briefs, accustomed to debate, familiar not only with the law but with business operations, assured merchants and manufacturers of being ably represented.

From 1789 to 1840 all but three United States senators from Massachusetts were members of the legal profession; the three exceptions were merchants. Almost an equivalent percentage of members of the House of Representatives from the state had legal training. In 1840 eight of the eleven were lawyers. Not all were Federalists or Whigs. The outstanding exceptions in Massachusetts, Elbridge Gerry and Robert Rantoul, represented the Jeffersonian tradition. Rantoul, an eminent lawyer in Boston, crusaded with notable ability for free trade, labor reform, and temperance. Probably no one in the United States spoke more ably on behalf of free trade than Rantoul. Although he enjoyed the reputation of being the most formidable man in Massachusetts among the Jacksonians, Rantoul failed to persuade the people of his state to join the democratic crusade.

The rapid expansion of trade and the accumulation of great fortunes in New England's seaports left almost no mark on the region's interior until after the War of 1812, when improved roads, canals, and finally railroads appeared. Roughly 90 percent of the population made its living on farms averaging from 100 to 200 acres.[15] Families in the interior were largely self-sufficient. The farmer and his family produced the items necessary for a very simple diet and also devoted time to spinning, weaving, and sewing clothes. Life was, to use a contemporary term, "comfortable" but simple. Only those in the vicinity of the seaports sold produce in the commercial market. Farmers were slow to introduce improved methods, and the land itself was of low quality except in the few river valleys.[16] The most important crops were corn and rye that could be ground into flour and used for fodder.

Timothy Dwight, president of Yale, who traveled over New England several weeks each year over a ten-year period, provided a detailed and delightful description of rural life. There were villages, such as Lancaster in Worcester County, Massachusetts, with large and lovely mansions, but most homes were modest. In the Connecticut valley, near Springfield, Massachusetts, the farmers prospered more than in less fertile areas. Dwight wrote of the locale, "No county in the state has uniformly discovered so firm an adherence to order and good government, or a higher regard to learning, morals, and religion." People were industrious, wrote Dwight, and "possess that middle state of property which so long has been termed golden, because in this situation the best character and the most sincere enjoyment are usually found." Few, he observed, were poor and few were rich.[17] Yet poverty was present and the appropriations for poor relief were considerable.[18]

New England towns with their well-established order of society, based less on birth than on the confidence and respect earned among neighbors, offered, as Carl Bridenbaugh observed, a way of life. The strong family unit owed its strength "as much from its economic and social as from its moral and religious significance" for it was also a principal unit of agricultural, industrial, and business life.[19] Leadership in the family had its parallel in the church, in the town meetings, and in the economic life of the town, and the town squires saw "to it that the town thought as they thought, and acted as they would have it act."[20] As Bridenbaugh put it so well, ". . . in New England the town meeting, church, and tavern formed a sort of trinity." Unfortunately the snug quality of the town also bred a smugness that endowed New England with a parochialism that created ill-concealed contempt for other sections of the country and a rigidity that nurtured suspicion of new ideas and of their apostles.

New England society, urban and rural, was united by the network of Congregational and Presbyterian churches. Dwight reported that there were 869 congregations in Massachusetts, New Hampshire, Connecticut, and Vermont.[21] A vigorous Protestantism, led by Congregationalists, provided a common view of the dictates of the creator and the frailty of men, as well as a reverence for learning and an ever present sense of duty. Ministers instilled in the community not only a reverence for God but for law and stability, and an admiration for the ordained social stratification. Until the dissension between Congregationalists and Unitarians early in the nineteenth century and the luxuriant growth of sects, Baptists and Methodists, during the same first two decades, Congregationalism ruled supreme, and its clergy enjoyed both intellectual and religious leadership. By the close of the War for Independence, the early Puritan doctrine of election had transformed itself into a view of society that sanctioned social stratification based on wealth and education. The harsh Calvinism of an earlier day gave way to a greater emphasis on God's mercy.

The clergy ranked near the top of the total structure, a rank they owed to their education and their vocation. Politics and religion were closely intertwined, and the clergy stood as the defenders of honesty, social responsibility, and traditional religious beliefs. When, by 1794, new religious views found expression, and French ideas came to the fore in Republican societies, it was only to be expected that the same clergy would mount a vigorous protest to defend the old order. They earned the praise of John Adams at the time he was elected president. Only the clergy, said Adams, had saved New England from being inundated by the radical ideas of the French Revolution.

The six states huddled together in the small northeastern corner of the vast republic confronted contradictory impulses: the pull toward parochialism on the one hand and, on the other hand, the pressing realization that their future as a region depended upon the success of the Republic at large. New Englanders needed the Republic for protection of their far-flung seaborne commerce, the defense of fishing rights off the shores of the British maritime provinces to the north, the creation of a stable system of currency and banks, and sturdy assistance in the area of foreign economic policy. New England without the Union would be less than a forgotten remnant.

The virtues of the region's people did not include a tolerance for subordination, nor were they willing to compromise their own drives in the interests of other sections. New England took great satisfaction in her supposedly unique virtues of morality, piety, and learnedness. Consequently a political barrier of sorts, at times of formidable proportions, existed between New England and the South and West. Rivalry and distrust thrived. Westerners—with good reason—could never feel secure placing their fate in the hands of Bostonians who saw their own importance diminishing as the West advanced. To add to the prevailing uneasiness New Englanders deplored the ruthless dispossession of the Indians. The Congregationalists went further. They sent missionaries who taught the natives both the gospel and agriculture, preparing them for the establishment of permanent homes. By the 1830s the missionary efforts on the frontiers of Georgia had created a political struggle between New Englanders, who supported the Indians, and the state government, which insisted on the removal of the missionaries. The state won the support of both President Jackson and the Supreme Court and imprisoned the missionaries who refused to leave. Other conflicts between New England, the South and West on issues of public lands and the tariff at times made New England a target for attack.

At the same time New Englanders were wholly dedicated to what they deemed republican principles and republican institutions. They disliked monarchies and landed nobility and gloried in popular government under a system of checks and balances quite as much as Jefferson and Madison, though at the same time they lived in mortal fear of what they termed "mob rule."[22] Their unlimited assurance that among highly competitive nations each must of necessity carefully calculate how best to advance its own economic interests carried with it the corollary that their own central government must serve as a benevolent friend of the entrepreneur who, in turn, provided employment, advanced the nation's economic well-being, and served as the leaven of enlightenment and stability.

# Emergence of the
# New England Federalists

The first session of Congress in 1789 initiated sharp sectional debates. Three questions dominated: import duties, the rate of discrimination against foreign vessels, and Madison's proposal to set a higher rate of discrimination on British ships than upon other foreign vessels.

The duty on molasses touched the nerve center. Molasses from the French West Indies provided New England rum distillers with an item for export to Africa and the southern states. Unless the New Englanders were free to import molasses France was likely to close her islands to fish imports. The islands provided the chief year-round market for fish and in the summer season the only market. Members of Congress from the South not only had no interest in the trade, they contended that rum was an evil that led to delinquency among the poorer classes.

Fisher Ames of Massachusetts did battle for his constituency of fishermen, distillers, and merchant-shippers with fervor. He portrayed the depressed state of the fisheries that had resulted from British restrictions; the hardships of seamen eking out a meager living; and the good work of distilleries in providing the only liquor poor people could afford. Protests that rum was a particular evil he dismissed as irrelevant. He declared with contempt: "I treat as idle the visionary notion of reforming the morals of the people by a duty on molasses." As a practical Yankee Ames announced, "We are not to consider ourselves, while here, as at church or school, to listen to the harangues of speculative piety; we are to talk of political interests committed to our charge. . . . Morality was not the business of Congress." Any discussion of morality should not be permitted to "confound itself with revenue and protection of manufactures."[1]

Elbridge Gerry, also of Massachusetts, turned the arguments of his western opponents around. They preferred to encourage the consumption of beer, alleging that it was less harmful. Gerry informed them: "There are no breweries in our country; it may be our misfortune, but the people there use molasses, with spruce and hops, as a substitute, and why should they be taxed for this inoffensive liquor more than the consumers of beer brewed from malt?"[2] And the proposed tax on molasses, said Gerry, was class legislation. Fishermen and their families would be paying the equivalent of a poll tax—"A poll tax towards which the poor contribute more than the rich."

Ames wanted low duties on imports. Those with shipping interests could scarcely be expected to prefer high duties that would curtail foreign trade. Ames, supported by Benjamin Goodhue and Gerry, defended the fisheries: because of her rock strewn fields, New England found the way to agriculture closed, and therefore her noble and heroic people, blessed with ingenuity, turned to the sea. Now there were those who would cut off this one escape route from economic poverty. Ames eloquently depicted the fate of the poor in New England—". . . they are too poor to live there, and they are too poor to move. . . . Gentlemen, who contend for the encouragement of agriculture, should recollect that nature has denied us fertility, but she has placed along our shores an inexhaustible store." Why, he asked, should industry on the sea be taxed more than other pursuits?[3] These rhetorical flourishes added luster to the debates, but the heart of the argument as set forth by the delegates from Massachusetts lay in the contention that the fisheries and shipping and merchant interests all depended upon a low duty on imports of molasses.

During the early days of July in that first session of Congress, James Madison called for discrimination against British ships and outlined a program to free the new nation from British dominance of the carrying trade, credit facilities, and heavy dependence on imports from England. Herein lay the heart of agrarian economic policy, and Jefferson spelled it out and supported it with statistics in his famous report in December 1793.

New England's representatives in Congress dismissed the Madison proposal as unrealistic. At this early stage the Federalists had not yet become anglophiles. They rejected Madison's theory as visionary and fell back on their experience as merchants and shippers. Hamilton's far-reaching plans for the future probably escaped them, but they could readily agree that it would be costly to engage England in economic warfare. They were dependent on British credit, knew that only England produced the manufactures they imported, and fatalistically accepted British restrictions on their trade. The Federalists believed that both Great Britain and France, as major powers, would ruthlessly calculate their own interests, regulate trade accordingly, and ignore appeals from a young, weak nation. George Cabot described how the British treated America with brevity but then observed that this was to be expected as the British "considered our weakness and inability to injure her."[4] Merchants, whose daily transactions aimed at profit and who viewed the ups and downs of the marketplace and tense competition as the very nature of life, could hardly find competing nations to be diabolical because of their dedication to self-interest, nor could they entertain expectations that those same nations would be moved by friendship.

Madison's efforts to discriminate against vessels of nations not in treaty with the United States—more particularly Great Britain—and to promote closer relations with France, encountered firm opposition. Ames declared himself "strongly opposed to being led by the principle of gratitude in matters relative to the public weal." Referring to the treaty with France Ames laid down the rule that the obligation incurred "never required more than what its terms stipulated for; therefore, on matters of commerce and revenue, interest ought to be the predominating principle."[5] Gerry, who adhered to the same principle, warned against the danger of entering a commercial war and held that coercive measures ought not to be pursued unless there was moral certainty of success.[6] Wadsworth of Connecticut added that the discrimination would do little injury to Great Britain and would not coerce but merely irritate.[7]

A petition from Portsmouth, New Hampshire, early in 1790 asked for an increase in the tonnage duties on foreign ships. The ensuing debate led promptly to reconsideration of Madison's proposal for further discrimination against British ships, thereby encouraging an expansion of trade with France. Theodore Sedgwick of Massachusetts declared the measure to be "of very great impropriety." His hostility erupted into a denunciatory series of questions: "Who are concerned in the carrying trade? We are declaring against one country in favor of another; for what purpose? Do gentlemen expect that France will aid our carrying trade? . . . It is a useless declaration, an impotent measure of passion, not dictated by the understanding. . . ."[8]

The conflict emerging between the Federalists of Massachusetts and James Madison could be clearly foreseen. The difference between their approaches to relations with Great Britain and France was to lead to the organization of political parties and eventually to the War of 1812.

The assumption of state debts, recommended by Secretary of Treasury Hamilton, also provoked a sectional alignment. Those supporting the recommendation maintained that the debts were incurred in support of a course common to all the states and were therefore a common obligation. Massachusetts, with a large debt, New Hampshire, and Connecticut leaned heavily on the argument that, having yielded their revenue from customs receipts, they should not be saddled with these debts. The assumption of these debts, Ames observed, was already related to the funding system and was an essential part of Hamilton's larger plan.[9] Let the debts follow the funds, Ames argued. Sedgwick, the most violent in his attack on the opposition, had personally led armed men to track down the Shayites of Massachusetts who had organized against foreclosures on their farms. He referred to a speech by Madison on the subject, stating that it was designed to make an unfair and undue impression on the public mind and was a performance, in his opinion, composed of unfounded facts, monstrous premises, and inconclusive deductions. . . ."[10] George Cabot could not reconcile "Mr. Madison's present conduct with his former principles." Madison had stood for strong national sovereignty, and now he opposed assumption of state debts. Cabot "apprehended that the anti-Federalists may seize the opportunity of attaching all the State creditors to their cause by providing honestly for them. . . . If they should do this in the State Legislatures, the government would be ruined irrecoverably."[11]

The long debate, carried on in the midst of great public clamor and excitement, was not resolved until 26 July 1790.[12] James Jackson of

Georgia, strongly opposed to federal assumption of state debts, placed the argument on moral grounds and moved for rejection of the measure. The motion lost, 32 to 29, with the representatives of Connecticut, New Hampshire, and Massachusetts casting 13 of the 32 negative votes. Of all the New England representatives, only two voted against assumption of state debts—Nicholas Gilman and Samuel Livermore of New Hampshire.[13] No change took place on the final vote two days later. Unfortunately, the two New Hampshire representatives did not explain why they cast negative votes. Gilman, a wealthy man, had been a member of the Constitutional Convention and a vigorous supporter of ratification. Livermore of Portsmouth differed from his Massachusetts colleagues on other points. For instance, while he favored redemption of the federal domestic debt, he argued that the interest rate should be lowered.[14] While men like George Cabot, Fisher Ames, and Theodore Sedgwick were the unquestioning lieutenants of Hamilton, Gilman and Livermore were more independent.

New England married herself to the secretary of the treasury, Alexander Hamilton. Her representatives supported his recommendations as if they were their own. Only one representative of New England in the House of Representatives, Jonathan Grant, voted against a bill to establish a national bank. Whereas Jefferson and Madison were devoted to political ideals and republican principles, the New Englanders devoted their energy to financial and economic problems. They were no less anxious than the Virginians to have the new central government succeed; they, too, had faith in the Republic, but, perhaps as a result of the countinghouse society out of which they emerged, they believed that its success or failure was dependent on undergirding the government with sound economic institutions. In this area they were both skilled and intelligent. The business careers of the New England leaders placed a premium on careful, even meticulous calculations. The rewards were as proportionately large as the penalties that could result from a lack of scrupulous attention to detail.

Fisher Ames epitomized the strengths and the weaknesses of the New England coterie. Ames, an able lawyer whose many speeches in Congress read like legal briefs for a client, was deeply conscious that the new political structure was a frail instrument, yet he wanted to believe that sound reasoning could harmonize different sectional interests. [15] Even so, he could not understand the theories or the visions of a Madison. As his son, Seth Ames, wrote of his father, Fisher Ames identified democracy with the public passions and lived in dread that they would burst through the barriers of the system of checks and balances. Madison troubled Ames. On the one hand he had a grudging admiration for Madison as "a man of sense, reading, address, and integrity"; yet, on the other hand, he distrusted Madison because he found him "Very much Frenchified in his politics." [16] Some weeks later he noted, "But I see in Madison with his great knowledge and merit, so much error, and some of it so very unaccountable, and tending to so much mischief, that my impatience may have tinctured my letter with more gall than I can remember." [17] Madison, he concluded, looked upon politics as a science rather than a business: "He adopts his maxims as he finds them in books, and with too little regard to the actual state of things." [18]

Ames bolstered his already strong sense of respectability with harsh judgments of those who disagreed with him, but he mellowed as thoughts of his beloved Boston passed through his mind. Commenting on his native city he wrote: "I believe that the New England people are better taught than any other, and Boston better than any other city." No other city had ". . . such judicious expedients for repelling barbarism, supporting government, and extending felicity. . . . Boston might be an Athens, and I would wish to make it a London." [19]

No aspect of Madison disturbed Ames more than the Virginian's persistent campaign to establish discriminatory duties on goods arriving in British ships. Ames believed that the proposal could only lead to economic war, or war itself. The New Englanders were men of business, and as such they desired stability. In a mood of despondency Ames asked:

But are we Yankees invulnerable, if a war of regulations should be waged with Britain? Are they not able to retaliate? . . . Is it not more prudent to maintain a good understanding with Great Britain, and to preserve a dignified neutrality and moderation of conduct towards all nations? [20]

The same view of the Jeffersonians occupied the mind of George Cabot, senator and wealthy Boston merchant. The people in Boston, he wrote,

". . . have but one wish respecting the national peace—and that is that it may be preserved. . . . Our commercial and maritime people feel themselves deeply interested to prevent every act that may put our peace at hazard. . . ." [21]

The rupture between New England and the South and West was wider than they knew, for it was not only a question of discriminating against British ships but also a matter of intellectual orientation and social values.

When Congress assembled in Philadelphia in March 1793 the western world was experiencing the turbulence of the French Revolution. The Jacobins and Robespierre ruled Paris, the Reign of Terror was nearing its peak, and France, the nation in arms, was at war with her neighbors. The reports of the execution of Louis XVI and the horrors of the guillotine caused many to turn their backs on the French crusade for liberty, equality, and fraternity, but the ideas set forth in the Declaration of the Rights of Man continued to awaken dreams of a more democratic order. Not only in the United States but in other countries, particularly in Great Britain, the French Revolution caused a sharp political division between the defenders of the status quo and the apostles of change.

In Great Britain a reform movement was underway, and in 1792 a London shoemaker founded the Corresponding Society which promptly adopted Thomas Paine's *Rights of Man* as its platform. Another society, Friends of the People, also called for reform. As the French Revolution moved to extremes with the execution of Louis XVI in February 1793, a backlash took place, and war began between England and France. Suppression of individual liberties on a large scale followed. The reform societies continued their campaign, opposing the war and advancing the idea of a government by and for the people. The parallels between the British radicals and the republican societies that came into being in the United States in the same years are striking. [22]

The French Revolution set off a similar movement in the United States where republican societies advocating related ideals came into existence. The Federalists promptly labeled them Jacobin and equated Jacobinism with anarchy. The republican societies in the United States included few workingmen. They were made up of craftsmen, merchants, and a scattering of public officials, clerks, professional people, innkeepers, and printers, who saw in Hamilton's program the domination of the new federal government by an elite group and the betrayal of republican principles.[23] These societies usually took a friendly attitude toward France while perpetrating the hostility toward England that had existed during the War for Independence. Great Britain's continued occupation of eight military forts from Niagara to Mackinaw, all within the American boundary set by the treaty of 1783, and her ties with Indians on American territory did little to diminish hostility toward the British.

Differing political ideals and a related difference in attitudes toward foreign policy opened a wide political gulf between the two parties in the United States that eventually erupted in a controversy marked by heated vilification. In New England foreign affairs became the paramount issue. Even there there were those who sympathized with France. Resolutions adopted by the republican societies in Massachusetts and Maine proclaimed that the future of the American Republic depended upon a French victory in Europe.[24] Just as the British radicals denounced their government's decision to go to war against France, the American republicans denounced the British war against France as an effort to destroy liberal principles.

Factions could compromise or at least avoid rancor on questions of duties on molasses, interest rates, and tonnage duties, but the question of relations with England and France introduced issues involving important differences in political ideals, morals, and religion. The gate was now open for a contest involving foreign policy.

Federalists had worried about French influence even before the crisis of 1793. In October 1792 George Cabot worried about the opposition in New York and Pennsylvania and the efforts underway to displace John Adams as vice-president. Cabot wrote to Theophilus Parsons: "The ruin of Mr. Adams would be a triumph of the *Jacobins*, and would be an important step toward the general overthrow of our establishment which is evidently intended."[25] The Federalist heartland of Boston had not escaped the French infection, and Cabot worried about Samuel Osgood of Massachusetts, who was "deep in the principles" of the opposition party.

In Philadelphia the Jeffersonians, beginning in 1792, spread their doctrines and views through Philip Freneau's *National Gazette*. Freneau was an ardent poet of the Revolution who had suffered aboard a British prison ship in New York harbor. He gained the support of Jefferson who, it is almost certain, set him up as editor of the newspaper. Hamilton, victim of Freneau's venomous attacks, held the *Gazette* to be an "incendiary and pernicious publication."[26] Other leading Federalists joined in denouncing the editor. Fisher Ames warned, "The manifestoes of the *National Gazette* indicate a spirit of faction that must soon come to a crisis."

Ames did not have long to wait, for developments in 1793 and 1794 funneled all political controversy into the debate over relations with England and France. The trap was set when England and France went to war in February 1793. The arrival of the new French minister, his spirit stirring with the leaven of the rights of man and French nationalism and free of the restraints of traditional diplomacy, promptly became the rallying point for the opponents of Federalism. The Frenchman's enthusiasm penetrated to Boston. The *Independent Chronicle* of that town also sang the praises of Freneau:

As the friends of civil liberty wish at all times to be acquainted with every question which appears to regard the public weal, a great number of gentlemen in this and neighboring towns have subscribed for Mr. Freneau's *National Gazette*.[27]

In July 1794 a Jacobin club was organized in Boston. Fisher Ames expressed his revulsion in a letter to Thomas Dwight, United States attorney for the district of Massachusetts:

They were born in sin, the impure offering of Genet. They are the few against the many; the sons of darkness (for their meetings are secret) against those of the light; and above all, it is a town cabal, attempting to rule the country.[28]

Genet's brief term as French minister to the United States needs no retelling here. His attempts to make this country a base for recruiting and for French privateers soon led Secretary of State Jefferson to conclude, "Never, in my opinion, was as calamitous an appointment made, as the present minister of F. here."[29] Coinciding with Genet's exploits was a firm declaration of American neutrality, but this was followed by a series of British orders-in-council restricting neutral trade, including trade in foodstuffs, and seizures in the West Indies of some 250 American ships by March 1794.

Hamilton, seeing in Genet's ill-advised exploits an opportunity to weaken Jefferson and his following, entered the journalistic forum and under the pen name *Pacificus* engaged himself in discrediting the Jeffersonians. At the same time Jefferson and Madison reviewed the earlier scheme calling for a foreign economic policy of discrimination against British vessels. In December 1793 Jefferson, in one of his final acts as secretary of state, delivered his famous report purporting to prove statistically that the British carried a disproportionate amount of American exports and imports and thereby cut off the United States from a potentially flourishing trade with France and the continent.[30] Madison, the helmsman of the Jeffersonians in the House of Representatives, was assigned the job of steering the proposal through the legislative rapids.

Madison built his case in favor of discrimination against British ships on three points: Great Britain must be forced into a more equitable relationship, one that would admit American wheat, flour, and salted provisions; second, British dominance posed the danger that she would use her position to derange American commerce; finally, Madison spoke of the influence "that may finally ensue on our taste, our manners, and our form of Government itself."[31] The last of these three weighed most heavily with both Jefferson and Madison. They saw in the British political order rule by the well born and a few vested interests. And they feared, with reason, that many of their countrymen wished to reproduce the British system in the new Republic. Their highly vocal disciples in the House of Representatives, Wilson Cary Nicholas and William Giles, both of Virginia, carried the brunt of the speech making. In 1793 Giles introduced a series of resolutions charging Hamilton with misuse of funds. Madison, who supported Giles, was one of the very few to do so. Hamilton was cleared without difficulty. Giles, a raucous adversary, launched into the debates on Madison's resolutions in January 1794 with appeals to patriotism and valor. To those who counseled patience, Giles replied that "patience is an admirable beast of burden."[32]

The New England contingent attacked the resolutions with all the vigor that self-confidence bestowed. Benjamin Goodhue of Massachusetts saw only disaster ahead, for it would not be the British who suffered injury but his own countrymen. Samuel Dexter of the same state "could not see what advantage America was to reap by restricting the navigation and manufactures of one foreign nation merely to favor another."[33] Fisher Ames deplored the theoretical nature of Madison's resolutions. "If our trade is already on a profitable footing," he held, "it is already on a respectable one." Every nation, including the United States, restricted its trade so as to serve self-interest. Why seek to dictate another nation's policy? He warned that theories and paper schemes would poison public discussion.[34]

Ames deplored the nostalgia that evoked memories of former relations with France and postulated a future growth of trade with that nation. "This," he contended, "is not the form nor the occasion to discharge our obligations of any sort to any foreign nation, it concerns not our feelings but our interests, yet the debate has often soared high above the smoke of business into the epic region."[35]

Like a true Hamiltonian Ames pointed out that if trade was to be cut back with Great Britain, it would reduce the public revenue. And as the advocate of the assumption of debts and the funding system, Ames knew the dangers that might be confronted. In a final peroration he declared that if Congress voted down the resolutions it would "show to our own citizens, and foreign nations, that our prudence has prevailed over our prejudice."[36] We should be Americans first he argued, and not basely descend to a servile dependence on France or Great Britain.

The difficulty was, according to Madison, that the United States had already become servile to Great Britain. He particularly objected to the argument that implementation of his resolutions would reduce the revenue and endanger the public credit. While he had no desire to destroy the present funding system he held that "it never was either meant by Congress, or understood by the public, that, in mortgaging the impost for their security, it was to be hostage to foreign countries for our unqualified acquiescence in their unequal laws, and to be worn, as long as the Debt should continue, as a badge of national humiliation."[37]

Discussion of Madison's resolutions ended temporarily on February 5 and was not resumed until March. By that time British seizures of American ships in the West Indies had wholly diverted interest from

Madison's long-term measures to the more immediate question of defense. The spirited New Englanders deplored the injuries suffered at the hands of England. They now sponsored a bill to build a navy. Sedgwick led those favoring the measure. He immediately ran into strong opposition from Madison's adherents who feared that the Federalists might employ armed forces to suppress those who opposed Hamilton. On Monday, March 10, the bill was put to a vote and passed 50 to 39. Only two New England members of the House, Niles of Vermont and Wingate of New Hampshire, voted against the bill.[38] Niles was a Jeffersonian Democrat. Paine Wingate, brother-in-law of Timothy Pickering, stood on the Federalist side on most issues, but he was deeply concerned about federal expenditures and undoubtedly voted against the bill on this ground.[39]

Two measures came to the fore in April 1794, one calling for the sequestration of debts owed Britishers, another establishing an embargo on trade with Great Britain. The first proposal never came to a vote.

Three New Englanders, Zephaniah Swift of Connecticut and Samuel Dexter and Jeremiah Wadsworth of Massachusetts, led the opposition to the embargo. On the final vote approving of the embargo twenty of the thirty-four negative votes came from New England. Nicholas Gilman and John Sherburne of New Hampshire and Henry Dearborn and William Lyman of Massachusetts voted for the measure.[40]

Federalists argued that the embargo would merely serve to cause Great Britain to strike back with countermeasures to rectify the situation; it would be viewed as a threat. The proper approach was negotiation.

In debates over Madison's resolutions, the embargo, and steps proposed to provide defense both sectional and party alignments came to the fore. New England received support from New York, Pennsylvania, and Maryland, but there were also sharp divisions among representatives from those states. No such division appeared in New England; it was on the verge of becoming a one-party section committed to a sound credit and currency system, to economic stability, and to a government that would serve the merchants and shipping interests.

Fisher Ames found Madison's resolutions "mere moon shine." Zephaniah Swift charged the opposition with describing "insults and injuries in the highest colors to inflame our passions and to animate our resentment." It was, he said, "our duty to conduct with coolness, candor, and moderation."[41] Swift considered Dayton's sequestration measure "a declaration of war." Theodore Sedgwick believed that passage of the embargo and sequestration measures would "banish every prospect of negotiation" and bring on war.[42] Samuel Dexter denounced the proposed sequestration measure as a violation of law, one that would completely destroy Americans' credit, and bring disrepute "on our national character."[43]

The ensuing conflict involved issues related to basic attitudes and cherished values. Sectional loyalties, different understandings of the meaning of republican principles, different economic interests, and even variations in the styles of political rhetoric combined to create an atmosphere in which passions were as prominent as reason.

Republicans, and especially Congressman Giles, resorted to violent language in denouncing the Federalists. The New Englanders, who prided themselves on restraint and polite manners, were no less insulting in their attitudes of superiority. However, not all debate was undistinguished. Samuel Dexter and Zephaniah Swift, renowned lawyers, spoke as if they were presenting a brief for a client, examining every detail with care, and demonstrating both a willingness to look at the British side and a concern for how the British were likely to respond if the resolutions were adopted.

Madison did not suffer by comparison in these respects, but zealous followers, such as Giles, delighted in rashly denouncing opponents, charging them with evil motives and chicanery. Giles' coarse language merely contributed to the New Englanders' feelings of their own correctness. However much the early Federalists praised coolness and sagacity, in the next decade they were to outdo even the most extreme of the Madisonians in reckless accusations.

The New Englanders occupied a strong position and were clearly in the right. The proposed program of discrimination against England and in favor of France was not likely to either move the British toward a more generous policy or result in a major expansion of trade with France and the continent. France could not extend the credit on which American merchants were so dependent, could not furnish the manufactured goods imported from England, and would strongly oppose any American advantage in the carrying trade.

The financial position of the United States at this time also argued against entering into economic warfare. In 1793 the infant Republic stood on the verge of financial bankruptcy. Europeans owned a large number of American government bonds. The treasury was only able to meet the interest charges by negotiating short-term loans in London. The wars in Europe had created severe financial stringency. Bold anti-British measures might well have cut off further short-term loans.

The crisis in the winter of 1794 provided ample reason to fear war. Seizures of American ships by the British, their continued occupation of military posts, and their dominance of American trade, combined to create a climate of violent resentment. Republicans especially advocated provocative measures, such as the sequestration of debts owed to Britishers. Hamilton warned President Washington of the need to strengthen defenses and, at the same time, to preserve peace.[44] Two days later Senators Oliver Ellsworth of Connecticut, George Cabot and Caleb Strong of Massachusetts, and Rufus King of New York met to discuss how they might advise the president. Ellsworth was to inform the president that they recommended that defenses be strengthened and that an envoy be sent to England to negotiate.[45] The president agreed. Hamilton was proposed, but he wisely declined because he would be viewed with suspicion by the opposition. John Jay was appointed in his stead, in a move that did nothing to assuage the Republicans.

Hamilton not only wrote Jay's formal instructions but gave detailed advice in private letters. The secretary warned that the prospective treaty must remove the more serious grievances. He recognized that England would not cease their seizures of American ships. He proposed that a concession to the British on this point might be made more palatable to the Americans if placed between layers of concessions by the British, such as compensation for seizures, the opening of the West Indies to American ships, and a provision stipulating British withdrawal from the military posts on American soil.[46]

Jay departed for London amidst suspicion and charges that he was an anglophile. Whatever he might reasonably be expected to achieve was not likely to satisfy his critics. Jay, to be sure, favored England rather than France but was above all devoted to American interests, and it appears unlikely that he could have secured greater concessions than he did.[47] In January 1795 Sedgwick reported that the treaty had been concluded and he wrote: "Our disorganizers looked as if they had received a denunciation from above. Their countenances exhibited evidence that the 'pains of Hell had got hold of them.'"[48]

The treaty included stipulations so unsatisfactory that Hamilton entertained serious reservations. The article providing for the opening of the West Indies limited the admission of American ships to those of seventy tons or less and included a two-year limit after which it would be subject to negotiation. Hamilton also deplored the lack of a satisfactory definition of contraband and the ambiguity of Article XVIII concerning the circumstances under which noncontraband would be judged contraband. However, he contended "the truly important side of this treaty" lay in the fact that it closed the "controverted points between the two countries—and thereby gives us the prospect of repossessing our Western Posts, an object of primary consequences in our affairs—of escaping finally from being implicated in the dreadful war which is ruining Europe—and of preserving ourselves in a state of peace for a considerable time to come."[49]

While Hamilton sought to be objective in his detailed evaluation of each article—and his conclusion did constitute an honest, careful decision—he was, of course, speaking as the father of the funding system and as a man who prized conservative financial practices. Both depended upon peace and satisfactory relations with England. His judgment, however honest, reflected deeply held biases and pride in his own handiwork.

Gerald Combs, in his excellent study of the Jay Treaty, concludes that the concessions won by the United States were dearly bought.[50] Sober minds of great ability, men of the caliber of James Madison and Albert Gallatin, reached a similar conclusion at once. They analyzed each treaty article as dispassionately as did Hamilton, arriving at their evaluations with no less care. The treaty provisions were subject to more than one interpretation and more than one estimate as to their future effects. The door was open to honest controversy.

The Senate approved the treaty by the bare two-thirds majority necessary.[51] Of the nine New England senators only Langdon of New Hampshire voted in the negative. Washington decided to delay ratification until the British rescinded a recent order calling for seizure of neutral vessels bound for French ports that carried provisions that might be French property.

At this time another New Englander entered the stage, Timothy Pickering. A citizen of Salem, a lawyer and veteran of the Revolution, Pickering had purchased thousands of acres of land in Pennsylvania hoping to become wealthy. In the course of his attempts to promote settlement he achieved some acclaim by settling a conflict between Pennsylvania and Connecticut over land claims and mediating the Indian wars on the frontier. He is remembered by historians as an arch Federalist, but as late as 1794 he was still friendly toward France and distrustful of England. In that year Washington named him secretary of war. In that position he was the overseer of negotiations between General Wayne and the Indians who had been defeated at the battle of Fallen Timbers.

As secretary of war Pickering ardently championed the Jay Treaty, believing that when confronted with this treaty, the Indians would be amenable to a favorable settlement. Should the Indians find that the British had given up the frontier posts on American territory they would have no choice but to accept American terms. However, after the Senate approved the Jay Treaty, the president delayed final approval.

Fate and error came to Pickering's rescue. He learned of a dispatch to the British minister stating that Secretary of State Randolph in his negotiations with the French minister, Fauchet, was sympathetic to France and that he had sought a bribe from France. The evidence was flimsy at best but served the purposes of the unreliable and alarmist Pickering who chose to inform the president of his newly discovered conspiracy. Washington, after a heated cabinet meeting, chose to ratify the treaty. Actually, Randolph was innocent of the charges, but Pickering was not one to question his sources when it was to his advantage to believe the spurious.[52]

The public in New England's seaports protested with vigor. A public meeting in Boston attended by 1500 unanimously passed resolutions condemning the treaty. Stephen Higginson, shocked by the actions of the Jacobins in Boston and the antitreaty resolutions passed at a public meeting held in July, could only apologetically explain:

You know, that in a Town like this, upon a popular Subject, the minds of many may be suddenly agitated, by sudden and preconcerted addresses to their passions; and their feelings being once strongly excited, they are easily impelled to any absurd or improper conduct.

Approval of the treaty, he wrote, would check "the French influence in our Country." [53]

George Cabot, already heavily despondent over the "private vices" that led to sacrifice of public liberty, was convinced that a "wicked faction" had triumphed. He found that corruption had set in even in Boston. Driving into the city from his farm in Brookline on July 25 he found the treaty being condemned. Some of his friends saw the error of their ways, but they thought it futile to set forth the true facts given the current ferment "which was extreme and universal." [54] Cabot attributed the furor to John Langdon, the New Hampshire congressman who had recently been in Boston, and to the fact that Samuel Dexter had acknowledged that the treaty was not as good as he had hoped. But the merchants rallied to the treaty in Boston, Salem, and Newburyport before the first half of August was spent. By August 24 Cabot's composure returned and he assured his friend, Oliver Wolcott, "that New England will be calm and steady." [55] His certainty was short-lived, however, for on September 11 there were riots and mobs in the streets.

The Jeffersonians had no intention of yielding merely because the treaty had been approved by the Senate and ratified by the president. They maintained that as the treaty required an appropriation the House of Representatives had the right and duty to pass on the treaty.

The sharp differences among prevailing opinions gave rise to caucuses and motivated the organization of the Federalist and Republican parties. The battle lines were set for the next session of Congress.

Debate on the treaty began in the House of Representatives on March 7 and continued until April 30. Repetitious speeches on both sides of the question made use of every possible argument for and against the treaty. Madison and Gallatin analyzed the treaty article by article. New England representatives ardently supported the treaty. Most of them believed that the House would be violating the Constitution if it interfered with treaty making, for the Constitution clearly reserved this power for the president and the Senate. Others, notably Jonathan Dayton, a Federalist from New Jersey who had formerly been opposed to the treaty, contended that the central issue did not involve actual treaty provisions but rather, what might happen if the treaty were rejected. Dayton did not think war probable but observed that calamities "must be admitted to be possible." Some, he said, treated these as chimerical, but there were calamities, in addition to war, that could result from rejection, and these "very far exceed those which are to follow the operation of the treaty."[56]

It remained for Fisher Ames to make an appeal to national honor. His sickly, weak and haggard appearance so moved those supporting the treaty that they wept. The nation, said Ames, had entered into a sacred obligation. Is the treaty so really "fatal," he asked, ". . . as to oblige the nation to break its faith?"[57] The proper ground of the controversy, therefore, he held, ". . . is really unoccupied by the opposers of the Treaty; as the very hinge of the debate is on the point, not of its being good, or otherwise, but whether it is intolerably and fatally pernicious."[58]

Ames' argument carried weight. The credibility of the new nation's commitments would not have been enhanced by rejecting the treaty. This consideration, in addition to the dubious constitutionality of the House acting on a treaty, weakened the case of the Republicans.

The final vote in the House stood at 51 to 48 in favor of the treaty. Of the twenty-eight representatives from New England, twenty-two supported the treaty, four voted against it, and two abstained.[59] The four voting against the treaty, Henry Dearborn, William Lyman, Joseph Varnum, and Israel Smith, were all Republicans and followers of Jefferson. Party bonds, though still loose, influenced the voting.

The vote brought to a close one of the most heated debates in American history. The issues reached well beyond the merits and weaknesses of the treaty. The participants freely acknowledged that pro- and anti-French feelings entered into the controversy. Ames stated that the alarm "spread faster than the treaty itself." Those who opposed the treaty had opposed the negotiation, and Jay was denounced while he was still on his mission. Ames ascribed the controversy not to the treaty but to the state of public feeling.[60]

While this may have been true, the criticisms of the specific articles as offered by Gallatin were not emotional but the result of careful and responsible thought. They did reflect distrust of Great Britain, but they were not influenced by any pro-French feeling. Gallatin's distrust of Great Britain and Madison's fear that close ties with that nation would exert too great an influence in the public councils lay at the heart of the controversy. And now the treaty barred the United States from imposing restrictions on British trade. Gallatin observed that the United States had no fleet ". . . to oppose or to punish the insults of Great Britain"; she was no longer free to use her only weapon, for the treaty barred discrimination.[61]

The Jay Treaty ended the drift toward war and therein lay its great merit. Its provisions, taken singly, were subject to just criticisms, but the treaty as a whole prepared the way for a decade of constructive rapprochement.[62] Those who supported the treaty readily admitted that Great Britain had dealt harshly and sharply with the United States, but they were not ready to brace themselves for economic warfare. This would have interrupted the growth of trade and reduced the prosperity they had recently experienced. The New England merchant and shipping community dominated the section politically. But more was involved; their fear of the Jacobins and the Republican societies at home was greater than their fear of Great Britain.

The New England clergy entertained an equally great fear of what they called French infidelity. The Republic's survival depended upon morality. They saw portents of anarchy in the mob scenes and in the intrusion of French ideas of liberty. To the clergy liberty meant freedom to do what was right. Stability and an ordered society were necessary to curb license. As one student of the religious thinking that dominated New England in the 1790s has written, they sincerely believed that they were ". . . the authentic defenders of liberty's sacred cause."[63] This was the gospel heard by Boston's leading merchants, many of whom attended the famous Brattle Street Church. Jefferson and Madison and their followers were humanists who had great faith in man. The New Englanders believed otherwise. And by 1796, while Congress debated the Jay Treaty, the Reverend Jedidiah Champion of Litchfield, Connecticut closed a public prayer with the words: "O Lord: wilt thou bestow upon the Vice President [Jefferson] a double portion of grace, for Thou knowest he needs it." [64]

Spurred on by the heated controversy over the Jay Treaty in 1794 and 1795, political parties began to assume shape. The party divisions in Massachusetts occurred between the established Federalists and the followers of the revolutionary leaders, Sam Adams and John Hancock. These two spokesmen looked to the people at large as their constituency and, in the eyes of the conservatives, catered to the whims and passions of the multitude. There was also a handful of Jeffersonians: Dr. Charles Jarvis, a Boston physician, General James Sullivan, apologist for the French Revolution, Elbridge Gerry, a maverick merchant, Levi Lincoln, an able lawyer in Worcester, and the brother of Fisher Ames, Dr. Nathaniel Ames, of Dedham, who referred to the Federalists' stance as "prigarchy" and "pettifogarchy." Until 1794 the Federalists held complete control, but in that year Joseph Bradley Varnum, a dirt farmer, and Henry Dearborn, veteran of the Revolution and United States marshal for the district of Maine, were elected to Congress.

Questions of foreign relations deepened the rift. Both John Hancock and Sam Adams defended the French Revolution long after the execution of Louis XVI had led many to become wholly disillusioned. The affinity of the anti-Federalists for the liberal ideals at the heart of the French revolution and the dedication of the republican societies to those ideals challenged the most basic tenets and values of the Federalists.

The pious but not so holy trinity of the Federalists, George Cabot, Fisher Ames, and Theodore Sedgwick rallied to defend their political-religious creed and dismissed the opposition as Jacobins, demagogues, and dreamers. These men acted with a rigidity that prompted distrust of the slightest departure from their own norms.

New England had been reduced to a bastion of conservatism by the Federalists when John Adams' election to the presidency occurred in 1796. At the same time foreign relations came to the fore and dwarfed the controversy over Hamilton's domestic measures. The conservatives' anti-French foreign policy prospered, while, simultaneously, a new hysteria arose over the liberal ideas of the Jeffersonians.

The new president lacked the single-minded distrust of the Jeffersonians prevalent among his New England colleagues. His relations with Jefferson were friendly and, to the horror of Fisher Ames and the stalwarts of Massachusetts, when the time came to send a mission to France, Adams appointed none other than Elbridge Gerry. But Adams, wholly distrustful of France, was determined to be firm. Given his dictum that resentment was a duty when others threatened to exploit any sign of weakness, he could only act with vigor.

The nation Adams confronted in 1797 was deeply divided. France at that time was ruled by the Directory. Authority had passed from the monarchy to the hands of a limited monarchy, to Robespierre and the Committee of Public Safety, to the Directory, with the army as the final residuum of power. France, it appeared, had reached a new peak of glory. Her armies had triumphed over Austria and the Italian states, Spain had been reduced to a client state, and Prussia had been appeased by the assurance that she was to dominate the German states north of the river Main. Only England remained between France and achievement of complete hegemony in Europe.

The outward facade of military omnipotence temporarily obscured from view the collapse of the French economy. Her armies lived off the lands they conquered; government employees went without pay; merchants and shipowners cut off from foreign trade by the British, lingered in the vestibules of bankruptcy. The greater the victories abroad the more adversity triumphed at home. John Adams, well informed as to the true state of affairs, thanks to the reports from Charles Cotesworth Pinckney, Major Mountflorence, and his own son, John Quincy, was not about to be intimidated by French military glory.[65]

In the years immediately preceding Adams' election, France highhandedly insisted on the right of French privateers to bring their captures into American ports and the right of French consuls to hold court and rule on the legality of seizures. In so insisting, the young French minister Genet was asking the United States to relinquish mastery of her own household. A succeeding French minister, Jean Fauchet, transgressed further by seeking to influence the outcome of the presidential election of 1796.[66] His successor, Pierre Adet, commissioned Victor Collet to make a survey of the states west of the Alleghenies to determine the nature of the terrain from a military point of view.[67] The expedition became public knowledge. In brief, Adams had good reason to distrust France.

Upon the conclusion of the Jay Treaty France took serious offense, charging that, in surrendering the principle that equated free ships with free goods, the treaty violated the alliance between the United States and France. The French then sought to intimidate James Monroe, the American minister in Paris. When Monroe, believing he was avoiding war, advised the French to delay on the basis that a defeat of the Federalists would work to the advantage of France, Washington recalled him. In turn France chose to interpret this as an unfriendly act. At the same time French seizures of American ships caused even deeper concern and Monroe's successor, Charles C. Pinckney, not only met with rebuff, he was ordered to leave Paris or face arrest. French hostility was a result of the war she was fighting with England. Because the British had cut off French trade, the French hoped to cut off British-American trade.

Talleyrand of France looked for no cooperation from the United States. The Americans, he wrote, were tied to the British economically and would be guided solely by self-interest.[68] To Talleyrand the Jay Treaty confirmed the fact that the Americans had cast their lot with the British.[69] In the meantime wholesale seizures of American merchant ships by the French replenished the empty coffers of her merchants. On 2 March 1797 the Directory issued a decree declaring enemy goods on neutral ships subject to seizure.[70]

Adams, possessed by a strong sense of national honor, declared that to make the reception of Pinckney dependent on prior accession to French demands "is to treat us neither as allies nor as friends, nor as a sovereign state." Worse still, said Adams, the French government was seeking to alienate the American people from their own government. In a message to Congress he demanded that France cease attacks on American ships, called for the establishment of a navy, and recommended the arming of merchant ships and armed convoys. Then he sadly took note that some Americans were serving on French privateers and firmly asked that Congress outlaw the practice. Adams' critics denounced his message as a call for war.[71]

Adams insulted the Republicans by implying that they were the dupes of France. John Nicholas of Virginia, member of the House of Representatives, responded by asking for proof.[72] To this Nicholas added in tones of alarm that the president's message could only lead to war rather than to any reconciliation. Nicholas and his fellow Republicans, already resentful over Hamilton's measures and the Jay Treaty, believed that the United States had acted unfairly in favoring England at the expense of France. Adams' message appeared to Nicholas to give blanket approval to the program of the Washington administration.

The House debated for almost an entire month on the terms of the reply to be sent to the president. Republicans called for amendments that would appease the French. The Federalists, led by Harrison Gray Otis, a newly elected congressman from Boston, defended Adams. Divisions in the House followed party lines and the members from New England supported the president with near unanimity. A major consideration of the New England merchants who had suffered losses was the collection of spoliation claims, and nothing was to be expected unless the United States took a firm posture on this issue.

Albert Gallatin of Pennsylvania spearheaded the attack on Adams' proposal to build a navy. The cost of a navy, he contended, was prohibitive and, moreover, unnecessary. Citing that the amount of revenue collected during the previous twelve months was $7,400,000, and the fact that the country's circulating medium totaled no more than $8 million, he argued that the country was in no position to support a fleet.[73]

Sewall of Massachusetts denounced Gallatin's analysis as a mere subterfuge and an abject refusal to protect a major economic interest. He then sarcastically observed that farmers had no reason to pay for a fleet and suggested that if the commercial people demanded a fleet for protection they should secede from the union.[74] This was the first mention of secession in Congress. The bill to create a navy passed the House, 78 to 25. Varnum of Massachusetts and Coit of Connecticut were the only New Englanders to vote against the bill.

New Englanders frequently expressed dismay at the coarseness of representatives of other sections and were particularly shocked by the not infrequent duels, but during the course of debates in the spring of 1797 two of their own group engaged in a brawl. Roger Griswold of Connecticut, an ardent Federalist, entered the House and found Matthew Lyon of Vermont, a Republican, sitting in his chair writing. Without warning he beat Lyon severely with a hickory stick. Then the two wrestled each other to the floor. A vote to expel them lost, and later a vote of censure met the same fate.

Adams' dealings with France may have reflected New England interests and political preferences, but they revealed even more accurately Adams' own convictions and his independence of mind. In his message he had announced that he would send a commission to France. Shortly afterwards he named John Marshall of the Supreme Court, Pinckney, who was still in Europe, and his old friend, Elbridge Gerry as delegates. The story of their encounters with Talleyrand, the request for a bribe, Gerry's remaining after the departure of his fellow emissaries, and the release of the XYZ papers, needs no retelling. What is deserving of note is that Talleyrand's efforts to secure a loan were rejected by the three Americans on solid Hamiltonian grounds. A loan would have involved the United States in a war with England. The United States, said the three American commissioners, was still dependent on agriculture and could not suddenly shift to producing the manufactures it needed. Therefore, the United States could not surrender their foreign commerce and, given the state of the world, these supplies could not be completely furnished without the aid of England.

Adams, after the tumult caused by the release of the XYZ papers had quieted down, continued his search for peace against the opposition of his fellow Federalists from New England. Gerry's reports and reports from Victor Dupont, who had recently gone to Paris, convinced Adams that Talleyrand was ready to negotiate in good faith. In late 1798 the president decided to appoint a minister to France. Distrusting his own cabinet he did not consult them. Secretary of State Pickering, an extreme partisan, convinced that continued hostility to France strengthened the Federalists, and Secretary of the Treasury Wolcott, vigorously opposed negotiation. Faced with strong opposition to the appointment of William Vans Murray as minister, Adams circumvented his opponents by appointing a commission consisting of William Vans Murray, Oliver Ellsworth, and Governor Davie of North Carolina. The more conservative Federalists in Boston loudly deplored the president's decision to appoint envoys to France. Abigail Adams informed him:

There has not been any measure of the Government since you have been placed at the Head of it, which has so universally electrified the public as the appointment of Mr. Murray to France, not the man, but the appointment, it came so sudden, was a measure so unexpected, that the whole community were like a flock of frightened pigeons.[75]

Cabot and Ames called Adams a man of violent prejudices and denounced his move to negotiate with France, claiming it showed a willingness to deal with "the vilest and wickedest ambition the world has ever seen."[76] The break with France in foreign affairs had served the Federalists well, for it discredited the Republican opposition. Cabot observed: "Our preachers and orators almost universally expressed a joy at the separation from France, and a confident hope that we should keep aloof from influence, poisons, and plagues; and I certainly do not know one in twenty among the Federalists who thinks there is any apology for attempting to renew the intercourse in any shape."[77] The break with France had robbed French ideas of their appeal and saved the country from French infidelity and Jacobinism.

Fisher Ames felt certain that Adams' creation of a peace mission would split the Federalists and give new life to the Republicans. Cabot saw in Adams' action the end of good government. The president, he wrote, "would part wider and wider" from the real Federalists, the public would no longer support measures of defense, and yet the dangers would remain undiminished.[78] Above all Cabot foresaw that negotiations would split the northern and southern Federalists, for the former would oppose the mission and the latter, given southern opinion, would support it.

The New Englander, Timothy Pickering, fought Adams both inside and outside the cabinet. Washington had appointed Pickering to be secretary of state. Adams retained him in spite of great doubts concerning his fitness for the office. Pickering's most notable characteristic was a lack of coolness and patience. Any difference of opinion with an opponent prompted his flight to an unreal realm of sinister motives and conspiracies in which he conceived of himself as the defender of the

Republic and therefore justified in adopting any means that would serve his ends. He thrived on illusions that France and the Jeffersonians were partners in a diabolical conspiracy.

Adams eventually chose to overrule objections by his secretary of state and search for peace. Suspicion of Adams' motives urged the uncontrollable Pickering to even greater extremes. Gerry's appointment to the commission sent to France for purposes of negotiation caused Pickering to confront the president in a manner reflecting his mistaken view that cabinet members were independent of the chief executive. When Adams was finally satisfied that France would receive an envoy and earnestly sought peace, he appointed an envoy. Pickering did his best to undermine Adams' peace efforts and to promote a decision to go to war, believing that while France might negotiate, she could not be trusted. Eventually, in May 1800, Pickering was dismissed.[79]

The treaty negotiated by Adams' envoys freed the United States from the treaty of alliance negotiated in 1778. The original alliance, which had never been undergirded with economic ties, stood at cross-purposes with American economic dependence on England. The new treaty canceled all claims of both nations against each other. The French had been adamant on this point and would not have agreed to a treaty that did not provide for this. Yet it was this clause that made the treaty objectionable to the American merchants and shippers who had suffered losses at the hands of French privateers.[80] The treaty encountered strong opposition in the Senate. After suffering defeat initially it was finally approved subject to future discussion of the cancellation of claims.[81]

# 3
# The Emergence of New England Defiance

New England's defiant spirit was in part a response to the public image of Thomas Jefferson. He became the symbol around which the New England Federalists joined hands in frenzied opposition. The president, as his eminent biographer, Dumas Malone, pointed out, was peculiarly vulnerable to being misunderstood.

To resolve all the apparent contradictions of this complicated man would be difficult indeed, and he would lose much of his fascination if reduced to stark simplicity, but a distinction can be made between what John Marshall referred to as the "general cast" of his political and social theory and his working philosophy as a responsible statesman. The latter he well summed up at the beginning of his presidency, that "no more good must be attempted than the nation can bear."[1]

Jefferson the deist, the critic of clergy, the visionary, these were the aspects his enemies concentrated upon. Unfortunately some of the distortion was attributable to Jefferson himself. In practice he was a cautious and politically wise statesman. This is not to say that he did not make mistakes.

Since the days of the Revolution, Jefferson had held the view that the Republic had most to fear from England, a nation with a powerful navy and many merchants. Close ties to British merchants in trade would, he thought, lead to an erosion of republican principles in the United States and give control to the merchants. Merchants, Jefferson believed, by virtue of their daily immersion in countinghouses, thought solely in terms of profits, were speculative rather than productive, and gave little or no thought to the welfare of the community.

In the crisis of 1798, when Congress passed the Alien and Sedition Acts, Jefferson ruefully observed that the most farsighted politician "could not, seven years ago, have imagined that the people of this wide-extended country could have been enveloped in such delusion, and made so much afraid of themselves and their own power, as to surrender it spontaneously to those who are maneuvering them into a form of government, the principal branches of which may be beyond their control." Why this had happened, Jefferson found easy to explain. It was because the commerce of England "has spread its roots over the whole face of the country." "This," he wrote, "is a real source of all the obliquities of the public mind; . . . ."[2] This rather quaint analysis of human evil would scarcely stand the test of his lifetime.

His early ebulliency also led him to the conclusion that the new Republic represented a break with the past and that history had bestowed upon it a mission. His dream did not fade rapidly. Having been elected to the presidency he assured himself that the ship of state was to be put "on her republican tack." He saw the whole world being influenced by the example of American republican society. He joyfully assured an old friend, "A just and solid republican government maintained here, will be a standing monument and example for the aim and imitation of other countries" and the success of the Republic "will ameliorate the condition of men over a great portion of the globe."[3] However, this stimulating elixir did not stand him in good stead when he encountered the centers of world power.

What he wrote with his free flowing pen did not always accord with his response to immediate crises, but his words were more of a threat to his reputation at the time than his actions. But that same pen was to nourish the democratic dream for generations to come. His pro-French sentiments did not survive the French Directory. His observations of Napoleon led him to describe the French emperor as "the first and chiefest apostle of the desolation of men and morals."[4] His distrust of Great Britain survived, and after leaving the presidency he described her as "the tyrant of the ocean." The British, he held, were devoted to the principle "that force is right."[5]

Fortunately for the Republic, Jefferson as president disengaged himself from the luxury of his study and confronted the realities of public office. For all his dreams he was an ardent nationalist who erred most often by failing to surmount the limited perspective of an ardent apostle of republican principles.

In New England the opposition to Jefferson promoted the image of the president as the visionary, the deist, the enemy of commerce. Jefferson made no effort to answer the vile accusations made against him. He rightly believed that good government was the best antidote to misrepresentation. In fact the distrust might have been eroded had not the wars in Europe intervened. After his retirement he sadly noted: "It has been peculiarly unfortunate for us, personally, that the portion in the history of mankind, at which we were called to take a share in the direction of their affairs, was such an one as history has never before presented."[6] "All those calculations which, at any other period, would have been deemed honorable, of the existence of a moral sense in man, individually or associated . . . have been a matter of reproach on us, as evidence of imbecility."[7] And so it was. In the trying times when the belligerents, intent on victory, treated the United States in a high-handed fashion, there was no ready answer to the problems faced. Internal dissension flourished, distrust grew unchecked, and reason gave way to partisan emotionalism. In New England political, economic, and religious forces eventually combined to throttle all except the hardiest of souls.

But though the Federalists mounted a campaign of hatred and distrust, they were not wholly without a basis for their criticism. Both Jefferson and Madison failed to give due importance to the weaknesses of the United States as compared to the naval and economic strength of Great Britain. This was particularly true of Jefferson in 1806 when he shifted the responsibility for foreign policy questions to Congress. Furthermore, so strong were Jefferson's and Madison's convictions of the legitimacy of American complaints that they failed to give due weight to the arguments of their British adversary.

New England's violent opposition to the foreign policy of Jefferson and Madison and her eventual condemnation of the War of 1812 stemmed in part from party rivalry. Yet, opinion was also divided on the issue of who was entitled to the dominant voice in political decision making—the people at large or the upper economic and social strata. Finally, the confrontation that came to the fore after the embargo of 1807 was motivated in no small part by honest and reasonable differences of opinion as to how best to respond to the strangulation of trade by the belligerents. This final difference was not confined to rational argument; rather, it exploded into denunciations and stimulated the creation of a vile theory of conspiracy.

In the early phase preceding Jefferson's election, New England was divided by party rivalry and differences in political orientation. Political parties had come into being during the controversy over the Jay Treaty. This cleavage was, in turn, paralleled by conflicting responses to the French Revolution and to the new intellectual fashions sponsored by the Illuminati.

Federalists conceived of society as a growing organism with deep roots in the past. They equated the ideal of a well-ordered society with a belief in the primacy of reason over peoples' preferences and the need to calculate both individual and social interests with wisdom. Republicans, on the other hand, believed that the French Revolution would liberate man from the dead hand of the past and open windows to the fresh breezes of new thoughts. They held the opinion that liberation should allow everyone the opportunity to participate in a more fluid society.

In New England the Federalists ruled, but the new ideas of the Enlightenment gained adherents outside the legislative halls. This was particularly true in Salem where the Unitarian minister, William Bentley, after the French had captured Ostend, noted in his diary: "The people could not refrain from public expressions of Joy, and the Cannon were fired from the wharves before Sunset in the Town."[8]

When Daniel Appleton White entered Harvard in 1793 he found the college "under a flood of infidel and licentious principles" and "so generally had the French mania seized upon the popular mind in this country, and so susceptible of its fiery influence were the ardent spirits of young men, all alive to freedom of thought and action and indulgence, that reason and argument and persuasion had for some time no power against it."[9] On becoming president of Harvard in 1798, John Thornton Kirkland found the college swamped by admiration for the French, and he devoted his Phi Beta Kappa address to counteracting this evil. George Cabot, a leading Boston merchant, who shared Kirkland's fears, had a thousand copies printed for circulation.[10]

Frightened by the invasion of new points of view, the clergy and the

Federalists joined hands and fought what they viewed as a dread disease—French licentiousness and Jacobinism. The New England Congregational clergy had for several decades believed that their responsibility included instruction in appropriate political doctrine. Ever since the Seven Years' War the clergy had turned from the promotion of piety to the political problem of promoting public virtue.[11] They sought to create a Christian commonwealth that would preserve liberty, the freedom to do what was right. Assurance of this freedom was dependent upon a government committed to upholding piety and virtue. The clergy were convinced that in the absence of such a government anarchy would result in the moral sphere and tyranny would triumph. Republicans who believed in the separation of church and state and whose leaders, Jefferson and Madison, did not attend church, were therefore seen as a threat. The clergy, as they saw it, faced Armageddon and felt called upon to do battle for the Lord.

By 1798 the Illuminati represented the most immediate danger. On May 9 of that year the well-known Congregational clergyman, Jedediah Morse, sounded the alarm in a sermon before his congregation. Morse claimed to have possession of documents that proved that a small group of anarchists had plotted the French Revolution and were now at work to overthrow the established order in New England. Morse launched a crusade. One historian of the movement concluded "there was probably not a solitary Federalist leader in the United States who did not believe that French ministers and agents were in secret league with influential representatives of the Democratic party."[12] Both parties labeled each other with abusive epithets. Fisher Ames countered his brother's earlier reference to the Federalists as the "prigarchy" by speaking of people who attended Republican meetings as "rabble."[13]

Timothy Pickering and George Cabot gave way to bitter invective. Pickering acknowledged current economic prosperity but charged that his fellow Federalists were dissatisfied because "they see the public morals debased by the corrupt and corrupting system of our rulers." Men, he said, are not only becoming apostates to Federalism "but to virtue and to religion and to good government."[14] Cabot deplored the fact that even in New England "where there is among the body of the people more wisdom and virtue than in any other part of the United

States, we are full of errors, which no reasoning could eradicate, if there is a Lycurgus in every village." To Cabot a good government had as its first and greatest responsibility to "maintain the empire of principles against the assaults of popular passions."

Bentley, of Salem, who earlier had observed that society gave license to persecute anyone who was not anti-French, four years later noted that hatred of England and France had given way to hatred of domestic opponents. He wrote: ". . . letters are sent, the presses smoak [sic], and conversation has the tang of politics." [15] Emmons, the Congregational clergyman referred to Jefferson as "Jeroboam, the man who made Israel to sin." The sermon was printed and distributed gratis. [16]

Emmons represented the theological outlook of the conservative Congregational clergy. The sovereignty of God, the sinful nature of man, and the approaching day of judgment were as real to them as the soil beneath them. To men of this cast of mind the deism of Jefferson and current questioning of the Bible were powerful evils. And Emmons warned that judgment was close at hand: "We live in the last days, in which scoffers have actually come, who not only call in question the inspiration of the Scriptures, but the immortality of the soul and a future day of retribution." [17] The clergy, mindful of the biblical injunction that they were ordained to maintain the purity of the faith once delivered to the saints, believed that it was no less their duty to make war on the Republicans and Jefferson.

The political schism became even more extreme with the election of Thomas Jefferson to the presidency in 1800. The Federalists of Boston were now certain that the men of talent and probity had been dethroned and replaced by the party "of the worthless, the dishonest, the rapacious, the vile, the merciless and the ungodly." [18] Jefferson's administration did nothing that justified such fears, for it was far from revolutionary. Jefferson became ever more popular. By 1804, in spite of the energetic efforts of the Federalists, he carried all of the New England states except Connecticut.

Federalist leaders chose to do battle in more mundane ways. The Republicans were the first to appeal to public opinion, to build political organizations, and to make use of the printed page, but, as David

Hackett Fischer has shown, the Federalists, after 1800, quickly learned the importance of mass campaigning.[19] Eminently practical men, they were more concerned with winning elections than with maintaining the purity of the faith. On election day in Salem in 1802, according to Bentley, they played "dirty tricks," giving vouchers to men who did not live in town or who owned no property. The wages of sin in this instance were paid by a Federalist victory.

The party's efforts ordinarily adhered to less specious methods. Harrison Gray Otis, the most able of Federalist orators, saw the need for organization. He wrote: "If we mean to preserve the commonwealth and New England, our organization, must be more complete and systematic."[20] Fisher Ames stressed the need of creating a Federalist press. He wrote to his friend, Jeremiah Smith: "The pen will govern, till the resort is to the sword, and even then the ink is of some importance, . . . ."[21] Before long there were statewide, county, and local organizations and a lively publishing campaign.

In this strange and frightening new world, the sudden acquisition of Louisiana raised new specters of danger. Ames believed the acquisition to be mean and despicable. He saw no need for the negotiations as control of the Mississippi was already a fact. That river had served as a useful limit and "Now by adding an unmeasured world beyond that river, we would rush like a comet into infinite space."[22]

Ames enjoyed his dark forebodings; they convinced him further of his astuteness. He could not possibly believe that the present leadership could "contemplate a republican form as practicable, honest, or free, if applied where it is so manifestly inapplicable to the government of one third of God's earth."[23]

Cabot professed he could not understand John Quincy Adams' support of the acquisition of Louisiana "when it is so obvious that the influence of our part of the Union must be diminished by the acquisition of more weight at the other extremity."[24] The same fear led a handful of the more extreme Federalists, including Pickering of Massachusetts and James Hillhouse, Uriah Tracy, and Roger Griswold of Connecticut to make a plan for removing New England from the Union. However, they made no progress and the plan remained a secret until 1828 when John

Quincy Adams publicized it. John Quincy Adams was the only New England Federalist to vote in favor of the annexation of Louisiana.

Not until 1805 did the country come face-to-face with the question of the rights of a neutral country to carry on trade between the colonies of a belligerent and the belligerent. The reexport trade now exceeded the trade in American exports and imports. A British admiralty court in the *Essex* case virtually decreed an end to that trade in its interpretation of the Rule of 1756. That unilateral pronouncement, a half century before, had decreed that colonies closed in times of peace could not be opened in time of war. Americans had not challenged closure of direct trade between France and her colonies but asserted with boldness that goods carried from a French colony to the United States could be reexported to the mother country. The admiralty court decision severely restricting this reexport trade was followed by British seizures of American ships engaged in this trade. In turn the merchants in the port cities of the United States dispatched memorials to Congress protesting these seizures. However, their protests carefully avoided condemnation of the British and called for no more than polite remonstrance and negotiation.

Jefferson and Madison, on the other hand, held strong convictions that ruled out any submissive note. They viewed the new British ruling as a clear violation of the Law of Nations and as an infringement on American sovereignty. The president, in his annual message to Congress, stated that the Republic was now confronted by an injurious and novel doctrine endangering American neutral rights. In a second message he spoke of "new principles, derogatory of the rights of neutrals, and unacknowledged by the usages of nations." Secretary of State Madison wrote a lengthy and learned article showing that the British ruling was in conflict with earlier ones and wholly inconsistent with the conclusions of such distinguished authorities as Grotius, Pufendorf, and Vattel. Copies of Madison's weighty analysis were distributed in the Senate.[25]

Federalists did not equate neutral rights with sovereignty. They took a more realistic view, arguing that neutral rights were fine in theory but never honored when powerful nations engaged in war and believed they were fighting for survival. George Cabot preferred practical expediency to legalism. He wrote:

But we cannot be insensible that actions in themselves strictly lawful are often highly inexpedient. In the use of the clearest rights and in the preservation of unsullied honor, prudence guides the individual, and policy must guide the nation.[26]

Cabot dismissed Madison's pamphlet on neutral rights and the reexport trade, maintaining that Madison's arguments, while honestly held by many, were based on preconceived opinions and marred by prejudice, including animosity toward England. At this time, February 1806, prior to the severe restrictions of 1807, Cabot hoped that even with "large deductions for blockades and contraband, the total of our trade would be much enlarged and its profits *doubled* by a war between France, Holland, and England." At the same time Cabot saw the struggle in Europe in terms of a test of civilization's strength. England, he wrote, "is in the greatest extremity defending the independence of the civilized world; and the necessity of the case would justify her in saying to neutrals, if you will not help us in the battle, you shall not hinder its success under a cover of neutral pretentions."[27]

Fisher Ames shared these views. He, too, decried Madison's insistence on upholding neutral rights. Madison, Ames wrote, relied on cases that occurred in past centuries and "He might as well show that neither Aristotle nor the laws of Solon make any mention of such a principle." Ames claimed that "A new state of things exists, and a new case requires a new application of old principles."[28]

Jefferson hoped to enter into negotiations with the British. In turning to Congress he sought to affirm his own position in order to strengthen his bargaining power. He knew too, given the controversy that the Jay Treaty had evoked, that he must tread carefully and not take an advanced position the country would not support.

The Committee on Foreign Relations submitted its report on February 12. Bold phrases found their way into the resolutions. British actions were labeled "unprovoked aggressions," an "encroachment on national independence."[29] The report was approved by a unanimous vote, but this hasty action was followed by almost two months of heated debate in both houses of Congress.

Confusion ensued. A proposal to restrict British imports became the central issue. Some congressmen appealed to national honor, particularly those from Pennsylvania who had little to lose by the proposed restriction. Southerners voiced alarm. Cutting off British imports would invite Britain to retaliate by shutting their market to southern cotton and tobacco. Party lines determined opinion as much as sectional interests. George Campbell of Tennessee and James Jackson of Georgia argued in favor of the measure, but Joseph Nicholson, a powerful party leader, opposed a total ban on imports from England on the grounds that it would cut off supplies available nowhere else, would endanger the market for cotton and tobacco, and seriously upset the existing channels of trade.[30] The measure, he said, would call for undue sacrifices from the South and little from other sections. Nicholson's resolution, introduced early in the debates, would only prohibit imports of goods that could be produced in the United States.[31]

In the House the only New Englander to enter into the debate with feeling was Barnabas Bidwell of western Massachusetts, a follower of Jefferson. He took issue with those colleagues of his who minimized the importance of the carrying trade. That carrying trade, Bidwell contended, was an essential link in the nation's commerce, intimately associated with the exports of native products, and a major means of paying for what was imported. He applauded Jefferson's stance on neutral rights, arguing that these rights were "too evident and too important to be surrendered." The president, Bidwell asserted, planned to negotiate and had left it to Congress to determine what actions should be taken in aid of the negotiation.[32]

The New England Federalists sat quietly by during those long debates in March 1806. What they heard was disquieting. The protest of southerners who argued that they should not be made to pay for the interests of a few merchants confirmed the Federalists' belief that they would be sacrificed. They heard speeches describing the importance of the carrying trade as limited to a few merchants. However, a degree of philosophical tranquillity was induced by the sharp divisions that appeared among the ruling party. John Randolph spoke in contemptuous tones of the administration and denounced Madison severely. The Federalists also heard that many southern Republicans were not ready to support the president. Consequently the Federalists could sit quietly by and enjoy seeing their opponents tear themselves apart.

What then did the Federalists want in the way of protection for the carrying trade? They did wish to have the administration seek to rectify their grievances, including impressment, but they were opposed to taking any steps that could lead to a break with England. The watered-down Nonimportation Act of 1806 was finally passed by the House on March 25. The act merely limited nonimportation to a few articles, and it was not to go into effect until November 15. The Federalists sought to weaken it still further by postponing the effective date of the act until January 1 of the following year.[33] On the final vote in the House seventeen New Englanders voted against it.[34] However, seven representatives from Massachusetts, all of them Jeffersonian Republicans, voted for the measure, showing that the Federalists had yet to win complete dominance.

Early in 1806 Jefferson sent James Monroe and William Pinkney to London to negotiate. Their instructions laid down as a *sine qua non* British surrender of the practice of impressment and revision of the policy laid down in the Rule of 1756. Despite Great Britain's struggle against Napoleon, the importance to her of her fleet, and the jealousy with which British shipping interests viewed the growth of the American merchant marine, the British unwisely refused to compromise. The two envoys faced a bargaining table where neither justice, the threat to limit British imports, nor arguments resting on the Law of Nations were likely to carry the day. The negotiations were conducted in a friendly spirit, but the cards in the contest were unequally distributed. The British contended that to surrender impressment would make of the American merchant marine a "floating asylum for all British seamen who, tempted by higher wages should quit their service for ours."[35] Americans saw impressment as the equivalent of enslavement. The United States was willing to outlaw British deserters serving on American merchant ships, but the British doubted that this could be made effective. Confronted with a life and death struggle with Napoleon, the British were in no frame of mind to tolerate deserters. On the other hand the Americans knew only too well that young British navy lieutenants boarding an American ship looked upon all suspects as easy prey.[36]

When no progress was made on this issue, Monroe and Pinkney stated that according to their instructions they could not continue negotiations. The British then proposed that a note be attached to the treaty committing the British government to instruct sea captains to observe the greatest caution and assuring Americans that "the strictest care would be taken to preserve the citizens of the United States from any molestation or injury." Considering this a gain and placing value on advantages bestowed by other articles, Monroe and Pinkney signed the treaty. They sadly underestimated Jefferson's determination to end impressment.[37]

In the closing days of the negotiations the British appended a note to the treaty stating that the crown would not be bound by the treaty provisions if the United States failed to show resentment against France and her recent Milan Decree. Attaching this condition was tantamount to stipulating that the treaty would only be binding if the United States entered the war against France. Jefferson had no real choice but to reject the treaty. He did not send the treaty to the Senate for approval. His action offended his old friend Monroe, and his opponents were later to charge him with having rejected a reasonable settlement. However, to have approved the treaty would have been to acquiesce to British dictates and to have surrendered the right to retaliate against British rulings by discriminating against British imports. Jefferson hoped to continue negotiations. His hopes for success rested on his belief that the kaleidoscopic change of fortunes of the belligerents would eventually bring about the day when the British would be ready to meet what in his opinion were the just demands of the United States.

Events soon proved Jefferson's sanguine view to be unrealistic. In June 1807 the British warship, the *Leopard*, under orders from Admiral Berkeley at Halifax, a naval officer who felt a mixture of hate and contempt for Americans, set out to uphold British honor in Norfolk. Reports from there indicated that British deserters were about to enter the American service on the warship *Chesapeake*. The British consul at Norfolk protested their enlistment in the American navy. His protests were turned aside by Stephen Decatur, the local commander, and finally by Secretary of State James Madison. British frustration mounted as they heard of other deserters in Norfolk who boasted of their escapes from British ships.

The presence of several other British warships in the waters off Norfolk added to the warlike atmosphere as Captain Barron, under orders to go to the Mediterranean, sailed forth. Stores had not yet been put away when the *Chesapeake* was ordered to stop, and a British lieutenant came aboard to search for deserters. When Captain Barron rejected the order, the fifty-gun *Leopard* opened fire, seriously damaging the *Chesapeake*, killing three seamen, and wounding eight others. Captain Barron then lowered his colors, and a British officer boarded the ship to search for deserters. Three alleged deserters, all of whom were American, and one other, clearly a British subject, were taken.

To stop a warship and search it for deserters was unprecedented. The British captain had gone beyond the bounds of previous British practice. Following the incident, remaining British ships maneuvered in ways that provoked fears that a British armed force was about to land.

In Washington and the country at large the uproar of hostility justified Jefferson's observation that not since Lexington had the country been so united. War appeared inevitable, but weighty considerations forced a delay. Jefferson called for an apology and reparations and issued an order barring British warships from American ports.

Only in Boston, among the high Federalists, did anyone rise to the defense of the British. Among those who did was Judge John Lowell, friend of Timothy Pickering and a dedicated anglophile. When Lowell met John Quincy Adams, who was lecturing at Harvard that summer, he promptly delivered a defense of the British action. Adams, on the other hand, proposed to some Federalist friends that a public meeting be called to give expression to the public's resentment. They rejected the suggestion. When the opposing party did call a meeting Adams not only attended but helped draw up resolutions of protest. A few days later the Federalists, sensitive to the public uproar, called a meeting and passed resolutions.[38]

The vigor of John Quincy Adams and his readiness to take issue with his closest friends cut short his career in the Senate. He became more determined when he found the most conservative of the Federalists, the

Essex Junto, passing around a letter from the governor of Nova Scotia stating that Napoleon sought to promote war between the United States and Great Britain and that Jefferson was party to the plan.[39] Should the war take place some members of the junto were ready to take the side of Great Britain.

In the meantime the country faced the extensive blockades of the continent by England and Napoleon's Berlin Decree declaring a blockade of the British Isles. Finally, in November 1807, England issued an order-in-council requiring neutral ships to stop in England and buy a license before proceeding to the continent. In turn, Napoleon issued his Milan Decree declaring that any ship stopping in England thereby denationalized itself and would be subject to seizure on entering any continental port. American ships now faced the dilemma of subjecting themselves to seizure by either the British or the French or remaining at home. By September 1807 few ships escaped seizure and insurance rates quadrupled. America, a seafaring nation, found the sea lanes closed.

Confronted with this dilemma and fearful for the safety of the American merchant marine, Jefferson finally resorted to enforcing the Nonimportation Act of 1806. This was hardly an adequate response to the crisis. If American ships exposed themselves to capture, war was likely to prove inevitable. Faced with this situation Jefferson met with his cabinet and proposed an embargo. Albert Gallatin, mindful of the sacrifices it would entail, expressed the view that an embargo could only be justified as a temporary measure, preferable to war. James Madison thought that the provision affecting foreign ships posed dangers. Jefferson, at this stage, viewed it as the one way to protect American ships and avoid war. He wrote to Gallatin: "What is *good* in this case cannot be effected; we have, therefore, only to find out what will be *least bad*."[40] There were no viable alternatives. War, given Jefferson's strong preference for peace and the vulnerability of the country's seaport cities, received only the most incidental consideration. In addition, silence and acquiescence in the face of Republican outbursts of anglophobia and the fact that silence could only be interpreted as partiality for England ruled out this as an alternative.[41] In Congress the embargo received the prompt approval of the Senate. A House committee that included John

Quincy Adams as one of its members, concluded that there were no options, and the House gave its approval.

Among the members of the administration, only Madison expressed the view that the embargo would enable Jefferson to put pressure on England.[42] Not until two months later did Congress add amendments with an eye to giving the embargo such a coercive aspect. These amendments called for a closure of all imports. By withdrawing American ships from the high seas the embargo could be defended. Once the aim of coercing England was stated, the measure of the embargo's success was altered, and it became vulnerable to sharp attack. However, its real test was to be whether or not the public would bear the hardships it imposed.

# 4

# From Internal Dissension to Foreign War

The transformation of the embargo into a coercive measure and the injurious effects of that measure at home, both economical and political, led to such violent party warfare that the central issue of how to protect national interests in the face of the struggle occurring in Europe became, to a considerable degree, subordinate to preserving peace at home. The nation was divided on basic principles; the division between New England Federalists and the Jeffersonians reached down to the very taproots of political, social, and even religious thought. Now, as a result of the European holocaust, it acquired a new dimension.

The Federalists saw England as the last barrier to Napoleon's complete victory. England was, in their eyes, fighting America's battles. Should she be defeated, the new Republic would be sucked into the European vortex. This view had its supporters long before the enactment of the embargo. As early as January 1804 Samuel Taggart, Congressman from Massachusetts, wrote: "If England should fall, I see nothing short of an almost miraculous interposition of Providence that can save the United States. . . ."[1] Two years later Taggart repeated his doleful fears: "The British fleet . . . , is the only barrier in the way of our being swallowed up in our turn by the tremendous vortex which threatens to devour everything."[2] The embargo seemed to portend the catastrophic end, and the day it was enacted Taggart wrote mournfully: "Should I say that the die is cast, that my country is no longer independent; we have been legislating under an imperial decree of the Emperor of France and sanctioning a plan matured in Paris it would be saying no more than I fear it will be realized."[3]

Scores of New England Federalists shared Taggart's views. Although they appear to have been held by less than a majority, the embargo redeemed the Federalists from oblivion and gave the party new life.

On the opposing side, men of equally strong convictions held that opposition to British "tyranny of the sea" offered the only hope of avoiding becoming a mere puppet dominated by England. John Quincy Adams trumpeted the danger with a vehemence equal to that of James Madison. Both men were ardent nationalists who dedicated themselves to a policy that demanded respect from abroad and promoted national feelings of resentment when the Republic suffered arbitrary treatment. Both were anxious to promote unity at home.

Jefferson and Madison are often accused of being too sanguine and of exaggerating the strength of the new Republic's bargaining power. This may be so, but there were weightier reasons for the position they took in standing up against the British. The alternative to firm opposition to English policy was acquiescence, and this, they believed, would destroy the public's respect for themselves and their nation, reduce them to puppets of the British, and make them accomplices of England in the war.

No one put the case more forcefully than John Quincy Adams in his review of a collection of Fisher Ames' writings collected by friends of that pro-English Boston aristocrat. Adams denounced Ames and his group for viewing themselves as having a monopoly of "all the virtue, and all the talents, as well as all the wealth of the American continent" and for looking at "the rest of the people" as "a mere herd of Sodom, to be saved from the fire of Heaven only by their transcendent merits."[4]

If the pro-British party could convince the people of America "that they have no right to claim a free trade with the colonies of Britain's enemies, in time of war," wrote Adams, then "they would never assert it; they would without a struggle, surrender the trade, wherever it might suit the purposes of the British cabinet. . . ." To those who would rely on the British navy, he stated, they must prove "that the protection of the British navy would be a safe reliance." The British had played a shrewd game with nations who relied on their navy. Those nations had become allies, fought England's wars, and after defeat had been reduced to French control. For the United States to have accepted impressment and the British order-in-council of November 1807 would have meant surrendering neutrality, for this would have reduced the United States to a partisan role.[5]

As a result of the expectation of war in the fall of 1807, the embargo was promptly enacted by Congress. The law not only forbade American ships to go to a foreign port, it also prohibited foreign ships from taking on goods other than those already on board when notified of the act.

The future unveiled greater difficulties than anyone foresaw. The probability of England yielding was slight. In view of the war in Europe and the importance Britain placed on showing no sign of weakness to her allies, and given the uncompromising opinion of British shipping interests and the power wielded by these interests in the House of Commons, the embargo had little potential as a coercive measure. Nor did anyone predict that the sacrifices exacted of American shippers and merchants would eventually create danger of internal disorder. And little did anyone foresee that this attempt to resist British strangulation of American trade set a course from which there could be no turning back.

At first, with the exception of Connecticut, town meetings throughout New England supported the embargo with firm resolutions.[6] William Bentley, Unitarian minister in Salem, wrote on the day that news of the embargo arrived: "The merchants had already laid one in our port as few vessels ventured abroad so that this measure has excited no surprise or particular alarm at present & it is yet a secret whether the cause be from English or French measures."[7] On 3 May 1808, James Winthrop wrote to Mercy Warren defending the embargo and stating that while many merchants acknowledged its wisdom, a political faction opposed it merely "to gratify a few traders, who depend on the commercial credit given them by Great Britain."[8] Two leading shipowners of Salem, Jacob Crowninshield and William Gray, defended the embargo. Gray held that a greater part of American vessels would be seized if they went to sea.[9] The tripling of insurance rates during the fall bore out this view. The hostility against Gray became so intense that he moved to Boston, left the Federalist party, and in 1810 was elected lieutenant governor as a Republican, a position from which he extended loans totaling $600,000 to the federal government in support of the War of 1812. The Crowninshields remained loyal to Jefferson in spite of severe business reverses. As late as October 1808, the Republicans in Salem, at a town meeting, were able to defeat a Federalist resolution condemning the embargo.

In Boston Federalist opposition began almost at once. The newspapers, the *Columbian Centinel* and the *Palladium*, strongly partial to England before the embargo, immediately attacked the measure. By spring the opposition threatened to become general. John Quincy Adams, on his return to Boston in May, found Chief Justice Parsons "totally devoted to British Policy" and wholly opposed to the embargo. The Federalists could not resist making political capital of the situation. Timothy Pickering addressed a letter to the governor denouncing both Jefferson and the embargo. His aim was to prevent the reelection of John Quincy Adams to the Senate. In this letter Pickering charged that the embargo was proposed by Jefferson in response to orders from France. According to this conspiratorial theory the embargo was no more than an adjunct to Napoleon's continental system. The letter was printed and circulated by the thousands.[10] Adams wrote a long letter to Harrison Gray Otis explaining his position in which he decried Pickering's use of the crisis to seek his party's advantage. The administration, Adams asserted, had no alternative. He viewed the embargo as an experiment; whether it would be successful remained to be seen. He believed the administration should have his cooperation.[11] Although the embargo was only an expedient, he felt it deserved a trial.

John Quincy Adams, who voted for the embargo knowing he would be punished, became the first victim. Rather than wait for Adams' term to expire, the Federalists in the state senate scheduled the election three months early, passed resolutions condemning the embargo, and elected James Lloyd, an unknown friend of T. W. Perkins. Thereupon Adams resigned. Adams, who had taken the lead in criticizing the British after the *Chesapeake* affair and served on the Senate committee recommending the embargo, was charged with having betrayed the Federalists. Fisher Ames once described John Quincy Adams as "wild as a kite without a tail." The Federalists in the spring of 1808 viewed him as wholly unreliable. The attacks on Adams brought forth streams of violence and vengeance; he was called a "Lucifer," "party scavenger," "popularity seeker," "apostate," and one of "Bonaparte's Senators."[12]

In the House of Representatives, both in the spring and again in the fall of 1808, Josiah Quincy and Edward St. Loe Livermore, of Newburyport, led the fight against the embargo. Both men were forceful and sharp. Livermore stressed the distress and unemployment the embargo imposed, its crippling effects upon the merchant marine, and the futility of believing that England could be coerced. Merchants and shipowners should be left free to decide if it was safe to venture to sea. Many would undoubtedly find ways to evade the orders-in-council and decrees, and others would pursue trade where the channels were still open—in Asia, Africa and parts of the Mediterranean. Livermore closed one of his many speeches stating: "I am compelled upon this occasion to say, that from necessity, our only course of safety is peace with Great Britain and opposition to the boundless ambition of the Emperor of the French." [13]

In the Senate James Hillhouse of Connecticut presented the Federalist case. Hillhouse, a conservative with long experience in the Senate, did not resort to name-calling, nor did he engage in charging the opposition with conspiracy. He contended that idle threats of economic coercion could never serve to defend neutral rights. The way to protect neutral rights lay in negotiation conducted with firmness and reasonableness. The embargo, he held, represented an abandonment of neutral rights, and such a retreat weakened the position of the United States in negotiation. A highly popular president had promoted the embargo. But, he noted, eleven months after its enactment, the measure was so unpopular it was thought necessary to call out armed forces to enforce it. [14]

The sober and reasonable arguments in congressional debates scarcely measured up to the heated feelings of the Federalists in Connecticut and Massachusetts. Shipping interests were of great importance in both states and the embargo clearly imposed a hardship on both. The distress of the public in the seaport cities played into the hands of less scrupulous politicians who distrusted the administration for more reasons than the embargo and who were willing to exploit the more general public distrust that was rooted in aristocratic attitudes and religious thinking that made the liberal and secular attitudes of Jefferson their target. Both states were conservative and hated the more democratic views of the Republicans. Connecticut, the land of sturdy people, was even more firmly in the hands of the conservative Federalists than Massachusetts.

In January 1809 the Federalists took further action. T. H. Perkins, Boston's leading merchant, called a meeting to discuss measures to be taken. A petition to the General Court stated that Massachusetts was "not voluntarily to assist in carrying the Embargo Act into execution and all who should do so ought to be considered as enemies of the Constitution of the United States, enemies of the State of Massachusetts and hostile to the liberties of the people." [15] In Congress Josiah Quincy moved that it be printed. His motion lost, 53 to 20. [16] The resolutions of the Massachusetts legislature spoke of England's glorious struggle against the tyranny of France and Napoleon's efforts to dominate the world.

The legislature in Connecticut passed resolutions condemning the embargo, and in February 1809 Governor Jonathan Trumbull called an extra session of the legislature to consider it. In his call he declared the embargo unconstitutional. [17] Republicans in Connecticut and those in Massachusetts, after the legislature in that state adopted resolutions, responded by charging that it was unconstitutional for state legislatures to seek to dictate foreign policy, an area delegated to the national government. In both states the Federalists used the foreign policy question to put down their opponents and prevent them from gaining control of the state government.

Not until the last day of November 1808 did the arch Federalist, Timothy Pickering, senator from Massachusetts, enter the prolonged debate in Congress. An able speaker, well versed in foreign affairs, and one who had read the diplomatic correspondence in search of Jefferson's guilt, he began with a cautious and judicious survey of relations with England. Prepared to be attacked for being pro-British, he sought to disarm his listeners by cataloguing the injuries suffered at the hands of England from 1773 to 1806. He followed this with a factual portrayal of how Napoleon implemented his continental system through a large part of Europe. Finally he came forth with his conspiracy theory. He cited a letter from the French minister of foreign affairs received by Jefferson on December 14 and read into it a request that Jefferson help make the continental system effective by cutting off trade with England, a charge that would not pass close examination. [18] Pickering held that Jefferson was a willing accomplice of Napoleon and asserted that France was the dangerous enemy of the American people. Spurious as this charge was, it was to be repeated hundreds of times and believed.

Josiah Quincy accepted Pickering's interpretation as a fact. He contended:

France, by her edicts, would compress Great Britain by destroying her commerce and cutting off her supplies. All the Continent of Europe, in the hands of Bonaparte, is made subservient to this policy. The embargo law of the United States, in its operation, is a union with this Continental coalition against British commerce, at the very moment most auspicious to its success. Can anything be more in direct subservience to the views of the French Emperor? [19]

The embargo served Napoleon's purpose, for in closing the American market to the British the United States plugged one of the few remaining openings to British exports.

Quincy, an astute and able man, but an irresponsible senator, skewed the evidence to suit his purpose, that is, to undermine the Republicans. In the same speech he attacked his Massachusetts colleague, Ezekial Bacon of Stockbridge, a Republican, who had reported that in his travels throughout the state he had found no hardship resulting from the embargo. Bacon, significantly, was elected for two more terms, evidence of the fact that Massachusetts was far from a one-party state, but Quincy was correct in saying that Bacon had not taken into account conditions in the towns along the seacoast where unemployment and soup kitchens prevailed.

Thanks largely to the embargo the Federalists were able to reverse the Republican political trend. Other sections suffered along with New England but did not turn against the Republicans. The conservative character of New England society helps explain the difference in response to the embargo. However, on the central question of neutral rights the Federalists were guided by deep political biases and by expediency.

Jefferson and Madison, fervent nationalists when it came to foreign affairs, could have no sympathy with the Federalist anglophiles. They equated neutral rights with independence and sovereignty. No American equaled Madison's expertise in the law of nations. As secretary of state he wrote a lengthy pamphlet on the rights of neutrals and displayed a knowledge of earlier authorities and of the rulings of British courts over a period of more than a century. To compromise on neutral rights, in his opinion, was to yield to the illegal aggressions of powerful nations who would see surrender as weakness and push for further concessions. Second, Madison, not without reason, believed that the jealousy of British shipping interests of the rapid growth of the American merchant marine was the real force behind British restrictions.

Federalists saw all things British through friendly eyes and the British restrictions on neutral trade in 1806 and 1807 did not erode this bias. In turn, this helps explain their violent opposition to the embargo. They convinced themselves that Jefferson's embargo added up to senseless self-flagellation. They argued endlessly in congressional debates that were it not for the embargo they would be free to trade with other parts of the world where British restrictions did not apply. The embargo, not the British, cut off their trade connections in India, the East Indies, South America, and the Mediterranean, plus their coastal trade.

Southern planters faced a different situation, as James Burwell of Virginia explained, for their prosperity depended upon freedom to sell their produce in both England and on the continent. If the British closed the markets of the continent, as they did, then the British market became glutted, and prices for tobacco and cotton fell below what it cost southern planters to grow these products. This basic difference between New England and the South further widened the gap between the two on the question of neutral rights.

When the Jefferson administration in January 1809 proposed extremely stringent measures to prevent all evasions of the embargo, at least seventy town meetings in Connecticut and Massachusetts, passed fiery resolutions condemning the proposed laws in which members threatened to nullify the acts by refusing to obey them and to use force to resist enforcement. As these poured into Washington the president, now almost ready to retire, wrote: "I felt the foundation of the government shaken under my feet by the New England townships. . . ."[20]

Well before the Federalists held their meeting in Boston at which they declared they would have no part in the enforcement of the embargo and would censure those who did, thoughtful men had come to realize that the embargo was reducing the country to warring camps. As early as November 1808 John Quincy Adams wrote to Ezekiel Bacon, that he would prefer abandoning the embargo and substituting a nonintercourse law prohibiting commerce with the two belligerents. The latter, he believed, would avoid the risk of war at home.[21] Albert Gallatin was likewise ready for a change, and with his usual care he drew up a ledger listing the pros and cons of giving up the embargo, substituting a nonintercourse law, or arming merchant ships.[22] Members of Congress had also reached the conclusion that the embargo must be abandoned.[23] The embargo had caused a dangerous split at home and, though both Jefferson and Pinkney in London maintained otherwise, there was no prospect of its success as a coercive weapon.[24] It was the domestic opposition that turned the tide. Whatever gains the embargo offered in the way of security for American ships or as a coercive measure, these gains were more than outweighed by its divisive effects.

The evils of the embargo were resolved by the passage of the Nonintercourse Act in February 1809. The law prohibited trade with Great Britain and France. Many agreed that the law was little more than a token gesture whose chief significance lay in the fact that in the eyes of the Republicans it offered an alternative to acknowledging submission to British dictates. The law relieved New England's economic paralysis. This, in addition to hopes inspired by the Erskine agreement of a settlement with Great Britain, elevated Madison to something approaching a statesman in Federalist eyes. The respite was brief, for Canning rejected the Erskine agreement and then poured salt into the wound by appointing Francis J. Jackson, popularly known as Copenhagen Jackson, as minister to the United States.

Jackson's tenure ended after a few months when he accused Madison of acting in bad faith during the Erskine negotiations. The Federalists admired Jackson while the Republicans despised him. He closed his stay with a visit to Boston where he was greeted with adulation and praised for his gracious manners and charm.

The Nonintercourse Act expired on 1 May 1810 and, in turn, Congress enacted Macon Bill Number Two. The new law reopened trade with all the world, but it stipulated that if one of the belligerents canceled its decrees and the other did not, the United States could prohibit trade with the recalcitrant. Napoleon, in the summer of 1810, declared his decrees canceled. The administration was sceptical for

French seizures did not cease, though from time to time France admitted a ship and thereby kept the administration in suspense. Finally, in February 1811, Congress chose to believe that France had met the conditions laid down by the Macon Bill and President Madison cut off all trade with England. By October 1811 President Madison, seeing no indication that England would yield on either impressment or freedom of trade, concluded that war was inevitable.[25] The New England Federalists adhered to their antiadministration and pro-British position. They did not believe that Madison would lead the country into war, preferring to believe he was too weak to take such a drastic step. However, in June 1812 the president called on Congress for a declaration of war. The country had lived in a state of half-war—half-peace for more than four years.

New England, during these years, was largely Federalist, tied to shipping, and out of step with the predominant Jeffersonian party. Its leaders did not lack grounds for challenging the foreign policy of the Jefferson and Madison administrations, but they closed their eyes to the prevailing mood of the times, becoming ever more parochial and so pro-British that they did not see the injuries imposed by the British. Of course, the Federalists were by no means alone in opposing the war.

In 1811 and 1812 the Boston Federalists resorted to ridicule and ignored the fact that both belligerents treated neutrals with disdain. Although Josiah Quincy at one point paused to question whether his party had not gone too far in aligning itself with Great Britain, he did not change course. In the opinion of Samuel Eliot Morison, the Federalists could have changed direction, for "No Federal president could have done more than Madison to obtain the good will of the British government."[26]

New England was almost equally divided between Federalists and Republicans in the years before the outbreak of war in June 1812. In 1810 the section had a population of 1,213,189 and 41 representatives in the national House of Representatives. Massachusetts almost equaled the total population of the rest of the New England states and, likewise, their representatives in Congress. Only in Connecticut did the Federalists maintain uninterrupted control. When the Eleventh Congress met in 1809 all of New Hampshire's five representatives were Federalists, but two years later all of her representatives were Republicans. In the Eleventh Congress Massachusetts had fifteen representatives; seven were Federalists, five were Republicans. In the Twelfth Congress there were seven Federalists from Massachusetts and eight Republicans. Two of the latter were from Maine, one from Stockbridge, one from Haverhill, and one from Scituate, but in Boston the Federalists reigned supreme. Of the four representatives from Vermont, three were Republican. Ten New England representatives voted for war; nineteen voted against it. The votes of Connecticut were unanimously against war. In Congress at large the vote was 92 in favor and 62 opposed. The vote largely followed party lines, though 22 Republicans voted against war.[27]

The War of 1812 promptly became known as "Mr. Madison's war." Given the federal form of government and dependence on state militia, the war had to be carried out with the cooperation of state governments. This left Massachusetts and Connecticut in a position to continue their opposition to Republican foreign policy. Opposition to the war by Massachusetts became possible when Elbridge Gerry, the Republican who held the governor's chair for two terms, in 1810 and 1811, was defeated by Caleb Strong. The state senate remained in the hands of the Republicans, but the lower house was in control of the Federalists.

Caleb Strong—a lawyer of some distinction, former congressman, ardent Calvinist, and a well-known moderate—denied that the war involved national interests. To Strong the war was nothing less than a conspiracy on behalf of French infidelity and Napoleon.

At the same time the war did have support from some prominent citizens. In Plymouth, Mercy Warren, vibrant champion of republicanism and talented writer of poetry, history and plays, identified Strong, the Federalists, and her nephew, Harrison Gray Otis, as blind admirers of English monarchy and as enemies of freedom. To her, the scene in Europe had a different meaning: France represented liberty and England the decaying order of privilege.[28] And her friend, James Winthrop, a Harvard librarian, far to the left of the mainstream republicanism, wrote of the weakness and absurdity of the old establishments in Europe and deeply mourned Napoleon's defeat in Russia.[29] He professed to see biblical prophecy fulfilled in Napoleon's conquests.

Elbridge Gerry, representing the broad stream of Republican opinion, wrote at the close of 1812:

The reelection of Mr. Madison was in my mind an event of vast magnitude; for had it been defeated, G. Britain would have had a well founded prospect of a triumph over our liberty, and with all the Powers of Europe, would have considered her corrupt influence over us, as being paramount to our political Virtue, and to our sense of national honor.[30]

Abigail Adams, too, believed the war justifiable. When Massachusetts defied the national government she wrote:

The conduct of our State Government cannot surely meet the approbation of any real American. I should much rather chuse, that the Name of my Family should be blotted out from the page of History, than appear upon Record as the proposer of such a Resolution as past the Senate in their late Session."[31]

John and Abigail believed the war necessary to protect injured rights and the security of the Republic's independence.

The voices in defense of the war increasingly became voices in the wilderness. Opposition to the war made itself felt in other sections, too, but nowhere did it reach the proportions it did in Massachusetts and Connecticut. One week after war was declared the lower house of the Massachusetts legislature passed a resolution calling on the public to resist the war effort. Governor Strong set aside July 13 as a day of fasting "to ask God to forgive their sins," and to protect the people "from entangling and fatal alliances with those governments which are hostile to the safety and happiness of mankind." On August 6 a Boston town meeting condemned the war; in frenzied anger members denounced the Republicans as enemies of liberty and property and held them responsible for the breakdown of domestic relations and civil institutions.[32] Governor Strong denied Madison's request for militia, as did the other New England governors with the exception of Governor Gilman of New Hampshire. In spite of this powerful political opposition to the war, the five New England states contributed nineteen regiments of volunteers for the national army.

And while the clergy and political leaders denounced the war, others had no hesitation in making full use of the opportunities to profit it offered. Shipowners eagerly embarked on privateering, while merchants profited by high prices received for goods smuggled in. Owners of privateers in Salem and Marblehead netted about $650,000 in sales of goods captured.[33]

The outburst of public feeling against the war revealed underlying fears and frustrations. The traditional society now bordered on a new and very different era. New England, particularly Massachusetts, was in the first stage of modern development. Urbanization on a modest scale was underway. Boston increased in population from 18,038 in 1790 to 43,940 in 1820; Salem from 7,917 to 11,346; Providence from 6,371 to 11,767.

The new factory system made its appearance first in Providence in the 1790s, and then in seaboard Massachusetts. In 1809 the nation's cotton mills employed 4000 workers of whom 3500 were women and children. By 1810 Lynn was producing more than a million pairs of shoes and boots annually.

Religious changes were also underway. Congregationalists were divided between Trinitarians and Unitarians. Dissenting Baptists and Methodists, often led by itinerant ministers with little education, disturbed members of the upper class and, more particularly, the clergy of the state church. Emotional revival meetings, presenting a sharp contrast to the staid and well-ordered services of the state supported Congregational churches, aroused fears for the established church. The Reverend William Bentley of Salem complained regularly about new religious groups who were both ignorant and fanatical. Some of the leaders, Bentley claimed, were unprincipled fellows and guilty of "licentious invectives."[34]

The clergy was prompt in reporting a decline in morals. Bentley noted that there had been many unexpected deliveries of infants even in good families, but the height of scandal came when a woman of ill fame delivered a child in church during the religious service.[35] And in 1813 the defenders of morality in Charlestown founded an association to combat license. In a public announcement the association observed: "Some late occurrences having attracted the attention of many respectable citizens of this town to the state of morals among the children and youth, it was found that extraordinary measures were necessary to guard the rising generation." [36] Even all the trumpets extolling industry, sobriety, and good behavior in pious Boston could not eradicate delinquency. The workhouse in Boston averaged 500 occupants, not all from Boston; half the number were foreigners. Three hundred and seventy-two were there more or less permanently. Some thirty-four women and twenty-three men were held as drunkards. [37] The *Clergyman's Almanac* warned: "The relaxed state of domestic authority and government, at this period of *licentious equality* is one of the most alarming symptoms of the degeneracy and approaching ruin of our country." The editor deplored the loss of "salutary control" by "parents and masters" which they ought to exercise "over those, whom providence has placed in their care and guardianship." [38]

While reports of departure from established norms of behavior were not peculiar to the years immediately before and during the War of 1812, what is noteworthy is the fact that the public believed this to be the case. And more significantly, from the point of view of the student of New England's near revolution against the federal government, during that war the conviction that the decline was due to the triumph of Thomas Jefferson—and with him the triumph of his latitudinarian principles—was widely held. Pious New Englanders saw the war as a first step toward an alliance with Napoleon. They looked upon Jefferson, Madison, and the Republicans as the advance troops of French infidelity.

Jeffersonianism, New Englanders concluded, imperiled the Republic. And not without reason did the New Englanders, with their obscurantist ideas, view their own parochial establishment as in peril. Neither Jefferson nor Madison was a churchgoer; neither proclaimed fast days for prayer and meditation. Both were emancipated from traditional orthodoxy and viewed the world as verging on being freed from the dominance of a nobility of birth and the priesthood. Both genuinely believed in popular control of government. They found the new age exhilarating and the future bright with hope. Their faith in men, once emancipated from the trammels of the past, was unbounded.

The dominant class in New England held to fundamental intellectual and social doctrines of a very different cast. Whereas the frontier turned other sections inward with joyous anticipation of expansion, the people of the Northeast were tied to Europe—more particularly, England—economically, culturally, and psychologically. Expansion and the frontier posed a threat. The new lands drained off their sons and undermined New England agriculture while at the same time robbing them of their rightful place as the dominant group in the federal government. While Jeffersonians could be ebullient over a new era, the New Englanders could not. They, like Edmund Burke, saw society as an organism of slow growth in which the present was closely knit to the past, and the future tied to the age-old institutions of the present. Whereas Jefferson placed his faith in progress, New Englanders indulged in gloomy forebodings and lived in fear of the destructive potential of public passions.

Carl Bridenbaugh called the New England town a way of life; self-help and self-sufficiency were idealized. Yankees ran their towns efficiently, and the towns were close-knit units centered around the family, the church, and the local inn. The inhabitants "rationalized themselves into believing" theirs was the "only way possible and right." Bridenbaugh concluded: "It followed therefore, that they had nothing but contempt for those benighted souls to the south and west who did not order things as they did in New England." Theirs was a local patriotism rather than national pride.[39]

New England Federalists' revolt against the war had deeper roots than mere political partisanship. It was a sincere, warmly felt drive to turn back the clock to the time when, in their nostalgic view, virtue had not been faced with the danger of extinction. The Reverend Samuel Cary, in a fast day sermon delivered at Kings Chapel in Boston, reaffirmed a premise that lay at the base of all conservative New England thought. In a republic, where all the traditional restraints inherent in a monarchical society had been removed, virtue depended on the individual. Virtue, as Cary defined it, was dedication to the welfare of all of society as opposed to self-interest. Patriotism and virtue were synonymous terms. Cary gave his reasons for what he judged to be the decline of patriotism: first, the size of the country—it was so large and heterogenous that people were strangers to one another and had no common interest; second, the want of integrity of government officials who substituted the promotion of special interests for the interests of the whole. Demagogues flattered the public and exploited public envy of the best men in the community. People saw that the rulers used their power "for the most unhallowed purposes." Cary had only one comforting thought: "In this part of the country at least, the wise and good men are in authority, and like the best patriots of Rome are struggling for the commonwealth and for liberty." [40]

Men in politics saw the issue more in political terms. The Massachusetts Federalists addressed the national House of Representatives, charging that the Madison administration manipulated the Republic into the war under the cover of secrecy. In Congress the device of calling for the previous question had been employed to silence the minority. Congress had been called into secret session to decide the question of war and the president's message had revealed nothing that had not been previously known. The Massachusetts address warned that an experimental republic should not embark on a course that could only result in division. Moreover, the address stated, "that if we entered upon this war, we did it as a divided people; not only from sense of inadequacy of our means to success, but from moral and political objections of great weight, and very general influence." [41]

The antiwar hysteria fed not only on the distrust of Jefferson and the fear that the old order was about to be overwhelmed by demagoguery, but upon hatred of the bugbear Napoleon, the embodiment of all that was evil. The specter of an alliance with Napoleon, however unreal, received more attention than any of the several hobgoblins of the antiwar party. An ode written for the 174th anniversary of the Ancient and Honorable Artillery Company of Massachusetts set the tone.

> But the mania of Gallia now palsies the state,
>> And the evils of Europe Columbia await.
> At the nod of her Tyrant Embargo appears,
>> And whelms a whole nation in sorrow and tears.
> Napoleon's fierce soul, can now not control,
>> Ambitious and steady, for prey ever ready,
> Till the world is his Empire—A World Is His Goal. [42]

The passions of war let loose the wildest conjectures, and two groups took on the burden of instilling in the public mind the dangers at hand.

The Washington Benevolent Societies, which had little relationship to the first president and even less to benevolence, may well have been the first of those many superpatriotic societies that have made frequent appearances in American history. It first appeared in Rhode Island in 1810 and was established by the Federalists. Within two years the society had branches in all of the New England states and thousands of members.[43] Each state had its own officers. The Massachusetts society wrote in its platform that it was dedicated to restoration of Washington's principles and measures. Arnold Welles served as president. The six vice presidents included William Sullivan, Josiah Quincy, Captain Henry Purkitt, Colonel Daniel Messenger, Francis J. Oliver, and Major Benjamin Russell. Boston critics, in a satirical attack subtitled *The Book of Knaves*, held that the society covered their designs with the broad mantle of charity "but Charity disavows a disgraceful connection."[44]

Meetings took place throughout the year, but Washington's birthday offered a special opportunity to call back to the fold those who might have strayed into the ways of Republicanism. The dominant theme of these sessions was that the war was contrived by the Jeffersonians in support of Napoleon. The United States and France were now both fighting against the British bastion of liberty. The Republic, proclaimed William Sullivan, had "joined with the Despot, who had struck from being, nations, empires, republics, and the rights of man, and helped him to crush the last hope of European commerce and liberty."[45]

In an oration at Templeton in celebration of the country's independence, Lewis Bigelow told his audience: "It was not enough, that in compliance with requisitions of France, we had given her fifteen million dollars for a territory she never owned, and from which we can derive no possible advantage. . . . Now we were pledged to France to make war on England." Our people, he declared, have been corrupted by French politics.[46]

Richard Dana, representing Cambridge in the state legislature of Massachusetts and one of the most eloquent of the orators, in a meeting at Cambridge, declared that the French Revolution represented the triumph of visionary ideas and that these same ideas had made progress in the United States. Prominent among these ideas was the notion that man's errors and crimes were attributable to despotic government, "that

distinctions in honors, wealth, and rank were alike an insult to understanding, and an unauthorized assumption over the person of man—
that the sceptre should be broken in pieces, the ribbon torn from the
breast, and the very land marks of property trodden down. . . ." The
malignant enthusiasts, said Dana, looked forward to the destruction of
the fabric of society, the end of property, and the end of religion: ". . .
vain of their own mad systems, they heeded not the pain, the poverty,
and heavy sorrows which awaited the human race." He closed on a
nostalgic note, claiming that now that Napoleon had been defeated
"Licentiousness will no longer be called liberty; nor well-balanced liberty, slavery." As a result, Dana declared: "May we return to the good
way in which we walked, and be blessed, as we once were blessed."[47]

In a speech before the Washington Benevolent Societies of four towns
in the neighborhood of Dartmouth College, Josiah Dunham reached
new heights in his indictment of the war. Dunham called on his listeners
to pray for a British victory. "It becomes our duty if our war is unjust,"
he declared, "to pray for the success of our declared enemies." The
British cause he held to be the cause of Americans. He implored: "The
good citizen, consistently with his duty as a Christian, can do no other,
than pray for the triumph of a righteous and just cause, *however that
triumph may affect his country, his friends, his family or HIMSELF.*"[48]

The clergy's opposition to the war had its antecedents in the alarm
that took hold in the 1790s over the infiltration of the ideas of the
Illuminati. With the outbreak of war in 1812 the clergy in the Congregational church launched a crusade. The Reverend Elijah Parish,
repeating a frequent theme, called on his audience:

Rise in the majesty of your unconquerable strength, break those chains
under which you have sullenly murmured, during the long, long reign of
democracy; batter down those iron walls, which have incarcerated your
souls and bodies so long, and once more breathe that free, commercial air of
New England, which your fathers always enjoyed.[49]

A large portion of the clergy looked upon both Napoleon and Jefferson as enemies of the Republic. In a sermon preached at Brookfield, the
Reverend Thomas Snell did not name Jefferson directly but the implica-
tion was clear. He could not doubt "that some invisible hand, with

consumate art, has been moving the whole of government to bring us where we are." Snell feared "the loss of God's favor, by making cause with the atheistic and despotic power of Europe, against the foe she is trying to crush." Snell closed his sermon with a reference to France— "Her moral and religious character augurs no good to her or to her allies. . . . Can it be safe to league ourselves with that anti-Christian power, the volume of whose history is written with lamentation, and mourning, and woe!" [50] The sermons usually began with the warning that God was now punishing the people for their sins, more often Sabbath breaking and the election of deists. After a recital of past wrongs of the government, the preacher would warn that usually when two countries were fighting a third they soon became allies.

The Congregational minister in Medford on the Sunday after the declaration of war could find no cause for going to war and therefore concluded that it could be accounted for "on no other principles, but the imperceptible influence which the author of all evil, the spirit that worketh in the children of disobedience, had been permitted to exert in the hearts of the dark minded, cool, deliberately wicked authors." Those who had declared war, he concluded, were obviously men of hardened hearts, seared consciences, and reprobate minds. [51]

The decline of morals furnished a consistent theme for the many sermons delivered in opposition to the war. The minister in Colerain in western Massachusetts listed the major sins of the day. These included the wide prevalence of drunkenness, the gross violation of the marriage covenant, and the making of common cause with the enemies of God and religion overseas. The last of these led him to observe: "It can neither be denied, disguised, or concealed that we are in danger of an entanglement at least, if not making common cause with the conqueror, or rather the tyrant and oppressor of continental Europe." He viewed Napoleon as antichrist and warned that if an alliance should take place, it would have fateful consequences "to our prosperity and happiness, and even to our national existence and independence." [52]

The clergy had a strong voice. They spoke with divine authority. The clergy were not only ministers of the state church; in the public eye they were as one with the civil authorities. On occasion both appeared on the same platform. The defeat of Napoleon in Russia was celebrated everywhere. A special service was held in Boston in "Honor of the Russian Achievements over Their French Invaders." The program included the singing of the Hallelujah chorus, an opening sketch of how France had dictated American foreign policy, and a prayer by the Reverend William Ellery Channing. Harrison Gray Otis gave the main address. The United States, too, said Otis, had almost been a victim of Napoleon's intrigues. Otis repeated the familiar theme: "The history of our government, for several years, has exhibited a coincidence in the measures, and a conformity to the plans of Napoleon, too plain to be mistaken." [53]

The clergy did meet opposition. William Plumer of New Hampshire warned that they were tools of a political faction and that an alliance of the clergy and the Federalists would produce a dangerous union. He declared: "You have used every means in your power to prevent enlistments in the army and subscriptions to loan money to support it—and many of you, without evidence, have with unblushing effrontery declared, that the Administration of our country was governed by foreign influence. . . ." [54] The Congregational minister in Dracutt on Cape Cod, a Republican stronghold, held his fellow clergy guilty of using trumped up charges against the administration. [55] The Congregational minister in Fitchburg defended the war and held that Great Britain had left no choice other than war. [56] There were a few others who defended government policy but they were a small minority.

A unique occurrence took place in Harvard, Massachusetts. When the Reverend Stephen Bemis preached against the war, the Jeffersonians, a minority of the congregation, took issue, appealed to the town meeting, and he was dismissed. [57]

Crusty John Adams summed up the situation in a letter to his friend, Dr. Benjamin Rush:

There is an alliance between our Essex Junto and our New England theologians—Unitarians and Athanosians, Hopkintonians and Freewillers and all. *Bos, fur, sus, atque sacerdos,* (ox, thief, pig, and priest) with a few exceptions. . . .

The object of all this spiritual and temporal bluster is to get Madison out. But who to get in? . . . I am less anxious on this point because I know that, bring in who they will, he cannot essentially or materially depart from Madison's present system. . . .

I know not whether you have read the Address to the People of the State by our House of Representatives, or that of the minority in Congress to the People of the Union. I wish my eyes would suffer me to write commentaries on these two studied compositions. . . . I am really grieved; I am ashamed, I am confounded to read such sophistry, such insincerity, such want of candor or want of information in such bodies of American citizens.[58]

Federalist opposition to the war stemmed from a variety of sources. Ever since the Jay Treaty and Jefferson's election in 1800, Federalists had consistently opposed the Republicans on all measures, domestic and foreign. They were less than responsible in their party zeal and permitted reason to give way to rancor. Their distrust and suspicion of Jefferson and his party pushed constructive criticism and sober analysis offstage. Federalists permitted themselves to become apologists for England at a time when the United States suffered serious grievances at British hands. Thereby they helped convince the British that disunity in the Republic would prevent Americans from taking any firm action.[59]

## 5

# A New Era and a New Englander
# as Secretary of State

A Massachusetts newspaper editor coined the phrase "Era of Good Feeling" that has since served as a label for the years immediately after the War of 1812. The editor of the *Boston Patriot and Daily Chronicle* joyfully acclaimed the change that took place and announced that "the sons of New England are now as ardently alive to our present and future greatness as their brethren of the South and West." He wrote

There was a time, perhaps, when a bright vision of our national glories was in some degree hidden by the mists of party prejudice and foreign partiality but the cloud has cleared away, and the Genius of the Western world displays himself at present in all his beauty.

The editor correctly estimated the character of the postwar era, though good feeling and unity were not universal. The now wholly dominant Republican party served as a facade, temporarily obscuring from view the factionalism within its ranks. The maneuvering and manipulation that had been motivated by personal ambitions in the Monroe administration included undercutting the president. What John Quincy Adams saw taking place led him to write in disgust: "This Government is, indeed, assuming daily more and more a character of a cabal, and preparation, not for the next Presidential election, but for the one after—that is, working and counterworking, with many of the worst features of elective monarchies." [1]

If "Era of Good Feeling" was a misnomer, nevertheless, the rivalry between sections moderated and President Monroe's dedication to promoting the healing process quieted angry sectional passions. Shortly after his inauguration, Monroe made an extensive tour of New England. The warmth of the reception he received went far beyond what respect for his office demanded. The president's friendly gesture helped open the door to New England's taking its place once again as a responsible member of the Union.

The end of the War of 1812 marked a major turning point. Since 1789—and particularly since 1806—the nation at large had lived in the shadow of the wars in Europe and suffered from divisive domestic politics and the factionalism that was rooted in the frustrations of dealing with the belligerents. True, the Treaty of Ghent that ended hostilities did not resolve American grievances concerning neutral rights, but the return of peace eliminated them from practical and immediate concern. The nation was free to actualize the dreams nourished by its incomparable potential in land, resources, navigable rivers and seaports. Nowhere did the bright new prospects of peace receive more acclaim than in New England.

However, in Congress New England faced distrust and bitterness stemming from her failure to support the war. On the national scene, Federalists of the extreme Brahmin wing suffered disrepute and were identified with the Hartford Convention. Federalists continued to be elected in the years immediately following the war but faced total eclipse after 1824. The section's representatives in Congress were no longer the vocal and belligerent spokesmen they had been prior to 1812. Even the great orator, Senator Harrison Gray Otis, rarely spoke. When representatives of the section did have proposals to make or faced measures not to their liking, they often preferred to have allies from New York or Pennsylvania do the speaking. The representatives immediately after the war were not formidable figures. Harrison Gray Otis, though able, suffered from the stigma of having been a leader in the Hartford Convention. Daniel Webster had yet to make his name. Edward Everett and Robert C. Winthrop were not yet on the scene.

Economically the section was in a state of flux. Shipping no longer flourished as it had, and manufactures had yet to receive the support of a protective tariff. However, New England did take a lively interest in trade with the British West Indies, the problems of piracy, and the Florida question.

A new era beckoned on the horizon. New England served as the forerunner of modernization, setting the pace in industry, modern banking, and improved means of communication. Other states—New York, Pennsylvania, and Ohio—moved in the same direction, but the importance of agriculture in those states and sharp political divisions compromised their Whiggery. New England, with a declining commerce and an agriculture that gave no promise of a bright future, was more ready to commit herself to a new age.

Rapid industrial development between the War of 1812 and the Civil War replaced the old order of agriculture and commerce. The prewar industries—the cotton mills in Rhode Island, the shipbuilding industry along the coast, and the shoe industry in Massachusetts—suffered a severe decline during the War of 1812, but after hostilities, owing largely to the invention of the power loom and other improvements in spinning and weaving, farsighted New Englanders envisioned a future of factories, greatly expanded production, improved transportation, urban growth, and, in addition, a host of new institutions ministering to the handicapped and a universal system of public education. Men dreamed of a more productive, enlightened, and comfortable society. The imagination of young New Englanders—scholars such as Edward Everett and business entrepreneurs such as Abbott Lawrence—looked to a bright future, their vision as yet undimmed by the social dislocations and the social cost of the transition. How could rational men deny the benefits to be derived, the riches to be gained, the excitement of speedy transportation?

The vision gave New Englanders confidence in the future at a time when outward signs suggested that their role in the political and economic life of the nation was diminishing. In 1790 the six states of the Northeast, with a population of 1,009,522, contained approximately more than one-fourth of the country's population; by 1820 their population of 1,660,071 constituted only one-sixth of the total. By 1850 New England had grown in numbers to 2,728,116, but the country's total population had reached 23,191,876. Between 1790 and 1850 New England's proportion of representatives in Congress dwindled as the following figures indicated: in 1790 she had 21 representatives in the House of Representatives out of a total membership of 88; in 1816, 37 out of a total of 159; and in 1850, 31 out of a total of 232. In 1816 New England had no representatives on the House Committee on Foreign

Affairs. In 1818 David Daggett, of Connecticut, served on the Senate committee. By the 1830s and 1840s New England had gained a powerful voice in foreign affairs. She provided a number of forceful orators in Congress: Edward Everett, scholar and great orator; John Davis, of Worcester, one of the foremost lawyers of his day and spokesman for industrial interests; Isaac Bates, an extremely able speaker; Peleg Sprague, of Maine, distinguished legal scholar; and, of course, Daniel Webster.

The exodus of New England's sons to the fertile lands of the West and the ever present prospect of declining influence caused concern, but the rapid economic development of the northeastern section of the country counterbalanced these fears. New Englanders could no longer threaten secession, for they recognized that their economic well-being was tied to the Union.

The national capital provided an attractive social life, but the rudeness and roughness of some gave cause for dismay. In 1832 Sam Houston beat a fellow member of Congress with a cane and was censured by the House. In December of that year Duff Green and James Blair, both of South Carolina, fought in the House and Green was severely injured. A few weeks later Blair pulled out a pistol in a theater and fired at an actress. Everett noted in his diary that Blair appeared in Congress the next day acting as if nothing had happened. Edward Everett also detested the crudity of political bargaining and the catering to the passions of the multitude that occurred.

A combination of fortuitous circumstances saved New England from becoming a backwater area. Because New England's agriculture offered little promise of a bright future the roots to the rural past held less firmly. As the once prosperous shipping trade declined, shipping interests transferred their capital into industry. At the same time, New Englanders' experience in the business operations of shipping, merchandizing, shipbuilding, and smaller home industries provided an orientation toward private enterprise. Moreover, the region was not torn by internal dissension. A highly homogeneous population, roughly 80 percent of whom were of English origin, and not only Protestant but Congregational, made for a strong sense of identity. In Massachusetts, the central committee of the Whig party, made up of a handful of upper-class Bostonians, controlled all nominations for Congress and made the Massachusetts legislature into its handmaiden. New corporations readily received generous privileges. To hasten change the legislature provided state funds for the building of the first railroad to Worcester and, later, to the Berkshires and to Albany.

The opening of the Boston Manufacturing Company in Waltham in 1815 initiated a drive that soon made the waterfalls and smokestacks of the many textile mills as much a part of the landscape as the older white church steeples. Capital from Boston turned quiet rural hamlets into the bustling mill towns of Lowell and Lawrence in Massachusetts, of Dover and Somersworth in New Hampshire, of the towns along the lower Maine coast from Portland to Portsmouth. The Blackstone River Valley between Worcester and Providence soon became an almost continual lane of textile company towns. By the end of 1834 the Appleton Company, the Lowell Company, and the Suffolk, Tremont, and Lawrence companies were opening nineteen cotton mills in Lowell alone with 110,000 spindles and 4,000 looms. Victor Clark, in his monumental history of manufacturing, termed the 1830s "the most remarkable decade of progress, in a single place and industry, as yet achieved in our manufacturing history."[2]

New England became a citadel of business enterprise. Production and profits occurred in tandem with new intellectual currents, changes in communication, and social changes. Scholars who studied in Europe, men of distinction such as George Ticknor, Edward Everett, George Bancroft, and William Prescott, opened a broader world with new ideas that challenged traditional religion, broadened the popular concept of democracy, and introduced more scientific concepts of the origin of the universe that paralleled the innovation of economic life. To label the intellectual movement a new renaissance is to overstate the case, though the participants found exhilaration in challenging older ways. James Truslow Adams helped deflate popularly held notions of the quality of the philosophical and literary manifestations, stating that the so-called New England renaissance did not mark "America's maturity nor even its coming of age, but its adolescence—the sudden discovery of romance, of culture, of altruism, of optimism, of self-reliance, and the sense of one's own individuality."[3]

The new intellectual and social ideas, without denigrating their merit, did not constitute the main course of historical development of New England. They were largely eddies in the mainstream that swirled about them, responses, in part, to a wider world of learning and likewise to the dislocations accompanying rapid modernization. The fact remains, as historian, Carl Russell Fish, stated:

The youth growing up between 1800 and 1830 were indeed exhilarated by the breaking of barriers to thought and the wide new world of speculation; but the discipline of Calvinism was left, with its social order and habits of orthodoxy. However wild the views accepted, the habits of the newly liberated stood in this generation comparatively unchanged, and as this movement centered in the intellectual middle class, these were the habits of "plain living and high thinking."[4]

This new New England retained much of the heritage of an independent spirit, and this was best embodied in John Quincy Adams. Measured in terms of influence on national politics no New Englander rivaled John Quincy Adams, secretary of state from 1817 to 1825 and then president. Adams was more than an implementer of policy; he had a farseeing eye that enabled him to formulate policy in long-range terms. The harassment of day-to-day problems of great magnitude did not cause him to lose his composure.

Adams' appointment as secretary of state by President Monroe came as a surprise. The post was generally viewed as the stepping-stone to the presidency, and there were prominent figures such as William Crawford, Henry Clay, and John C. Calhoun waiting for Monroe's blessing. Monroe chose to avoid the trap. John Quincy Adams at the time was not identified as a presidential aspirant. Monroe was an advocate of the importance of healing breeches between sections. Adams, a New Englander and a moderate Federalist who had supported the war, would give his administration a needed national dimension. Equally important, Monroe, as secretary of state, had read Adams' many reports from Europe where Adams had served at several posts. Here was an experienced and highly qualified man for the position in Monroe's cabinet. He chose wisely. Adams was to have a distinguished career as secretary of state. To New Englanders his appointment offered joy and an occasion for a glorious dinner attended by its most prominent and wealthiest leaders.

Monroe and Adams worked together in harmony. The president respected Adams and gave him considerable freedom to conduct foreign affairs, but kept his own hand on the throttle, checking and making suggestions on all important actions taken. Adams, in turn, deferred to the president, saw him more frequently than did any other cabinet member, and loyally gave first priority to national interests and the success of the administration. However, on major policy Adams led the way, and Monroe usually limited his observations on drafts of dispatches to minor matters. At the same time Adams had to live with the fact that the president brought all important foreign policy questions before the cabinet to decide, and there Adams had to do battle with such powerful figures as John C. Calhoun and William Crawford. Adams, in the words of his finest biographer, Samuel Flagg Bemis, did not dominate the president.[5] However, his ability made him a power in his own right.

Adams brought an iron will, skill, and good judgment to the office, along with a dour personality. A fellow New Englander observed after Adams became president:

This same President of ours is a man that I can never court, nor be on very familiar terms with. There is a cold, repulsive atmosphere about him that is too chilling for my respiration, and I shall certainly keep at a distance from its influence. . . . He wants heart and all those qualities which attract and attach people strongly to him. An interested support he will get from many, but a warm and hearty one from none.[6]

Leverett Saltonstall, after attending a reception in honor of Adams prior to his inauguration as president, wrote to his wife: "You can hardly conceive the strange appearance he makes—so cold—so unbending. . . ." Saltonstall thought it "a miracle that he has been chosen President of the U. States." He asked, "Is it an invisible proof of his eminent merit, or the result of a singular concurrence of fortunate circumstances?"[7]

Abigail, John Quincy Adams' mother, worried about her son's inability to display a spirit of friendly cordiality, and though Adams worried about it, too, he did not change. Others, among them P. C.

Brooks, Everett's wealthy father-in-law, found him fiercely independent and, once convinced, stubborn to the point of bullishness. Neither party nor sectional loyalty could restrain him which made New England leaders consider him unreliable in politics. To Adams, seemingly all the world was foreboding, including both men and nations. He relentlessly disciplined himself and hoped others would practice the same self-discipline. He read avidly, especially Cicero and Tacitus. While he did enjoy the theater, he confided to his diary that he was happiest at work.

Adams exhibited a nationalism that exceeded that of any of his contemporaries. He was willing to bend all domestic policies in the interest of developing a strong nation. Therefore, while he favored a protective tariff, he would also compromise to conciliate its opponents. He favored a strong central government and used its power to promote the interests of diverse groups but did not allow the groups to become his masters. The New England Brahmins won his support but not his allegiance. His attitude toward foreign affairs was similar. There were times to compromise and times to be firm. He prized national honor, not of the flag-waving variety, but with a firmness that won respect.

John Quincy Adams defies easy categorization. He ardently promoted Whig principles, such as the protective tariff, internal improvements, and a national bank, but his commitment to the party did not keep him from attacking its leaders or acting in ways that challenged party stands. He was a regular churchgoer but aligned with no denomination—a man who referred to God as a kind of first cause but was utterly indifferent to theological questions. Religion was important to the extent that it affected the conduct of men. If a deist could be pious, Adams was just that. His integrity was not to be challenged. Sensitive to moral issues, he could, at the same time, subordinate moral considerations to considerations of statesmanship. He lived amid an endless cycle of contemporary political problems. Finally, he was a nationalist more than a New Englander, a man who rose above sectional interests.

Adams could be harsh in his judgments of men. At the time of Alexander Hamilton's death a memorial service was held at Chapel Church in Boston. Adams refused to attend and explained to his wife, "Neither the manner of his death nor his base treatment of more than one of my connections would permit me to join in any outward demonstration of regret which I could not feel at heart."[8] More than once his frankness overruled his sense of propriety. He once described Edward Everett as a man who "has largely contributed to raise the standard of this class of composition [oratory] and his eloquence has been the basement story of his political fortune—as yet, one of the most brilliant ever made in this Union."[9] Later he wrote, quite unfairly, that Everett's lack of firm devotion to moral principle made him unfit for political life when the pressures were strong. In 1835, when he believed Everett had made a deal to get himself nominated for governor, Adams said, [Everett] "is a double hearted man if there is one on the face of this earth."[10] He could never accept Webster as anything more than a self-seeking opportunist and on one occasion took him severely to task for misrepresentation. In 1841 he wrote concerning Webster: "Such is human nature, in the gigantic intellect, the envious temper, the ravenous ambition, and the rotten heart of Daniel Webster."[11]

On taking office as secretary of state in September 1817 Adams confronted pressing problems in foreign affairs. The Commercial Convention of 1815 with England was scheduled to expire in 1819, leaving the commercial interests of the country in a distressing state of limbo. In addition, the question of sovereignty over Oregon, the dispute over the fisheries (which had a high priority with Adams), and the issue of trade with the British West Indies confronted him. Equally pressing and offering little hope of easy solution were the questions of piracy, of the emerging republics of South America, and the issue of Seminole warfare in the Spanish Floridas.

Adams' first task was to open negotiations with England. Of the several difficulties he faced, two pressed for prompt settlement. The fishermen in New England encountered peremptory orders from British officials and naval officers who, on occasion, seized American fishing vessels. The British maritime provinces, having profited greatly in the absence of the Americans during the war, were of no mind to permit the restoration of the rights enjoyed by Americans under the provisions of the Treaty of Paris of 1783. To Adams, on the other hand, fishing rights were the equivalent of the right to American political independence. He needed no prodding to rise to their defense.

To Secretary of State John Quincy Adams, British prohibitions against American ships that traded with the British West Indies constituted an evil monopoly. Complete freedom of trade ranked first among Adams' prescriptions for a just and peaceful world, and he felt deeply about British restrictions. The issue was already a matter of heated concern when he became secretary of state, and Congress was about to adopt either countervailing duties on British ships engaged in the trade or go even further and prohibit those ships from entering American ports.

Cyrus King, of Maine, pushed the fat toward the fire in January 1817 during a debate on a new navigation bill in the House of Representatives. The bill included a provision that would prohibit entry of English ships going to or coming from the West Indies. King called it a bill "to retaliate upon foreign nations some of their injurious impositions." King complained about England: "All our ports are open to her; one-third of her ports are closed against us." And, King contended, "it is principally by this colonial trade of Great Britain, the decided advantage which that affords, which enables her almost to engross the direct trade between this country and Great Britain—the advantage of double voyages." [12] George Bradbury of Maine termed the bill the most important to come before Congress "in this session" and emphasized that his constituents had a deep stake in the outcome. [13] The final bill came before the Senate in April 1818, and Rufus King, now of New York but previously a resident of Massachusetts, the distinguished brother of Cyrus King, led the fight. Fearful of losing their export market in the British West Indies where their annual sales were valued at more than $6 million, southerners originally opposed the bill. However, the bill finally passed the Senate by a vote of 32 to 1. Thus, Congress acted before negotiations began.

Adams, after less than two months in office, wrote to Richard Rush, the new American minister in London, informing him that the United States sought a new commercial treaty and wished to reach a settlement on the question of colonial trade. By May 1818 the situation was altered in order to hasten negotiations. The British foreign minister, Lord Castlereagh, had given indications that he favored relaxation of trade restrictions. Adams now informed Rush that he would be joined by the

highly experienced Albert Gallatin, minister to France, in the negotiations which began at Castlereagh's country estate on August 22.

The question of fishing rights, Rush reported to Secretary of State
Adams, proved the most troublesome.[14] The British contended that
the recent war had wiped out fishing rights. Gallatin and Rush, acting
in harmony with Adams' instructions, maintained the war no more
canceled the fishing rights in the peace treaty of 1783 than it canceled
American independence. Rush felt that they were not wholly successful,
but from the point of view of the maritime provinces this was not so.
The convention, negotiated by Rush and Gallatin in 1818, gave American fishermen the "liberty" of fishing on the southern shore of Newfoundland and off certain specified islands. It also granted the Americans
the right to dry and cure fish on yet unsettled shores of Newfoundland.[15]

Negotiations led to no resolution of the question of trade with the
West Indies. Adams, though not readily given to compromise, nevertheless agreed that failure to settle this question would not stand in the
way of a treaty.[16] He recognized that the British were rigid on this
question.

The American negotiators maintained a firm posture on the trade
question. Gallatin and Rush insisted that a treaty should be reciprocal,
that both parties should share equally in the advantages. This was,
likewise, a point of central importance to Adams. It was a matter of both
honor and principle. When the British proposed that trade might be
carried in American vessels if this trade were restricted to a list of
enumerated articles, Rush responded that British trade with the United
States was not so restricted. Moreover, held Rush, while the United
States was to be treated as one country, the British insisted on one rule
for the home country and another for her colonies. Anything less than
opening the islands, Rush maintained, was less than reciprocal.[17]
Adams, after a meticulous analysis of the British proposals, held that, if
approved, they would place an even greater percentage of the carrying
trade in British bottoms.[18]

Other points in the negotiation were readily settled. The British
agreed to renew the Commercial Convention of 1815 during the earliest
days of the negotiations. On the Oregon question, both sides dutifully
recited their respective claims based on discovery and exploration and

then promptly agreed to joint occupancy. The question of the Maine boundary was referred to the king of the Netherlands to resolve.

Adams never intended that Gallatin and Rush should include the impressment question. His experience as minister to Great Britain had convinced him that no satisfactory settlement could be reached. However, Lord Castlereagh raised the question, and a lengthy exchange of views took place in the early days of the negotiations. Rush, prior to the negotiations, suggested the possibility of a proposal whereby both nations would outlaw the employment of the seamen of the other. Castlereagh, however, laid down two conditions—that the treaty should be binding for a limited period of time and subject to termination after three months' notification, and that a British officer boarding an American vessel should have the authority to call for a list of the crew and should likewise be free, if he saw someone he suspected of being an Englishman, to make a record of the fact and refer it to his government who would pursue the matter. When the British proposal reached Washington, Adams and Calhoun opposed it. Monroe leaned toward accepting the first proposal but flatly rejected the second condition on the grounds that it would only give rise to public resentment. Adams opposed both conditions, contending that an agreement not to employ Britishers on American ships would cripple the American merchant marine.[19]

Adams, in spite of the failure to open the West Indies to American ships, wholly approved of the resolutions negotiated by Gallatin and Rush. Monroe raised objections to the renewal of the Convention of 1815, and Rufus King, in the Senate, wanted something in the way of freedom for American ships in the West Indies, but both gave their approval. It was now December 1818, and affairs with Spain had so absorbed the attention of the country that the new convention with England aroused little discussion and general approval. Congress readily approved it.

New England joined other sections in the excitement surrounding Spanish affairs, the most important development of the postwar years. The issue at stake, the future of the Floridas, had occupied public attention since 1803. The Jefferson administration claimed that the

Louisiana purchase included the territory east of the Mississippi river as far as the Perdido River. Then, in 1810, American settlers overthrew Spanish control in West Florida. During the War of 1812 British forces penetrated the Floridas, but an energetic campaign led by Andrew Jackson, culminating in his victory at New Orleans, ousted the British. Spain's hold over the Floridas after the war was precarious. She was in no position to maintain order in Florida, to promote economic development in the region, or to contest American designs.

Spain's power in Florida posed no threat, but the Monroe administration had to be concerned about possible intervention in South America by the postwar Quintuple Alliance in Europe led by Metternich. The alliance had promptly dedicated itself to keeping the peace in Europe. To do so, Metternich and the monarchies on the continent aimed to suppress revolution wherever it raised its head. Would the alliance suppress the revolutions in South America? What course would England pursue? Might Spain, if pushed by the United States, declare war and win support from other powers? These were questions facing the president.

At the same time Monroe and Adams encountered embarrassing developments in the Caribbean. Piracy raged there, endangering ships of all nations, and these pirate ships, flying the flags of the rebel governments in South America, were built in the ports of the northeastern United States. Many of the owners and captains were Americans, largely from Baltimore, and they enjoyed immunity from the law, thanks to influential political personalities.[20] Portuguese, Spanish, and French ships fell victim to piratical attack.

The Spanish minister, Don Luis de Onís, protested repeatedly against the failure of the United States to suppress piracy. Shortly after Adams took office Onís brought to his attention the fact that a pirate ship flying the American flag and manned by Americans had seized a Spanish ship. He called for "the most decisive measures for putting an end to the abuses practiced in the ports of the Union, by arming privateers, to cruise against the Spanish trade, thus prostituting the Flag of the United States by these predatory acts, . . . ."[21] Adams, already well aware that Americans were engaged in piracy and embarrassed, found himself unable to take action. He was similarly embarrassed by the fact that Americans were trading in arms with the republics in revolt in violation of American neutrality.

The readiness of the American public to equate the revolutions in South America with their own revolution posed another problem. The public had little awareness of the complex rivalries that existed among the rebellious states. Henry Clay made himself the leader of the popular cause, and he gave it a strength that threatened to force the hand of the administration into prematurely granting the rebels recognition, a move that could cause the allies to intervene and would certainly arouse even more hostility in Spain.

Adding complexity, the representative of Buenos Aires at one point informed Adams that his government planned to seize East Florida. His country would benefit by possessing a port in the Caribbean, and it would serve as a great annoyance to Spain.[22] Seizure of Amelia Island on the St. Mary's river, the boundary between East Florida and Georgia, by a band led by the Scotsman, Gregor MacGregor, posed additional difficulties. Ships captured by the pirates were hauled into Amelia Island. At the same time the island served shippers seeking to avoid American customs duties. MacGregor, too, as Adams soon learned, had prepared a project to take East Florida.

Adams took the lead in one of his first cabinet meetings by calling for an expedition to oust the marauders from Amelia Island. By 14 November 1818, orders were ready, and Amelia Island was taken by General Edmund Gaines. The Spanish minister, Don Luis de Onís, promptly entered a vigorous remonstrance. Adams replied that it was to the benefit of Spain to have the United States occupy it. After lengthy cabinet discussions, in which Adams contended in favor of holding the island, it was decided to do so. Onís continued to call for an explanation. Adams put him off by stating that the United States could only withdraw if Spain was prepared to move troops to the island at once.

Onís at the same time pressed Adams on the Florida question. Spain would concede East Florida, but in return she demanded that the western boundary of the Louisiana Purchase be set close to the Mississippi river. Onís was anxious to settle the question but, at the same time, determined to obtain the best bargain possible. Adams dismissed his proposals as not worthy of discussion and in an interview in March, advised Onís that the president saw no prospect "that the two parties would ever come to an understanding with each other." [23]

In the preceding months two happenings gave Adams new hope. In late January England offered to mediate between Spain and her colonies but did so with accompanying assurance from Charles Bagot, the British minister in the United States, that Castlereagh was determined to preserve peace and that, if discussions took place, Great Britain would take a liberal position toward the Spanish provinces in South America and favor opening their ports to all nations. The message relieved the administration of concern over a possible unfriendly interposition and, given British dominance of the seas, made it unlikely that allied powers would come to the aid of Spain.

Second, General Andrew Jackson had conducted a whirlwind campaign in Florida. Jackson was appointed in December. The impatient and peppery general first wrote to Monroe proposing that he take East Florida and promised he could do so in sixty days. He did. He took over two Spanish garrisons, Saint Marks and Pensacola and, in the course of his march, took as prisoner two British subjects, Robert C. Ambrister and Alexander Arbuthnot. After hurried military trials, he executed both men on the grounds that they were guilty of promoting the attacks on American settlers by the Seminole Indians. Jackson's military adventure had an immediate impact on negotiations with Spain and, at the same time, provoked controversy in the United States.

The reports of Jackson's adventure in Florida did not reach the administration until the middle of May. On the eighteenth Monroe brought the matter before the cabinet. "This, and other events in this Indian war, makes many difficulties for the administration," Adams noted. Monroe, very inconveniently from Adams' point of view, after a few days left for his home in Virginia, leaving Adams to deal with the inevitable inquiries from Bagot and Onís. The latter's note was so full of invective that Adams urged Hyde De Neuville, the French minister, and a friend of Onís, to advise him to take it back. Members of the cabinet, particularly Calhoun, were highly critical of what Jackson had done, and Crawford and Wirt sided with him.

Adams may well have disliked what Jackson had done, but immediate and practical considerations determined his course. To attack the popular general would raise a storm of criticism of the president; it would also be humiliating to publicly acknowledge error. There was also the danger that the president would be charged with making war without the authorization of Congress. In addition to these worries Adams was mindful that Spain might declare war. At first Adams, wisely, did not take a strong lead in defending Jackson before the cabinet, for firm opinions prevailed and his arguments were not likely to make much impression at the moment.[24]

By July 17 he was fully prepared to defend Jackson, contending that all his measures had been defensive. The next day a draft of the note he proposed to send was rejected by the cabinet. He returned to the fray the following day, explaining that while Jackson had exceeded his instructions, he was justified. Jackson's measures, he explained, were to be judged in terms of Jackson's intentions: the general entertained no hostility to Spain; faced with the hostility of Spanish officers, he had acted out of self-defense. Again, on the third day, he met with rebuff. Monroe and the other cabinet members continued to insist on disavowing Jackson. Monroe's and Adams' colleagues in the cabinet focused on the domestic side of the question. Adams gave attention to the domestic aspect, but he focused on relations with Spain. He saw clearly that Jackson's military campaign enhanced the chances of a settlement with Spain.

On July 23, following the serious debates in the cabinet, Adams sent Onís a reply to his protestations.[25] The letter corresponded with Monroe's original sketch but included a strong justification of Jackson.[26] Adams did recede from his initial recommendation that the United States should continue to hold St. Marks and Pensacola. The letter stated that both would be restored to Spain as soon as adequate Spanish forces arrived to assure order. This accorded with Monroe's ideas. Monroe held that only then could Spain maintain her honor and continue negotiations. Adams' letter acknowledged that Jackson had not been instructed to take St. Marks or Pensacola, thereby clearing Monroe of having gone to war without congressional approval. He held that, in light of what Jackson learned about the encouragement the Spanish commanding officers had given to the Seminoles in their attacks on white settlers, Jackson was wholly justified in going beyond his instructions.

Adams also faced inquiries from Sir Charles Bagot, the British minister, concerning Jackson's execution of Ambrister and Arbuthnot. The English public, Rush informed Monroe, was outraged. Adams held that the two Britishers were guilty of working with the Indians and of supporting the Seminole attacks on the white settlers. To support this judgment he gave to Bagot a bundle of documents containing incriminating evidence. The British government raised no further questions.

The debate at home and in Congress was not over. A Senate committee delivered a stinging report indicting both Jackson and Gaines for violating the Constitution, for taking brutal and inhumane action against the Indians when such action was wholly unjustifiable, and for arrogating to themselves powers reserved to the civilian branch of the government.[27] The Senate did not act on the report. A committee of the House of Representatives was appointed to study Jackson's activities in Florida. A majority report of the committee denounced Jackson for his execution of Arbuthnot and Ambrister. After lengthy debates in February 1819, the House, by large majorities, disapproved of the report of the committee.[28] Thirteen of New England's thirty-three representatives voted with the minority.[29]

New England was not united on the question of Jackson, but newspaper comment and private correspondence shows that the position taken by Adams had strong support. As early as January 1818, a letter to the Boston *Patriot and Advertizer* expressed impatience over Spanish procrastination and favored action. The same paper fully approved of the seizure of Amelia Island. In June the editor defended the execution of Arbuthnot and Ambrister, and on August 3 he praised Jackson's actions in Florida. The conservative *Columbian Centinel* did not lavish fulsome praise on the administration or Jackson but gave support to the manner in which the administration handled the Spanish question and thought the United States was entitled to the Floridas. Commenting on Jackson, the editor, quoting Shakespeare, observed: "To do a *great right* do a *little wrong*." Many Bostonians, noted William Eustis, former member of

Congress and secretary of war under Madison, had claims against Spain, but in spite of this, most people in Massachusetts did not want war with Spain.[30]

Adams, as secretary of state, kept his eye on obtaining a favorable settlement with Spain and quickly perceived that Jackson's campaign would put an end to Spain's procrastination. Others, led by Clay, were rocking his boat by crusading for what he considered a premature recognition of the South American republics. Adams had serious reservations about those republics, and he also had no wish to offend Spain unnecessarily until a treaty had been completed.

During the same days in July, while the cabinet debated the Jackson question, Adams was negotiating with Onís. In Madrid George Erving had fared no better in his negotiations than Adams. In July 1817, José Pizarro, Spain's foreign minister, had proposed that Spain cede the Floridas and, in turn, the United States set its western boundary on the west bank of the Mississippi. Onís had repeated the offer many times, and each time Adams had stated this was impossible. Spain wanted Texas. Adams was not unwilling to yield Texas if the eastern boundary was set at the Sabine river.

During these negotiations there remained the possibility that the Quadruple Alliance, then meeting at Aix-la-Chapelle, would decide to intervene in behalf of Spain. Letters from Richard Rush and Albert Gallatin soon eased that concern. Rush told of a conversation with William Von Humboldt, Prussia's minister in London, who had assured Rush that intervention was most unlikely.[31] The Prussian minister was highly respected and viewed as wholly trustworthy. A later letter carried a report that three members of the British cabinet now favored recognition of the South American republics.[32] On his return to Paris, after completing negotiations in London, Gallatin learned that Castlereagh had killed a mediation proposal by stating that England could not agree to the mediation without an express reservation that force would not be used.[33]

Throughout the summer and fall of 1818 Adams and Onís continued to bargain on the boundary question. Adams, aside from the Texas question, was determined to have the line limit Texas on the north and to have the line extend to the Pacific coast. The innumerable exchanges of the two men do not fall within the parameters of this study. What Adams gained won him great praise. His biographer, Samuel Flagg Bemis, wrote: "Even without Texas the Transcontinental Treaty with Spain was the greatest diplomatic victory won by any single individual in the history of the United States."[34] The United States gained the Floridas and a boundary that excluded Spain north of Texas and north of 42 degrees on the Pacific coast. The Senate unanimously approved the treaty on 24 February 1819.

In the midst of the fatiguing negotiations, Adams found it necessary to defend the administration's management of affairs with Spain from domestic critics. Clay and others were ready to launch a campaign against both Jackson and the president. Adams found his opportunity to counteract these critics in a message to Pizarro on November 28.[35] The message was widely circulated. Adams recited the horrors of Indian warfare; the culpability of Spanish officials in not only failing to restrain the Indians but actually encouraging them; the guilt of Arbuthnot and Ambrister; the failure of the Spanish to control the territory; and all this Spain had permitted in direct violation of a treaty in which she bound herself to preserve peace. No note of apology was offered. Instead Adams held that Spain must pay the cost of the expedition and the losses suffered by Americans. The Boston *Patriot and Daily Chronicle* called it "one of the most striking state papers we have ever seen." The editor hailed it as "written with an astonishing force of ingenuity, and adorned throughout with the most captivating eloquence of all descriptions."[36]

The Transcontinental Treaty with Spain was acclaimed throughout New England. The *Columbian Centinel* referred to the "immense acquisition of Pensacola," the finest port from the Chesapeake to Vera Cruz. And should war come that port "must be a point of terrible annoyance to the whole West India trade." Possession of it, wrote the editor, "cannot but operate most powerfully to induce the nations which own the West India Islands, to admit the United States to a fair and reciprocal trade; and to relax or abolish that selfish, narrow-contracted Colonial policy, which has been prosecuted in defiance of the soundest maxims of policy and permanent interest." To this he added that he had learned that the claims for Spanish spoliations "possessed in this town, exceed a million and an half dollars." One merchant owned more than three hundred and fifty thousand dollars, "besides an interest for fifteen years."[37] Henry Dearborn, popular anti-Federalist, wrote to Monroe assuring him that the handling of affairs with Spain "is universally approved in Boston."[38]

The troubled affairs with Spain did not give rise to sectional rivalry. New England as well as the other sections had much to gain by the treaty Adams had negotiated. Adams' success was due in no small part to his skill but also, as he would readily have acknowledged, to a set of fortuitous circumstances: the weakness of Spain, the widespread distrust in Europe of the capricious Ferdinand, the statesmanship of Castlereagh, and Europe's desperate need for peace after the devastation of the Napoleonic wars. Hyde de Neuville, French minister to the United States, also gave Adams a hand on several occasions. He was anxious to avoid a war and as a friend of Onis counseled him wisely.

In the course of the next four years Adams laid the foundations for the Monroe Doctrine. The secretary of state's actions and pronouncements clearly portended what Monroe was to say in his message of 1823.

Three years before Monroe stated that the United States would not entangle itself in Europe, Adams explained the American position in much fuller terms. In July 1820, Henry Middleton, newly appointed minister to Russia, received his instructions. Adams labored for several days preparing them. He anticipated that Russia would propose that the United States join the Holy Alliance. He explained to Middleton why the United States must reject the proposal. "The political system of the United States," he wrote, "is also essentially extra-European. . . . To stand in firm and cautious independence of all entanglement in the European system, has been a cardinal point in their policy under every administration of this government from the peace of 1783 to this day."[39] Then, in reference to joining the Holy Alliance, Adams emphasized that, "If the United States . . . could acquire a right to ask the influence of its most powerful members in their controversies with other states, the other members must be entitled in return to ask the influence of the United States for themselves or against their opponents." This statement reaffirmed his earlier one to Peter Poletica, the Russian minister in Washington. Their conversation had turned to the question of recognition of the South American republics. Adams informed him that the

United States would act independently of Europe. Poletica, Adams recorded, "appeared disposed to argue against this." Adams then told him "we must be the judges of our own policy."[40]

In October 1820 Adams enunciated his views in a conversation with Stratford Canning, British minister to the United States. Great Britain sought an agreement whereby she hoped to suppress the slave trade. The proposal included the establishment of a multinational court to try offenders. Other aspects of the proposal, especially that permitting search of ships suspected of engaging in the trade, also stood in the way of the United States' acceptance of the plan, but Adams once again chose to emphasize the two-hemisphere principle. The systems of America and Europe, he said, were too different to permit easy collaboration. It was best that the two remain separate "for if the United States should become a member of that body they would even now be a power entitled to influence, and in a very few years must become a first-rate power in the league. . . . They would bring to it some principles not congenial to those of the other members, and those principles would lead to discussions tending to discord rather than harmony."[41]

In 1823 Adams inserted into Monroe's message the noncolonization principle. This, too, had ample antecedents in Adams' thinking and in the expansionist dreams that were present even during the War for Independence. The secretary of state denounced the imperialism of the European colonial systems. Fearful of any move that could lead to the establishment of an American colony abroad, he strongly opposed promoting a colony for emancipated slaves in Africa. The project, although wholly a nongovernmental one, could, as Adams saw it, lead to the establishment of a colony.[42]

However, his imagination took wing whenever he contemplated continental expansion. At a cabinet meeting in November 1819, Secretary of the Treasury William Crawford told how, after a tour of England and France, William Lowndes of South Carolina found that everyone with whom he conversed "appeared to be profoundly impressed with the idea that we are an ambitious and encroaching people." Crawford thought this should be a warning that we ought to be "guarded and moderate in our policy." Adams dismissed the European feelings as a product of envy. Expansion to the Pacific was inevitable. This was not because of American ambition "but because it is a physical, moral, and political absurdity that such fragments of territory, with sovereign fifteen hundred miles beyond the sea, worthless and burdensome to their owners, should exist permanently contiguous to a great, powerful, enterprising, and a rapidly growing nation." Americans could not reason Europeans out of their belief; they simply had to wait until Europeans found it to be a "settled geographical element."[43]

In these two respects, nonentanglement and expansion, Adams' peremptory statements were well rooted in the American experience and did not originate with him. However, one important stand in his foreign policy was peculiarly his own. On the Fourth of July 1821, Adams delivered a major address in the House of Representatives. At first, in preparing his speech, he thought of simply making an innocuous speech in the spirit of the occasion. He gradually came to the conclusion that this invitation gave him an opportunity to air some of his private concerns about foreign relations. In his speech he expressed sharp criticism of Great Britain. Many listeners believed that Adams was foolishly, and, as secretary of state, quite improperly, rekindling hostility to England. Robert Walsh, well-known editor of the *American Register* who had written at length on the unfriendly attitude of British writers, wrote to Adams. Adams' response was highly significant.

Adams attributed the hostility of public sentiment in England to a spirit of revenge and envy. He did not hold the British government responsible. A recent writer, he observed, looked forward to a future war in which the British would completely destroy all populous towns and, while he admitted that this would be unfitting in a war against a monarchy, noted that it would be justifiable in a war against a republic. Adams saw future danger in this universal castigation of the British. He wrote:

It inculcates a political doctrine . . . of the most pernicious tendency to this country, and the more pernicious because it flatters our ambition—the doctrine that it is the duty of America to take an *active* part in the future political reformation of Europe.[44]

This, said Adams, was what he had sought to counteract in his address, and he was aiming at those who would reform South America as well as Europe. Just as a fanatical spirit accompanied the Reformation, passions in America, he clearly believed, could readily become missionary fervor. When he wrote this in 1821, Adams had in mind how the popular sympathy with the revolutions in South America had transformed itself into an exhilarating, crusading spirit with a battle cry for freedom. He had seen Henry Clay exploit these public feelings, blind the public to the realities of South America, and approach a position from which he could push for military intervention. How much more dangerous if such a crusade should fix on reforming some part of Europe.[45] There must be a barrier to such a danger, and he looked on the two hemisphere principle as such a measure. In 1823, when he firmly took a stand against Canning's proposal that the two countries join in their opposition to European intervention in the new world, Adams saw in joint action a first step toward involvement in Europe, a step that could open the door to a crusade on behalf of the Greeks or some other cause that would enlist American readiness to advance the cause of freedom. In his earlier writings he had once said that he did not want to go abroad "in search of monsters to destroy." This was the guiding light of all his thinking.[46]

Adams returned to this theme in 1822 in a letter to Edward Everett. He pointed to the efforts of one group to align the United States on the side of the Scottish Whigs and the view that "the supposed duty of the United States [was] to take an active part in the impending European conflicts between *Power* and Right."[47] This doctrine had endangered foreign relations at the time of the French Revolution, and now was being used by those who wanted America to become entangled in the South American revolutions. Adams saw this as a trend that endangered the future destiny of the country.

His aversion to becoming a champion of South American independence also had its roots in his experience in dealing with the agents sent to Washington. Their aim, to entangle the United States in a war with Spain, disgusted him. In Adams' words, they would reduce us to dupes.[48] Monroe, in his annual messages, invariably included kind words about the South American patriots, a practice he adhered to as a way of counteracting Clay's criticisms of the administration for not granting them recognition. Adams sought to eliminate Monroe's gestures, believing that they were inconsistent with professions of neutrality, and delayed Spain's ratification of the treaty.[49] In March 1821, shortly after Spain ratified the treaty, he had a long conversation with Clay in the course of which he remarked concerning the South American republics that he had yet to see any evidence that they would establish free or liberal institutions.[50] He further observed:

They are not likely to promote the spirit either of freedom or order by their example. They have not the first elements of good or free government. Arbitrary power, military and ecclesiastical, was stamped upon their education, upon their habits, and upon all their institutions.

Adams held out no hope "of any beneficial result to this country from any future connection with them, political or commercial." These convictions foreordained that he would be less alarmed in the autumn of 1823 by the possibility of intervention by the concert of Europe. Of course he did not expect intervention, but he believed that even if it took place it was doomed to failure.

There were other early indications as to what his course would be when Canning, in August 1823, proposed to Rush that the two countries join in a statement that they would not countenance European intervention. Adams had sought to promote good relations with England from the day he became secretary of state and a great improvement did take place. However, he firmly believed that the two countries could find themselves on a collision course. Should another war break out in Europe, there would inevitably take place another crisis over neutral rights. Cuba, too, posed future dangers. He readily acknowledged the strategic importance of Cuba to both Great Britain and the United States. If it fell into unfriendly hands, it would serve as a point from which to control or destroy England's extensive trade in the area. Cuba was equally important to the United States for the same reasons.

When the time came to consider granting recognition to the South American republics, Monroe presented the question to the cabinet. Others thought it would be wise to consult with England and that the two countries should extend recognition in concert. Adams promptly urged that it would be unwise to be pinned to the sleeve of England. He won his point and the United States acted independently.

Canning's proposal to Rush arrived in Washington in October 1823. His action was a response to the French invasion of Spain in the spring of that year, an action approved by the Quadruple Alliance. Canning was also undoubtedly influenced by the friendly spirit of the United States at the time and possibly saw the proposal as a way to prevent American seizure of Cuba. Fearful that once embarked on the military course French enthusiasm might lead her into a further adventure across the seas—this time on behalf of the Bourbon monarchy France restored in Spain—Canning was alert to danger of war. A frank pronouncement by Great Britain would dictate caution on the part of France. If agreed to by the United States, who had the same interest in the area as England, it would at least have the effect of inhibiting American distrust should England find it necessary to act. England had no need of American support in the case of war, but war would renew the old conflict over neutral rights and thus endanger good relations.

The gyrations in Washington in response to Canning's proposal did not assure the triumph of Adams' principles. Monroe consulted with Jefferson and Madison, and both advised a favorable response. Calhoun, when he heard of the French victory in Spain, expressed fears of an approaching invasion and looked favorably on joining hands with Great Britain. A note from Russia stating that she would not recognize the new republics, combined with a statement expressing Russian gratification that American recognition was coupled with a policy of neutrality in the wars between Spain and her colonies, caused some members of the administration to express fear that Russia planned to intervene. There was general concern outside the inner circles of government.[51] Adams believed European intervention most unlikely and thought that if it did occur would end in failure.

The discussions that followed in the cabinet and Adams' success have been narrated and brilliantly analyzed elsewhere.[52] Monroe was at first inclined to join with the British. The cordiality between the two nations found frequent expression, especially in the spring of 1823. However, at another point the president opposed taking a position that would give the appearance of being subordinate to Great Britain.[53] Adams held out against aligning the United States too closely with the British. In the final discussions of the reply to be sent to Canning, Adams again opposed joining hands with the British. England, he said, "negotiated at once, with the European alliance and *with us*, concerning America, without being bound by any permanent community of principle."[54] With the approach of the next meeting of Congress in mind, the president invited the cabinet to submit suggestions. Adams failed in only one respect. Monroe incorporated each of his principles but insisted on saying a friendly word in behalf of the Greeks who were in revolt against control by Turkey.

It would be an error not to give James Monroe a due share of the credit. The president had long contemplated making a pronouncement warning that the United States would view European intervention in the New World as an unfriendly act, but an appropriate moment for such a declaration had not presented itself. Moreover, it was the president who would have to bear the responsibility in the event of some unforeseen developments. As Dexter Perkins put it, the message was "a special pronouncement of the President himself."[55]

Monroe's now famous message was reprinted in all of the important newspapers of New England, but only one made any comment on the foreign policy parts. The *Boston Evening Gazette* alone took special note of the fact that the president stated: ". . . all attempts of the European powers to extend their system of government to any portion of this hemisphere, would be viewed as dangerous to our peace and safety, and be met by such a change of policy on our part as may be considered essential to our security." One week later the editor again took note and closed with the peroration:

We believe that the tone in which Mr. Monroe speaks of the interference of the Alliance with South-American neighbors is agreeable to every citizen of his country. We live in a substantial, plain house—and perchance it is not founded on sand—and we shall not patiently behold the erection of gothic palaces too near us—no grandeur of architecture—or splendor of ornament would reconcile us to dungeons and grates.[56]

Two weeks later the editor returned to the subject. He now spoke of the possibility that should the Holy Alliance intervene, the American and British navies would become partners in the war. "We should then be in the situation of allies in fact, without an alliance in form." He then added: "Such at least, we hope, is all the alliance we shall ever form with Great Britain or any other formidable power of Europe."

The silence of the press, with the exception of the *Boston Evening Gazette*, suggests that editors did not find the doctrine controversial nor did they disapprove. The major points were already accepted by most and certainly startled few.

However, the full implications of the message escaped many, and their understanding of it was no more sophisticated than that of the armchair editor in Boston. At the very time that the doctrine was laid down, New England, particularly Boston, was caught up in a movement to aid the Greeks in their revolution. A society for Greek relief, chaired by Edward Everett, raised $100,000.[57] The public sympathy stemmed from the reverence of the educated class for the ancient Greek philosophers and historians. The wider public saw the Greek uprising as a struggle for freedom from the despotic Turks. So popular was this cause that the governor of Massachusetts and Daniel Webster gave it their support.[58] The *Columbian Centinel* of Boston endorsed the Greek cause stating: "Sympathy for the oppressed and suffering Greeks, is what every man of liberal sentiments, and every hater of tyranny and cruelty, ought to feel and express." The *Essex Register* of Salem joyfully reported contributions collected in Hartford, Windsor, Glastonbury, Southington, East Hartford, and Manchester in Connecticut.

A month after the president delivered his message to Congress, an important group of Bostonians sent a lengthy and eloquent memorial to the national House of Representatives pleading for the cause of the Greeks. The memorial did not propose a course to be followed by the government and recognized that in the past the policy had prohibited interference in the affairs of Europe. If, however, "the peculiar and unprecedented condition of the Greeks should, in the opinion of the Government of the United States, form a case of exception to the rule of that policy, the measures which may be adopted shall receive their cordial support."[59]

On January 19 Daniel Webster made a strong plea for the Greeks. Webster, in extravagant rhetoric, denounced the czar for threatening to intervene. Russia was guilty, he claimed, of advancing "to check a Christian nation in resisting the bloodiest cruelty of a horde of

Mohometan Tartars." He called on the House to adopt a resolution in support of the Greeks. The people, he said, were ahead of their government. "Is not this whole people already in a state of open and avowed excitement of this subject? Does not the land ring from side to side with one common sentiment for Greece, and indignation towards her oppressors?" [60]

Webster helped create the feverish excitement that Adams so feared and that he had sought to guard against. A crusade in behalf of Greece could mean war with Turkey, and even if Greece should free herself of the Turks she would most likely fall under the domination of the czar. Adams argued against making any move in support of the Greeks.

## 6

# A Section Held Together by the Tariff Question

Before 1824 the section called New England gained its identity largely from its interest in foreign trade and shipping. After 1820, and especially after 1827, manufacturing replaced commerce as the dominant economic interest. This development brought with it an about-face on the tariff question after 1824. What might have remained a question of mere expediency, as it had been earlier, that is, a purely economic issue to be resolved after careful calculation, became instead a highly emotional conflict inflated by abstract rhetoric and fed by political rivalry. The final result was that New England became the scapegoat, a whipping boy for the South and West; in turn, New Englanders assumed the role of portraying the economic and social advantages of a manufacturing society. As agents of modernization they heralded the blessings of increased production, of free labor, of new economic opportunities, and of transportation. In a country where approximately 90 percent of the population were engaged in agriculture, New England faced the political problem of how to win support for the new economic sector from a government that had devoted its energies to promoting agricultural interests.

The first battles had to be fought in New England itself where commercial interests held control. The merchants engaged in foreign trade reacted with vigor as the new manufacturing interests set out to commit the state government to a protective tariff. In January 1820 Governor John Brooks of Massachusetts, a Federalist, called for a protective tariff, an omen of changes to come that alerted the merchants to the danger.[1] In Salem the merchants rose to the defense of the old order, protesting that a protective tariff would result in "a prostration of regular commerce." [2] The *Boston Centinel* rallied to the merchants' side, opposed a tariff in its editorials, and published "Letters of a Farmer," a series of letters from a subscriber that argued that if markets were shut off by a tariff, then prices would decline and both merchants and farmers would suffer. [3] In 1824 the merchants, speaking through their representatives in Congress, opposed the protective tariff bill. Determined to resist the new movement, the merchants of Boston, meeting in the Exchange Coffee House, drafted a vigorous memorial contending that the manufacturers did not need protection and "that the importing system gives a more extensive and more beneficial employment to American capital and industry than the manufacturing system, forced by high duties." [4] Theirs was a last gasp. In 1827 Daniel Webster, attuned to the changes taking place, reversed his position and emerged as the champion of protectionism in the tariff battles in Congress.

The new economy transformed New England's politics by creating an alliance between rural and urban areas. The situation in Massachusetts led to a one-party system with the Whigs in full control. The older division between coast and hinterland, never a sharp one, disappeared almost wholly as economic development created a tie between town and country. Woolen factories, by 1828, were to be found throughout the state on the streams that provided water power. In Massachusetts there were important mills in the central area of Worcester County in Dudley, Southbridge, Worcester, and Fitchburg; in the western towns of Springfield, Pittsfield, Northampton; northeast of Boston in Andover, Haverhill, and Lowell. Springfield, on the Connecticut River, was as dedicated to promoting manufactures and the protective tariff as Boston. In the western parts of the state almost every farmer began to raise sheep as the demand for wool increased. By 1830 the three northern states of New England had a total of 3 million sheep. [5] Equally important was the improvement of roads; and the coming of railroads enabled farmers to find an ever increasing market in the new industrial towns for their milk, butter, cheese, poultry, and meats. By 1848 sales of poultry in Boston's Quincy Market reached a total of $694,483 and for the city as a whole, more than $1 million. [6] Apples from the interior went to Boston and then to southern ports, the West Indies, and many to

England. Thousands of bushels—120,000 in 1855—were shipped to England. Cities and rural areas became interdependent.

Vermont left the era of the self-sufficient farmer and tied itself to the newly emerging economy. In 1811 William Jarvis, successful merchant and American consul in Portugal, shipped a load of merino sheep to his farm in Weathersfield, Vermont. For a time there was a merino sheep rage, based on the superior quality of their wool. Vermont soon became the most important sheep-growing state in New England. At the same time the state experienced a promising start in woolen manufactures. In 1820 Vermont produced $890,353 worth of manufactured goods; more than one-fourth of these were woolens.[7]

Rhode Island spearheaded the development of the textile industry. Commerce continued to be of some importance in that state until well after the War of 1812, but the first beginnings of the textile industry date back to 1790 and to Moses Brown of Providence, the founder of cotton manufacture. Providence and the Pawtucket river valley north of it became the center of the cotton industry. Woolen manufactures met with failure in the early years, but by 1832 the woolen industry had a capital of $335,000 and 380 workers. The cotton industry far surpassed it in importance. By 1832 it represented a capital investment of $5,590,190 and 9,071 employees.[8]

The new economic age reached the other New England states more slowly, but southern Maine, southern New Hampshire, and the river valley in Connecticut contained dozens of mill towns. Connecticut, after a brief flurry of reforms of the state government in 1818 settled in to preserve rule by the well born and to protect the state from the mad passions of the multitude, including Jacksonism. The state lived with a one-party system though the Anti-Masonic party challenged the National Republicans in the early 1830s. The modest beginnings of industry gave an impetus to protectionism, but Connecticut looked backward rather than forward, and the enthusiasm for economic development that characterized the leadership in Massachusetts was slow to develop. Ownership of land by aliens was prohibited by law, an indication of the state's conservatism. Foreigners could memorialize the state legislature for permission and after 1824 could appeal to the state supreme court. In both instances they had to offer testimony of good character.[9] Connecticut's representatives in Congress joined the followers of Adams and then Clay by supporting the protective tariff that assured the few advance agents of factory production that they were well represented.

Maine gained statehood in 1820 and there, too, the new impulses toward rapid industrialization were slower to be felt than in Massachusetts. Commerce continued to be important in the seacoast towns, and commercial interests there as elsewhere feared that a protectionist policy would lead to a decline in foreign trade. The high duties placed on molasses and hemp in 1828 concerned the merchants of Maine who had a direct interest not only in carrying molasses but in the distillery trade. As shipowners they also had an interest in low-priced cordage for their ships. These considerations moderated their enthusiasm for the general principle of protection. Massachusetts failed to steer Maine onto the rightful path of Whiggery, and the Democrats enjoyed considerable success. In 1827 and 1828 the Maine representatives in Congress opposed high duties on woolens. Albion K. Parris, senator from Maine and a Democrat, strongly opposed the tariff bill in 1828, contending that Maine with 174,000 tons of shipping would suffer.[10] He cited memorials from his constituency opposing a high tariff. In the House of Representatives, Peleg Sprague, distressed more particularly by the high duties on molasses, protested that they were all for the sake of the whiskey maker. He emphasized the importance of the merchant marine as the nursery of seamen and charged that the nursery was about to be sacrificed by placing a high duty on hemp.[11] However, the tide moved in the direction of manufactures, and by 1832 there was support for the tariff.

New Hampshire representatives picked their way through tariff bills that supported or opposed specific items but avoided general pronouncements. However, New Hampshire had forty cotton mills by 1830. The leader of the Democratic party in New Hampshire, Isaac Hill, editor of the *Patriot*, fought the protective system. Hill, a devout Jacksonian who liked to pillory the rich, charged that most of the people in the manufacturing states suffered from a high tariff. To call for more protection, he said, "is to benefit the rich and depress the poor—to enable wealthy manufacturers to swallow up the small manufacturers."[12]

By 1827 the protectionist policy—more particularly, high duties on woolen goods—won almost complete allegiance among the political leaders of Massachusetts. Governor Levi Lincoln, in his message to the legislature in 1827, warned that with the decline of shipping the future well-being depended upon agriculture and manufactures. The latter received his full support and he called on Congress to protect industry. The ruinous competition "with the insidious exportations of the calculating, or the forced sacrifices of the starving Manufacturers of Europe" made protection a vital interest.[13] The legislature responded promptly with a memorial to Congress.[14] Later in the year the editor of the *Patriot* called on his readers to acknowledge that it was the mechanic who was responsible for the new implements of the farmer, for the improvements in transportation, for "stately public and private edifices which adorn our cities and villages. . . . Who, in fine, gives motion to the world?"

The most prestigious figures in Boston readily acknowledged the importance of the mechanic—and the tariff. Daniel Webster reversed his position and in 1827 gave a lengthy oration in Congress in support of New England manufactures. Edward Everett, scholar, orator, and member of Congress, and Abbott Lawrence, leading woolen manufacturer, addressed a public meeting in the state house.[15]

In January of 1827 Rollin Mallory of Vermont, dedicated protectionist, with his detailed knowledge of the woolen industry, introduced a bill in the House of Representatives to raise duties on both wool and woolens. "The great capital now devoted to the woolen manufactures," he declared, "is now in jeopardy." England, he charged, sought to monopolize the trade of the world. John Davis of Massachusetts, close friend of Boston's elite, was also on the committee; he cited the evasions of duties under the *ad valorem* provisions of the 1824 tariff, pronounced the vast amount of capital invested in woolen manufacturing to be in danger, and called on his colleagues to give attention to the great number of memorials that "have been heaped upon our table from day to day."[16] Dutee Pearce of Rhode Island gave a lengthy speech calling for aid to the woolen manufacturers and wool growers.[17] Ichabod Bartlett of New Hampshire, tired of the long debate, observed that "terrible as speeches were, and they were sufficiently terrible," he must, nevertheless, defend Mallory's bill.[18] On February 7 the House remained in session all night. James Buchanan of Pennsylvania and George McDuffie of South Carolina led the opposition. On February 8 New England won a victory for woolens in the House, but the bill was defeated in the Senate by the vote of the Vice President.

In the summer of 1827 some one hundred people gathered at Harrisburg, Pennsylvania to study the tariff question. Many were not manufacturers. Among those attending was Rollin Mallory of Vermont, the well-informed and persuasive tariff advocate. The convention sent a detailed report that supported protectionism to members of Congress. Among the recommendations were several of the provisions Mallory had incorporated in his bill earlier in the year.

The stage was now set for the heated debates of 1828 and the next three years. The tariff question became an instrument to be used in the presidential election. John Quincy Adams preferred a moderate tariff; he also wished to make the central issue in the election the question of protection and to deprive the Jackson forces of a basis for their claim that Adams had made Clay secretary of state in payment for Clay's support for the presidency. The Jacksonians, in turn, wished to avoid the tariff issue, knowing that it would splinter Jackson's following. The debates in Congress in 1828 ranged far and wide, but their focus was the question of which section should have the upper hand. Basic questions did arise; virtually every economic vested interest from a few hemp growers in Kentucky, raisers of flax in New Jersey, those with sugar interests in Louisiana, distillers and importers of molasses in New England, and wheat farmers and distillers in the West who were anxious to encourage American production of whiskey, sought federal aid in the form of restrictions on imports. Members of the opposition in Congress wondered if every petty interest were to dictate national policy at the expense of national interest; however, Henry Clay, intent on leading an alliance of the East and West, euphemistically labeled his program of protectionism, internal improvements, and a national bank "the American system."

New England promptly became the target of opponents of the tariff. The debates concentrated on the proposed duties on woolens, whereas the many other new duties on bar iron, iron tools, hemp, and flax stirred little debate. The reasons for this originated, in part, in the fact that while duties on woolens were set at an extremely high rate, the duties on other items were modest. Second, southern opponents of the tariff expected to align the West on their side but entertained no hope of winning New England's support.

Consequently New England came under thunderous attack. She was seen as the center of aristocracy, and her people were viewed as the villains who now cried for a strong Union but had failed to support it in the recent war—the section of monopolists. Southern critics were joined by James Buchanan of Pennsylvania who asked rhetorically where the $40 million of capital was located: "Where? Is it spread over the regions of the West? or in the Middle States? Certainly not. But a small portion of this capital, comparatively speaking, exists out of New England."

"The greater part of it," he said, "is confined within a narrow space." Boston and Salem were the centers of capital of woolen manufacture. And, he continued, this branch of business was not conducted by individuals but by a few individuals who, with their tremendous wealth, had formed corporations. Woolen manufacturers in other sections would never be able to compete with them. If the bill passed, Buchanan warned, it would establish an eastern monopoly.[19]

George McDuffie of South Carolina led the opposition, calling the Mallory bill a perversion that aimed to oppress one part of the Union for the benefit of another. He labeled it an "odious and irresponsible tyranny. . . . What is it to my constituents, sir, that they are represented on this floor when Massachusetts, feeling power (which God . . . knows how she got) and forgetting right has the means of extorting from them, through the agency of this Government, the hard earnings of their industry, to swell the profits of a few wealthy manufacturers?"[20]

William Drayton, also a representative from South Carolina, sounded a similar note during the lengthy debate on the tariff in April 1828. Focusing on the American system he asked: "Can that, without mockery, be called an American System, which controls the citizen in the exercise of his lawful pursuits—which taxes labor for the profit of the capitalist—which imposes burthens upon commerce and upon agriculture to swell the coffers of the manufacturer. . . ?"[21]

Daniel Webster denied the charge that the tariff bill was promoted exclusively by and for the benefit of New England, and that it was "designed to gratify the cupidity of her wealthy establishments." The tariff of 1824, passed over the objections of New England, placed before her the question of the future, "What was she to do?" Webster continued: "She was fitted for manufacturing operations, by the amount and character of her population, by her capital, by the vigor and energy of her free labor, by the skill, economy, enterprise, and perseverance of her people." He pointed to the political designs of those who drafted this tariff of abominations. New England's critics expected New England to vote down the bill that protected woolens because the same bill placed high duties on molasses, "a tax, in my opinion, absurd and preposterous." Webster warned: "Sir, gentlemen mistake us. They greatly mistake us. . . . New England, be assured, will exhibit not submission, but resistance; not humiliation, but disdain." [22]

New England voted for the bill—the "Tariff of Abominations"—as Webster had threatened, and Jackson won the presidency as a result of his great popularity. The sectional controversy was to rage throughout his two terms.

The large migration from New England to the West caused almost as much concern as the tariff. On 30 December 1829, Senator Samuel Augustus Foote of Connecticut introduced a resolution calling on the Committee on Public Lands to inquire into the expediency of limiting the sales of the public lands for a certain period. Thomas Hart Benton of Missouri promptly declared the resolution "was one of infinite moment to the West." Foote's resolution assured that the year 1830 was to be one of heated sectional debate, a debate rich in recriminations.

Early in January 1830 the contest reached a climax after Thomas Hart Benton and Robert Hayne delivered speeches that rang with sectional appeals and attacks on New England. Thomas Hart Benton, senator from Missouri, leveled the most violent attack on New England on 2 February 1830 during a debate on the Foote resolution calling for limiting the sales of public lands. Benton, who denounced the protectionist policy, yet at the same time voted for protectionist duties on all items of interest to the West, was dismissed by John Quincy Adams as "a liar of magnitude beyond the reach of Ferdinand Mendez Pino." [23] Senator Benton portrayed at length New England's lack of patriotism in 1798 and in 1812. He struck at the upper aristocratic class "who thought it unbecoming a moral and religious people to celebrate the triumph of their own country over its enemy, but quite becoming the same people to be pleased at the victories of the enemy, over their country, who gave a dinner to him who surrendered Detroit." He denounced Daniel Webster for claiming that New England had always been friendly to the West. The contrary, he said, was true, and he listed fourteen occasions when New England had betrayed the West.[24] Benton's attack took the full attention of the Senate for three days.

What followed took on the nature of an oratorical festival as Daniel Webster entered the fray. His cause has been called dubious by his critics then and since, but no one could question his unrivaled skill as an orator. Behind the memorable address lay the awareness of New England's need for the Union. That Webster did not have to say. Confronted by a prospective combination of the South and West, he set forth an appeal to nationalism and reduced the sectional appeals to the category of petty self-interests standing in the way of a realization of noble republican dreams. The first day Webster spoke, he devoted his time to portraying New England as the friend of the West and the advocate of all that was beneficent and for the general good.[25] Hayne delivered a lengthy rebuttal making the same indictment of New England that Benton had made. Then, seven days after his first attack, Webster, in a three-hour speech, elevated himself to the position of defending the Union by demonstrating the depth of the abyss into which the country would fall if each of the twenty-four states should have the authority to declare an act of Congress null and void. In closing he pronounced the oft quoted words:

When my eyes shall be turned to behold, for the last time, the sun in heaven, may I not see him shining on the broken and dishonored fragments of a once glorious Union, on States dissevered, discordant, belligerent, on a land rent with civil feuds, or drenched, it may be in fraternal blood! Let their last feeble and lingering glance, rather, behold the gorgeous ensign of the republic, now known and honored throughout the earth, still full high advanced, its arms and trophies streaming in their original lustre. . . .[26]

The speaker became Mr. New England, the "God-like Dan'l." The original tariff question, so tawdry and dry, had first moved into the broader realm of federal powers, then into the nullification controversy, and finally into an emotional outburst of chauvinism. Webster's defense of New England's past role was based on a highly selective perception of events, but his fellow New Englanders never ceased to be grateful for the service he had rendered. P. C. Brooks was to write "I love that man." Edward Everett forgave Webster all his weaknesses. Amos Lawrence praised him and wrote that he doubted "if there be any man, either in Europe or America, his superior." The speech was published and 40,000 copies distributed.[27]

Webster did not stand alone. John Davis, member of the House and from Massachusetts, in a speech on 4 May 1830, spoke for one and a half hours in defense of the protective system and his native section. "I should fail of the duty I owe to my constituents, as well as to my State, to sit here in silence and hear them calumniated—to hear them called monopolists, because they insist on the right of this Government to protect its citizens—to hear them stigmatized as tyrants, because they refuse to return to colonial bondage."[28] Everett, a more soft-spoken man, defended the tariff and responded to McDuffie's charge that the capitalists controlled elections in Massachusetts. His district included the two textile centers, Waltham and Lowell. He affirmed that "if the suspicion could be infused into the minds of the people of that district, that their representative was under the influence of the moneyed capital invested in it, it would cost him his seat."[29]

The question of duties on woolens greatly strengthened the bonds that united New Englanders because it gave the great majority of her representatives in Congress a common cause. Rollin Mallory of Vermont, a master of detailed facts, provided the protectionists with a rationale; Dutee Pearce of Rhode Island, Isaac Bates, and John B. Davis of Massachusetts delivered the most able speeches in favor of woolen manufactures.

The Tariff of Abominations of 1828 provided both commercial and manufacturing interests with a common grievance. Commercial interests, most ably represented in the House by Peleg Sprague of Maine, a jurist of great distinction, and Ralph Ingersoll of Connecticut attacked the high duties placed on molasses and hemp. They did not criticize the high duties on woolens; in fact, they defended them. In turn, Webster,

Everett, and the spokesmen for the woolen interests sharply criticized high duties on molasses and hemp. The two major economic interests of New England, though rivals, were able to combine forces.

The debates in 1832, though New England was no longer singled out for attack, revealed bitter sectional feelings. The South now found itself deserted by the middle states and southerners in Congress repeatedly spoke of themselves as a minority. The nullification movement in South Carolina added to the tensions. The controversy increasingly took the form of an irreconcilable conflict between southern agriculture and northern manufacturing. Abstract principles came to play an ever greater role with the South asking for justice from a tyrannical majority and the North defending majority rule.

The explosive slavery issue, not openly discussed, lay just beneath the surface. The question of duties was beginning to give way before a vastly wider and deeper issue involving two kinds of society and two different political systems. George McDuffie, the southern extremist, in a speech before the House in May 1832, displayed deep emotion. His speech rang with such words and phrases as "outrage," "acts of violence," "injustice," "the taking away of property," "plunder," "the greatest of all absurdities," and "flimsy disguise."[30] The speeches of Mallory, Bates, and Davis did not employ invective, but those men were no less certain of the correctness of their position and spoke both as New Englanders and as the advocates of industrialism.

The passing references to slavery were ominous. McDuffie warned that it was his deep and deliberate conviction, "in the face of all the miserable cant and hypocrisy with which the world abounds on this subject, that any course of measures which shall hasten the abolition of slavery by destroying the value of slave labor, will bring upon the Southern States the greatest political calamity with which they can be afflicted. . . ." In a peroration he added that when the people of the South ceased to be masters "they will assuredly be slaves." The irresistible tendency of the system of protection would be "to precipitate us upon this great moral and political catastrophe."[31]

New Englanders generally avoided the slavery question, but it slipped into some of their speeches and more than one pronounced slavery uneconomical. John Davis, wholly uncompromising on the tariff and hostile to the South, compared the systems of slave and free labor. Slave labor had "nothing to hope or expect beyond the coarsest of food and clothing, and a hovel for shelter." The free laborer, Davis argued, labors for himself, and he aspires to objects beyond his physical wants: he aims at something higher and in that direction lies a higher civilization.[32] Nathan Appleton, a leading woolen industry entrepreneur, elected to the House of Representatives by the Boston district in 1832, favored treating slavery as a local problem, but in seeking to refute the arguments of McDuffie he raised the question as to why New England was prosperous and the South poor. "The facts, as they appear," he said, "suggest the inquiry, whether this cheap slave labor does not paralyze the industry of the whites? Whether idleness is not the greatest of their evils? Whether even the stimulus of the tariff is not sufficient to move this inert mass?"[33]

By 1832 the deep hostility of the South and the well-recognized danger of a breakup of the Union had instilled sufficient fear to moderate the demands for a high protective tariff. John Quincy Adams, chairman of the Committee on Manufactures in the House of Representatives, announced in January that compromise was essential.[34] With the support of Edward Everett and John Davis, he hoped to conciliate the South. Early in February Adams and Everett met with their friends to discuss the tariff: both men favored reducing tariff rates.[35] Everett was extremely anxious about the possible political effects of a high tariff. Nathan Appleton, now a member of Congress, also favored a limited compromise. He acknowledged that his own mills were not dependent upon a tariff. New England, he wrote, enjoyed certain advantages over the British: cheapness of water power compared with steam, the fact that raw materials were closer at hand, and cheapness of labor, resulting from the employment of farm girls.[36]

The manufacturers in Boston entertained no ideas of compromise. As Everett put it, they "do not think it safe to adventure upon any fresh reduction."[37] But John Quincy Adams, more sensitive to the seriousness of Southern demands, told Everett that "the minimum system ought to be and must be abandoned or there will be Civil War."[38] P. C. Brooks, Everett's wealthy father-in-law, and Boston's business community, worried about Adams whom they found to be fiercely independent and stubborn in pushing his own opinion.

As chairman of the Committee on Manufactures Adams presented a report suggesting that the time had come to reconcile the two major economic interests of the country. In it he said that the burdens complained of by the South should be alleviated. In so doing the interests of the manufacturers must not be sacrificed. Tariffs should be lowered or eliminated on all items not in danger of being ruined by foreign competition. Where manufactures faced foreign competition the duties should be no higher than necessary to enable domestic manufactures to compete. Manufacturing had received its start during the Napoleonic wars when the country, because of the embargo, was cut off from foreign supplies. This could happen again and the nation must, as a matter of defence, be prepared to furnish manufactures.[39]

Edward Everett agreed with Adams. Upon him fell the burden of avoiding a reduction that would endanger his home state industry. The investments in the woolen industry alone were somewhere around $100 million by 1832. He argued that the farmers of New England, with their capital invested in more than a million sheep, had much at stake. "It was not for the profit of capital, that will usually take care of itself, but to render capital profitable to the farmers. . . .", he maintained. Idle capital benefitted no one. Capital put to work in farming and in factories yield general wealth. Everett, the enthusiastic proponent of the beckoning era, held, "In converting this capital into a factory, the farmers and mechanics furnish the materials—stone, brick, lime, lumber, nails, glass, machinery, etc.; the labor of the mason, carpenter, millwright, blacksmith, etc. in exchange for capital; and the result is that the iron chest is emptied, its contents distributed among the people, and its owner in exchange becomes the owner of a factory."[40]

The great orator, once a professor of Greek and future president of Harvard College, also tied the tariff question to national security and economic stability. The recent Napoleonic wars had engulfed the country in a desperate controversy over neutral rights and brought on war with England. The country had been exposed to the vicissitudes of peace and war. "It is, in fact," Everett declared, "on general views desirable that events abroad, over which neither the Government nor the citizens of the United States have any control, should not exclusively decide the condition of the industry of the country."[41]

Everett was willing to promote compromise but not at the price of ruining industry. However, it would not be a compromise if duties were so lowered as to destroy manufactures. That would be sacrifice, "and this we cannot agree to." Nor did Everett wish to use the term "concessions" for this implied "a sacrifice of that pride of opinion which men are much more reluctant to make, than a sacrifice of their interests." He would ask, he said, to put "abstract principles aside, on which it is impossible for opinions to unite."[42] He called for a more practical approach: "Can we not all agree that the duties shall be reduced to the lowest point to which they can be brought without impairing great interests that have grown up under the laws of the country?"

John Davis and Rufus Choate, both of Massachusetts, also favored compromise, but they staunchly defended the protective system. Davis introduced an amendment to the bill presented by the Committee on Ways and Means that lowered duties but rejected the suggestion called for by the committee bill, namely, a tariff for revenue only. Rufus Choate supported the amendment. Choate, like Adams, recognized that the two most objectionable features of the existing tariff were the duties on negro clothing and cotton bagging, and the minimum provisions whereby a square yard of cloth was charged only the minimum in its price bracket even though its value was well above the figure set as a minimum. Davis' amendment would have exempted both from paying duties.

Rufus Choate, brilliant orator, master of the Greek classics, who read history avidly and who looked to history to guide him, was both a devoted New Englander and a nationalist. Choate insisted on maintaining the protective system and contended that none of the abuses that the free traders attributed to the protective system had been realized since it was adopted.[43] The southern states had prospered, and the degree to which prosperity had been diminished was a result of other causes. Southerners, he said, spoke of the current scene as one of tribulation, of a great crisis. Choate held: "All these things must needs be, and may very safely be. . . . They are only part of the price—how inadequate the price—which every nation pays for greatness and liberty." "The history of every free state, which ever existed," Choate affirmed, ". . . is an unbroken record of internal strife, and sharp civil contention, and the collision of interests and feelings which the good men of the time thought utterly irreconcilable, but which were yet harmoniously reconciled. . . ." This, said Choate, "is the language of one of the wisest of men and most accomplished men that ever lived."[44]

The representatives of Massachusetts were ready to compromise and seek to conciliate the South within well-defined limits only. Abbott Lawrence, the state's leading manufacturer, opposed all compromise. "Our friends here," he wrote, "are opposed to it." "It appears to me," he explained, "that we should say at once we will not give up the duty on Cottons, Wool, Woolens, Iron, Hemp, Sugar, etc., not a mill we concede. . . ." The southern enemies, he contended, wished to destroy the woolens industry. Abbott advised not to give way except on the one dollar minimum. He concluded, "The South cannot be appeased by any concession we can make and we only lose strong ground which we have fought hardly for, by making concessions to them for the sake of obtaining their good will."[45]

The 1832 tariff did include concessions but the protective system remained intact. For woolens, the system of minimums was eliminated. The duty on the coarsest woolens was reduced to 5 percent. On woolens of higher quality duties were raised to 50 percent. The rate on worsteds was reduced from 25 to 10 percent. The duty on hemp was reduced from sixty dollars a ton to forty dollars. Flax was placed on the free list. There was no change of duties on cotton goods.

The new tariff bill of 1832 split the votes in New England. Adams, John Reed, and Henry Dearborn voted for it. Choate, Everett, and Davis voted against it, as did representatives from Vermont and Rhode Island; only one representative from Connecticut voted for it.[46] Passage of the bill took Everett by surprise. In a letter to his brother he explained what happened:

The Southern men saw that the manufacturers would not vote for a bill, by which they would be sacrificed & they knew that if no bill passed, the whole South would be thrown into the hands of the Nullifiers. The Jackson tariff men of New York, therefore (acting under orders) allowed the bill to be so amended so as to sour the Woolen's interest, & the Southern members opposed to Nullification voted for the bill.[47]

In February 1833, in the midst of the nullifcation crisis, John Quincy Adams presented the report of the minority of the Committee on Manufactures. Adams wrote the report that was published in Boston. It stands as one of the most able state papers ever penned by him. Andrew Jackson's message to Congress in December 1832 provided the occasion. The importance of the paper lies in the breadth of its political perspective and its comprehensiveness. Here, more forcefully than in any other one document, is set forth the National Republican's concept of the role of the federal government.

The report made clear that New England's stand on the tariff was only one facet of a much broader view. New Englanders saw the opposition to a protective tariff as part of a general assault on their interests. If Jacksonisn had its way, the federal government would be prevented from encouraging rapid industrial development.

Adams centered his attack on the statement in Jackson's message: "The wealth and strength of a country are its population, and the best part of that population are the cultivation of the soil. Independent farmers are, everywhere, the basis of society, and true friends of liberty." This favored class clearly did not include the slaves and, as Adams chose to believe, included only the wealthy landowners, the owners of plantations. This, he held, had been the basis of feudal society. The cardinal principle articulated by Jackson permeated his entire program. It exhibited itself in the opposition to internal improvements. It would limit internal improvements to those that yielded benefits nationwide and rule out those that brought great benefits to a local neighborhood. To advocate giving away the public lands to the cultivators of the soil when these rightfully belonged to all of the states was to favor one class over another. Jackson, Adams argued, denied what was obviously true. The right of the nation's people to the public lands entitled them to compensation. The settlers on the new lands enjoyed protection from the Indians, the cost of which was paid for by all the people. To deny them this was to deny the right of property. Therefore, Adams held, it would be a grievous error to give away the public lands.

Jackson's system would deprive manufacturing interests of protection by limiting protection to what is necessary "for securing a supply of those articles of manufacture essential to national independence and safety in time of war." This principle, wrote Adams, was not applied "to other great though partial interests, namely, to the Southern planter and Western settler, to the merchant and the mariner." This principle, if applied, would abandon "the future interests of domestic industry to the mercy of foreign legislation, leagued with foreign competition" and, finally, consign all the great manufacturing establishment of the country to speedy and inevitable destruction.

Adams laid down the principle that the individual manufacturer was entitled to protection as a *right* in the same way that the southern planter, the shipper, and the western settler enjoyed protection as a right. He wrote:

In the formation of the social compact, undoubtedly the safety and independence of the whole are the ultimate object of every engagement undertaken by the community to protect the interests of every one of its parts; but that safety and independence are to be secured as much by the protection of interests, contributing to her well-being in time of peace, as by that of securing to herself a supply of the instruments of death, necessary for a battle or a siege.

It was the responsibility of Congress to judge every measure in terms of the welfare and prosperity of all the people. To rule out assistance to the economy because a particular activity, such as manufacturing, was concentrated in one area could only weaken the nation. The purpose of the founding fathers was "improvement of the condition of the whole." [48] The fisheries and navigation interests had benefitted in the past by government aid. Now that manufactures offered the area the only hope of future prosperity, why should government operate on different principles?

Other problems stirred up the ire of New Englanders during the remainder of the 1830s, particularly Jackson's attack on the National Bank and the removal of deposits. Debates on the wisdom and efficacy of protective tariffs were to continue, and New England remained protectionist in opinion. Manufactures continued to grow and New England became increasingly more industrial, more urban, and the citadel of the middle-class virtues of caution and stability. Successful business leaders remained firmly in control until the slavery issue disrupted the political scene. In foreign affairs, with the exception of New Hampshire, adventurous expansionism found little favor. Capital accumulations mounted and so did caution. By 1831 New England banks had a capital of more than $36 million, of which $21 million were in Massachusetts.

Early in 1833, to the dismay of New England, Henry Clay introduced a series of resolutions and a new bill calling for gradual tariff reductions each year for ten years. Webster and Everett sought to introduce a more moderate measure without success.[49] Everett met two New England manufacturers, George Bond and Charles Thorndike, who expressed disgust with Clay's compromise. In Boston Clay's bill caused dismay. P. C. Brooks wrote to Everett that Clay's bill "displeases them very much, and his speech not much less" and "his disregard of posterity they think unpardonable. . . . What is to become of us, my friend, if such men as Mr. Clay are to whiffle about in this way." Wholly dispirited, Brooks confessed he was ready to ask, "Is there an honest man on this ere [sic] earth?"[50] As he saw it, "Our Southern, and some of our northern gentry will now be easy." He wrote in disgust: "They have had their way—when they ought to have been hanged."[51] However, not all despaired. Harrison Gray Otis opposed Clay's measure but informed Webster that the manufacturers believed that it "would secure to them a better protection than they have been led to think it would be possible to obtain from this Congress."[52]

# Dedication to Stability at Home and Abroad

New England experienced a remarkable economic growth in the 1830s and 1840s. Boston functioned as the financial capital for the new industries and the rapidly expanding railroad system that tied the rural areas to her. By 1840 Lowell had $9 million in capital, 28 mills, 163,304 spindles, 5,094 looms, and a labor force of 6,470 females and 2,037 males. Worcester County, in the central part of Massachusetts, had eighty-four cotton factories and sixty-four woolen factories. Rhode Island was the site of numerous textile mills. By 1840 similar enterprises on a considerable scale dotted the valleys of Connecticut, New Hampshire, Vermont, and Maine. The rise of the textile industry was accompanied by manufactures of textile machinery. And in Massachusetts the growth of the boot and shoe industry and the paper industry paralleled that of textiles. A similar growth took place in banking and insurance.

The economic revolution led to a concentration of wealth and control. A complex network among entrepreneurs in the various fields developed. The leaders of industry served on the boards of banks, insurance companies, and railroads. The close-knit business leaders of Boston controlled a minor empire. Water power on the Connecticut and Merrimack rivers fell under their domain, and competitors, dependent upon water power, paid for its use. They collected royalties on patents they owned, owned canals and railroads, and other business concerns depended on their banks and patronized their insurance companies.

Intermarriage strengthened the bonds among the entrepreneurs. By 1840 Boston could boast of twenty-six millionaires.[1] Those who acquired great wealth were also the leaders in the establishment of beneficent institutions, hospitals, asylums for the mentally ill, schools for the blind, and homes for those in distress. Harvard, once largely dependent on state support and whose leadership was tied to the legislature, became increasingly the pet of rich philanthropists; they eventually took full control. Professors married the daughters of merchants and other entrepreneurs. Harvard became a much stronger institution academically and benefitted by the association, but it also led to an environment that stressed the genteel values.[2] The same enclave of wealth supported the Boston Atheneum, the Lowell Institute, and several other cultural societies.

Stewardship, the cardinal virtue, symbolized admission to the elect. In 1830 John Quincy, mayor of Boston, enumerated the list of charities and the gifts received. The gifts totaled $1,155,986. Charities included educational institutions, libraries, certain religious societies, and those making more direct contributions to the needy. The list was amplified in 1845, and the gifts by then totaled $2,938,021. S. A. Eliot, treasurer of Harvard and described by his biographer as "a public spirited and high minded aristocrat," who gathered the later statistics, saw charity as an obstacle to the growth of barriers between the rich and poor that could lead to revolution. In the spirit of the true Whig, Eliot wrote:

Where shall the line be drawn between the many for whom our state of society is good, and for the few for whom it is not good? In truth, there is no such line practicable; and it is one of the condition of things in New England, that it proves the identity of interests of all component parts of society. No one can say to any other, "You are not wanted; we can do without you." There is a mutual dependence far more widely felt, and not only felt, but acknowledged here than elsewhere, and as the political institutions of the country are adapted to continue this state of things, it may be hoped that it will long endure to produce the fruits which we have been contemplating.[3]

Many of the recipient institutions served the poor and needy. Others reflected the faith of Whigs in education and religion as instruments of social mobility.

Stewardship began with concern for the future security of the family. The elite married the elite and helped fortify the next generation. Two of the daughters of P. C. Brooks adhered to this well-established custom;

one married Edward Everett and another Charles Francis Adams. At the wedding of Patrick Tracy Jackson and Susan Loring, among the 300 guests there were no fewer than 120 first cousins.[4] Kenneth Wiggins Porter noted the importance of kinship in the business world:

Jonathan Jackson received his early business training in the countinghouse of Patrick Tracy: Jonathan Jackson's mother and Mrs. Patrick Tracy were both great-granddaughters of Maj. Gen. Daniel Gookin. Enoch Titcomb was a clerk in the firm of Jackson, Tracy & Tracy; his grandfather, and the grandfather of Mrs. Nicholas Tracy, Nicholas Tracy being the uncle of the Tracy partners, were brothers. George Cabot received his maritime training under his brother-in-law and later partner, Joseph Lee, Jr., entered business in the service of Joseph Lee, Sr.; and the latter's son, Joseph Lee, Jr., entered business in the service of Joseph Lee & Co., composed of his father and his uncle George. Henry Lee agreed to take into his store a son of Capt. William Farris; Mrs. Henry Lee's aunt, Mrs. John Tracy, was either the sister or the cousin of Mrs. William Farris.[5]

This was only an abbreviated account of the complexity of family relationships.

The leading families did not have a long heritage of wealth. Because they shared more austere backgrounds of parsonage or farm, they realized that disaster beckoned quite as often as opportunity. By 1845 the "Boston Associates," composed of the city's leading manufactures and financiers, controlled 20 percent of New England cotton spindles, 30 percent of Massachusetts railroads, 40 percent of the state's insurance companies, and a large share of the banks. Even so, these fortifications did not assure them of privileged standing in perpetuity.[6] Youthful rebellion and sharp business recessions, such as the one in 1840, were frequent enough to encourage sobriety and concern in every family household. Ironically, the greater the success and prosperity, the greater became the felt need for security and the greater the demands for caution.

The rapid rise of business was accompanied by the rise of the Whig party. After its organization in 1834 the party dominated four of the New England states. It viewed itself as the party of enlightenment and honesty, the guardian of stability, and the foe of corruption. The promise of the new economy was its guiding star. The party, including as it did the close-knit circle of business leaders, viewed the economic developments as the beginning of a new day. Above all, they were determined to promote and to protect both their economic interests and their elevated political and social positions.

The Whigs paraded under the banner of enlightenment versus ignorance and of expertise in management versus careless change for the sake of change. Newspaper editors of the Whig persuasion referred to the opposition party as "loco focos" or "tories." The former epithet identified Jacksonians as irresponsible and ignorant seekers after office, and the second implied that the opposition refused to accept the changes that had taken place. The editor of the *Boston Daily Advertiser* summed up the Whig view. The theory of the Whigs, he wrote, "is that offices are to be held for the good of the people, by men willing and able to administer to that good, while the declared theory of the administration is that office is the spoils of victory and the avowed object for concentrating masses into majorities." Equally important in the Whig constellation of virtues was that "they had not gone about, turning every existing and long established institution upside down, to discover whether its foundation is solid." Whigs, he declared, had no desire to change for the sake of change.[7]

These attitudes, enunciated in party rhetoric, were allied to immediate political aims. New England Whigs wanted a protective tariff, a stable currency, a national bankruptcy law, and protection for American shipping. In foreign affairs they advocated friendly relations with England. The thought of possible war with England was a hobgoblin of terrible mien. It was New England shipping on the high seas, New England sources of finance for carrying on trade, and the New England ports that would suffer should war occur. Regarding Massachusetts, Charles Francis Adams noted in his diary: "We are too commercial here to be warlike."[8] The Whigs likewise viewed any threats to the Union from internal disruption as disastrous. The new manufactures were exported to both South America and Asia but the most lucrative market was in the South and West.

The Whig ruling circle rejected the anglophobia so prevalent in other parts of the country and by no means absent among the general populace of New England itself. The reason, in part, lay in financial relations with

Great Britain. In 1839 when the western railroad was to be extended to Albany and a series of shorter lines were to be constructed in Massachusetts, the state legislature underwrote the loans needed by the private companies. The state issued $5 million in scrip for the use of corporations seeking loans; the script guaranteed payment by the state in the event the companies could not repay. Approximately $3 million of this amount were to be used in securing loans in England. The loan advanced by Baring Brothers for the project was the largest that had been advanced to an American enterprise. This was only one of many loans. The merchants of New England, in carrying on their foreign commerce, relied on advances in credit from British banks.[9]

Ties of other kinds were at least equally important. New Englanders, particularly the elite and distinguished, viewed England as the mother country, and their admiration for British institutions was as fresh as if they had recently migrated. Daniel Webster had long looked forward to serving as the United States minister to London but doubted his ability to afford the mission. In 1839 he went for a long visit, met many of the political leaders, was entertained in the homes of the most celebrated of the British ruling class and was delighted with his experience. Edward Everett appears to have felt more at home visiting the homes of the wealthy in England and conversing with well-known British authors than he did in Washington during his terms in Congress. He was treated as a celebrity in England. Upon his return he carried on an extensive correspondence with British leaders during the Oregon controversy and assisted in promoting mutual understanding. In 1839 Charles Sumner reveled in his travels in England and wrote in glowing terms of the people he met. A common political point of view, admiration for the British upper-class life style, and a fondness for British literature caused the American visitors to feel at home away from home. New England, like old England, was engaged in commerce; they shared common political traditions, and they were both Protestant.

New England in the 1830s and 1840s was in the throes of an economic revolution, but the old order did not change at once. Family and church engaged most people most of the time. Politics aroused minimal excitement. Voter apathy prevailed. In Massachusetts many rural towns, as had been true in the past, failed to elect representatives to the state legislature, thereby avoiding the costs of salaries and of travel. In 1822 a Boston newspaper reported that two-thirds of the towns were unrepresented in the state legislature.[10]

No one party dominated all of New England. The Jacksonians held control in Maine and New Hampshire. In New Hampshire the Jacksonians, led by Isaac Hill and Levi Woodbury, held sway by means of controlling patronage and were able to elect most of the state's representatives to Congress by perpetuating statewide elections that reduced the few Whig strongholds to impotence. In Maine the Jacksonians controlled the governorship and both branches of the legislature most of the years from 1820 to 1840. Elsewhere the National Republicans and, after 1834, the Whigs ruled almost without interruption. Vermont remained in Whig hands except for a span of four years during the first half of the thirties when the Anti-Masonic party ruled.[11] Connecticut, dominated by small rural towns who had equal representation in the legislature with the new cities, never strayed from the Whig fold.

Massachusetts, with 22 percent of the population of all New England, experienced sharp party strife. In the late 1820s the old Federalists in the National Republican party were at odds with the new leadership of the National Republicans. The hostility was so great they would not meet in the same room.[12] By 1831 the Anti-Masonic party controlled enough votes so that the Republicans no longer had a majority in the state. The Anti-Masons held the balance, and they were as prone to side with the Jacksonians as with the Republicans. In spite of difficulties, the Republicans and then the Whigs won the governorship every year until 1839 when Everett was defeated by Marcus Morton, judge of the state supreme court, who had been a Democratic candidate for governor for sixteen consecutive years beginning in 1828. Everett attributed his defeat in 1839 to the "fifteen gallon law," a measure aimed at curbing the drinking of the poor who could not afford to purchase so much at one time. Charles Francis Adams had a different opinion; the Whig party was on its last legs and deservedly so. Another year passed and the Whigs regained control, but in 1842 the Democrats regained control of the legislature. In most elections for governor no candidate received the required majority, and the choice was then made by the legislature. The Jacksonian party provided stiff competition. The new economic order created considerable discontent. The Jacksonians also enjoyed the advantage of controlling federal patronage.

Outside the political realm other stirrings came to the fore. Urbanization, the entry of new philosophical and scientific ideas from Europe, the general loosening of ties to the past, and greater openness to change led to a flurry of reform, rethinking, and freer communication. The old moorings held fast, but old ideas and traditional standards of value and behavior were now stretched to accommodate a changing environment. The clergy continued to serve as guides to truth and to ethical behavior, but they now competed with lyceums where the latest information on science, literature, and the problems of the day was dispensed. Ralph Waldo Emerson assured his friend Thomas Carlyle: "Boston contains some genuine taste for literature, and a good deal of reverence for it." [13] William Ellery Channing, the foremost Unitarian clergyman, sensitive to the changing social environment, turned his attention from theology to current social problems. His humanistic writings and sermons challenged current materialism.

Emerson called it "the goody, goody age." The philosopher of Concord was offended by the addiction of social reformers to self-advancement, but he shared their social concerns. He wrote:

We are all a little wild here with numberless projects of social reform. Not a reading man but has a draft of a new community in his waistcoat pocket. I am gently mad myself, and I am resolved to live cleanly. George Ripley is talking up a colony of agriculturalists & scholars with whom he threatens to take the field & the book. One man renounces the use of animal food; & another of coin; & another domestic hired service; & another of the state. . . . [14]

Charles Francis Adams, in 1840, labeled the reformers and new trends of thought "the mystical school who maintain the necessity of a further revelation." "Of fools," he wrote, "their name is legion," and New England, he said, had a large share of the same. He dismissed the apostles of idealism: "They will pass off like yesterdays and all of insects without planting any battery against them." [15] Adams was more concerned about the tenants on his father's property than with dreams of a future utopia, and was deeply moved when he found one tenant whose husband had deserted her, leaving her with two small children and a third on the way. Present evils interested him more than achieving some ideal society. Human motives gave no promise of a future utopia. After hearing a sermon by his close friend Frothingham on the sin of envy, he noted in his diary that a more pressing evil was the seduction of servant girls in the homes of the wealthy.[16] Adams, quite as much as Emerson, represented the conscience of New England.

The new stirrings of reformers and fresh intellectual innovations in the 1830s were only one aspect of the newly emerging society. New Englanders continued to give first priority to stability, the rule of law, and rank in society. Emerson took pride in the growth of Boston even while he noted its obscure garrets, damp basements, and "the victims of great suffering, poor men and women reduced by consumption or bed-ridden with rheumatisms, or worn with fruitless labors to meet demands the quarter day."[17] He took pleasure in seeing new Bostons spring up on the frontier, but he also hoped that these new cities would carry forward Boston's life of civil and religious freedom, of education, of social order and loyalty to law. These were the basic values of New England society that influenced the section's approach to foreign affairs.[18]

The same attitudes contributed to scepticism toward western expansion. Too rapid settlement of the vast frontier would mean the triumph of primitivism. Emerson noted that frontier pioneers were members of "the raw multitudes" and claimed that "men of respectability in mind and morals are rarely found." The frontier was being populated too fast "for its virtue & its peace."[19] Much the same attitude helped further the extensive home missionary movement of New England's churches. As the tumultuous 1840s approached, with their wave of expansion into Oregon and Texas, New England was not ready to succumb to the new spirit of manifest destiny.

Cupidity was flourishing as much in New England as among western land speculators, but it focused on the development of industry and trade. Boston's financiers invested in western railroads, and her shipping interests were much interested in the acquisition of seaports on the Pacific coast. Thomas Perkins and Daniel Webster joined hands in buying land for speculation in lower Michigan and central Illinois.

These activities did not appear to threaten traditional New England society. The family and church continued to be the centers of life. The concern of fathers for their children surpassed other concerns. John Quincy Adams and Abbott Lawrence labored incessantly at advising their children that in devotion to their studies, thrift, hard work, and bible reading lay the path to a useful life. Rich fathers endowed sons not only with wealth but with guidance to help them avoid the treacherous paths of undisciplined passions and the troughs of intemperance and wasted time. Self-indulgence had no place.

Not until the antislavery movement mushroomed in the 1840s did the leaven of reform make an impact on New England politics, but things were astir. Even the highly institutionalized realm of religion experienced tremors; never more so than when, in 1842, the impatient and impulsive Theodore Parker, Unitarian clergyman, delivered his famous sermon, "The Transient and the Permanent in Christianity," in which he discarded divine revelation as the basis of truth.

Antislavery feelings antedated the antislavery movement by decades. Leaders in politics viewed slavery as a moral evil but did not view it as a political question. In the early years of the century slavery was believed to be ephemeral. Later, as slavery continued to grow, much emphasis was placed on the slavery compromise in the Constitution, and this was accepted as binding, an agreement entered into in good faith. Many a New Englander was more concerned about the treatment of the Indians and, more particularly, the dispossession of the Indians of their lands. There was also a willingness to write off the evil of slavery as something that could not be remedied. No less a person than Edward Everett, in 1826, confessed that while he could not approve of slavery in principle, he believed that the master had a right to the service of one he supported until his death "in a society where general emancipation is impracticable."[20]

When Texas won its independence in 1836 and its annexation to the United States became an issue, a general turnabout took place. William Ellery Channing led the way with a public letter to Henry Clay denouncing the annexation movement as a conspiracy of slaveholders and land speculators. The rise of angry feelings so alarmed Everett that he thought the Union was on the verge of dissolution "and that we are approaching a state of things as calamitous as the world ever witnessed."[21] To another correspondent, William Jackson, he wrote at length explaining how the question of annexing Texas had completely altered the issue of slavery. Until annexation became a question slavery could be dismissed as an evil imposed on the colonists against their will. It had been sanctioned by the Constitution and therefore later generations were bound by the contract. The annexation of Texas changed all this. The extension of slavery would be a voluntary act, a positive move that would entail responsibility. If free Americans now stood by and consented to this extension then "We should stand condemned before the civilized world." If we agreed, Everett wrote: "It would be thought & thought justly, that lust of power and lust of gold had made us deaf to the voice of humanity and justice."[22]

In the 1830s New England confronted questions of considerable dimension in foreign affairs. Spoliation claims against France engaged the attention of shipping interests. The first set of these claims dated back to the period prior to 1800. The treaty concluded with France in 1801 canceled French responsibility for these. In turn the United States was released from the alliance with France. American claimants contended that this action imposed an obligation on the government of the United States to make payment. New England representatives in Congress pressed with no success. Edward Everett, who served in Congress from 1827 to 1836, repeatedly presented resolutions. Webster acted as the attorney for the claimants and served as chairman of the Senate Select Committee on Claims. It was said that Webster collected a fee of $20,000 in 1832 as an agent.[23] However, their efforts were futile. In 1846 Congress finally passed a bill appropriating $5 million but Polk vetoed it.

The larger set of claims arose out of French seizures of American ships during the Napoleonic wars. The United States did not press for payment immediately after 1815, recognizing that France, occupied by the victorious armies and laden with a bill for reparations of 700 million francs, could not pay. On becoming president, Andrew Jackson made clear that he expected payment, but he was not impatient. Jackson's minister to France, William Cabell Rives of Virginia, an able man, future distinguished biographer of James Madison, combined a tough negotiating stance with an affability that gained him the friendship of Louis Philippe and the queen. He had leverage from the fact that the American market for French goods surpassed all others. Warnings that this could be curtailed had a sobering effect. However, Rives did not readily penetrate the twisted threads of French politics. The French, not without reason, held that the claims were excessive. Moreover, the complex political network of forces opposed to Louis Philippe meant to control him. Rives dismissed demands that the claims be scaled down as insulting. He held out for $5 million, though Albert Gallatin had estimated that the amount of justifiable claims amounted to no more than $2 million.

After heated exchanges in April and May 1831 with Count Sebastianti, the French foreign minister, a treaty committing France to pay $5 million was signed. This proved to be a pyrrhic victory.

The French Chamber of Deputies controlled the purse and promptly demonstrated they, too, had a voice in foreign affairs. Members of the chamber refused to appropriate the necessary funds, charging that the amount provided by the treaty exceeded the justifiable claims. So determined was the opposition that the administration of Louis Philippe chose not to submit another request for the funds.

Rives' replacement in 1833, Edward Livingston, a legal scholar of some distinction, dismissed French protests and charged that failure to pay constituted a breach of faith. When the administration in France, in 1834, did ask for the appropriation, the chamber voted it down. Livingston now concluded that the time had come for action; early in the fall of 1834 he recommended to the secretary of state that the United States prohibit importation of French goods.[24]

President Jackson, who until this time had shown no disposition to take drastic measures, in his annual message to Congress in December 1834, called for sequestration of French property in the United States and reprisals. The United States, he said, had abided by the 1831 treaty and had lowered the duties on French wines. He declared further negotiations out of the question. War now loomed ahead.

New England faced a dilemma. It had an interest in the claims but it had, given its heavy involvement in shipping, an even greater interest in peace. The Whigs in Congress were in no mood to embark on what they labeled a $5 million war, nor did they choose to miss the opportunity to fasten on the president the label "military chieftain."

In the House of Representatives Augustus Clayton of Georgia led off with a declaration denouncing Jackson's recommendations as a war message. John Patton of Virginia introduced a resolution opposing the taking of any measures. Edward Everett, fearing war and anxious for peace, held that while the treaty should be maintained, the adoption of reprisals would be an error. The course of policy, said Everett, should exclude "all factious subjects of collision." He could admire the president's spirit "But spirit is not all that is wanted for the conduct of great affairs." Everett asserted that the people of New England wished for peace. He said, "The people are anxious; it is natural. There is a vast property afloat; our merchants have connections with every accessible port on the habitable globe. There are two entire capitals, not less than a hundred each in transit. . . . The people do not want war for five millions of dollars." [25]

John Quincy Adams' nationalism now came to the fore. While he had contempt for Jackson and permitted his hostility to blind him to Jackson's strengths, he now contended that the president, having made threats, should be supported. Adams pursued a course that was wholly out of step with New England's position. Fear, he exclaimed in fervent language, had so taken possession of some of his colleagues that they dared not resent French perfidy. The treaty, he declared, "before God and all mankind," was binding. The president, said Adams, "as the great representative of the whole nation in its foreign relations" had committed the nation and this was not the time to ask whether this was wise or unwise, spirited or rash." He referred to the Senate where a decision had been reached to do nothing. That body had refused to support the president and closed their eyes to "the great national interest at stake." He deplored the fact that some had sought to prove that there was no such thing as national honor. A nation, he held, must so act as to gain respect and exhibit readiness to defend the rights of its citizens. However, unlike Jackson, Adams did not rule out further negotiation. [26]

The House of Representatives proceeded to take action. Churchill C. Cambreleng, prominent New York congressman and one of Jackson's strongest supporters, took the same position as Adams. In the final days of the session Adams agreed to eliminate the phrase "at all hazards" from his resolution authorizing the president to take action, and Adams accepted Cambreleng's version. On March 3, by a unanimous vote, the House adopted the resolutions. The Committee on Foreign Affairs was discharged from further consideration of commercial restrictions or reprisals. The final resolution stated that "preparation ought to be made to meet any emergency growing out of our relations with France." [27] In the early hours of the morning of the final day the House voted $3 million "to be expended by the President, in the recess of Congress, if he should deem it expedient, for the military and naval service." [28] Adams voted for the appropriation, but nine Massachusetts representatives voted against it.

The Senate, it appeared, would simply ignore the president's recommendations. Clay and Webster simultaneously patted the president on the shoulder for his patriotic sentiments and slapped his wrist for the measures he recommended. Finally, on February 21, Nathaniel Silsbee of Massachusetts presented a series of memorials from New England recommending commercial restrictions as more appropriate than Jackson's drastic measures. [29] A heated debate then ensued. Daniel Webster expressed regret that the question had arisen, and the Senate moved on to other matters. In the final hours of the session, when the bill came from the House providing for an appropriation of $3 million, the Senate reduced it to $300,000.

A settlement with France was reached before Congress met again. When Congress did meet, Webster sought to place the blame on the House for failure to support the president. He did so in spite of the fact that it was the Senate that had reduced the House appropriation of $3 million to $300,000. John Quincy Adams, in a vitriolic attack, skirted the rules of the Senate and cited the facts in the case, placing Webster in the wrong on policy and calling into question his integrity. Adams not only gained the enmity of Webster but was charged by Boston's best citizens with being unreliable.

When it came to the fore in December 1834, the French claims question coincided with a political battle in Massachusetts. The political ambitions of Webster, Adams, and Everett crisscrossed. Adams hoped

to be elected to the Senate; Everett hoped to become governor; Webster
wanted the presidency. Webster dominated the Whig party in his home
state; he arranged for Everett to be a candidate for governor and the
popular John Davis, then governor, to run for the Senate against
Adams.[30] The former president had strong support in the state senate,
but he lost as a result of Webster's influence.

Adams' warlike stance on the French claims question was used against
him. P. C. Brooks was appalled by Adams' belligerence. In February
Brooks wrote to Everett, "For lands' sake avoid war." He predicted that
Davis would win over Adams "owing to late excitement caused by Mr.
Adams' course in Congress." "It is thought," wrote Brooks, "to throw
an air of uncertainty over his character—that alarms many of his
friends." He reported, "They say he is a party to himself—that no one
knows where to find him—and that, while they have a reverence for his
general character, they fear to rely upon him in politics." People were
also offended by Adams' attack on Webster in the Senate.[31]

The gulf between Adams and Webster deepened. In January 1836
Webster charged him with deserting the party and commented, "His
apostacy will do us no hurt."[32]

At the time Webster was, once again, in financial difficulty. He had
no means of paying a debt of $55,000. Each time the wealthy of Boston
had rescued him. This time Everett appealed to his father-in-law to
come to Webster's aid. Brooks refused, stating that those who had
loaned money to Webster knew he was a bad risk and should be prepared
to take their loss. Moreover, Brooks wrote, Webster would simply go in
debt again. In 1839 Webster's friends paid off his debts and then paid for
his trip to England.[33] Brooks was correct. In 1845 Webster again faced
bankruptcy, and his friends in Boston raised $37,000 for an annuity on
his behalf and another sum to pay off his debts.

# 8

# New England and the Maine Boundary Controversy

The victory of William Henry Harrison in the election of 1840 brought with it the appointment of Daniel Webster as secretary of state. Within a month Harrison died and John Tyler of Virginia entered the presidency. The ascendancy of Tyler ushered in a sharp split in the Whig party culminating in Tyler's veto of two national bank bills in his first months in office and the resignation of five cabinet members. Webster, however, remained, much to the distress of so-called ultra Whigs in New England. The only New England Whig in Congress who continued support of Tyler, Caleb Cushing of Salem, promptly found it would be futile to stand as a candidate in the congressional election of 1842.

Webster found Tyler a supportive and congenial ally. Tyler would have supported a bank bill of a different type, and Webster saw merit in his stand. Webster could also point out to his critics that, in 1842, a great Whig victory had been achieved in the enactment of a new protective tariff As he saw the situation, it called for union rather than the extreme demands of the "ultra Whigs." But it was, of course, the opportunity to achieve a higher standing, one that would strengthen his chances for the presidency, that led him to stay on with Tyler.

On assuming office Webster faced a serious crisis in relations with Great Britain. The *Caroline* affair remained unsettled. The ship that had been carrying arms to Canadian rebels on Navy Island on the Niagara river had been seized and destroyed by Canadian troops in December 1837. The British refused to make an apology on the ground that the action was taken in self-defense. At the same time Hunters Lodges and the Sons of Liberty were conducting raids into Canada. Peace was restored on the frontier, but the local uproar created a problem for the Van Buren and Harrison administrations that neither could solve. Alexander McLeod, a Canadian, was reported to have boasted that he had participated in the attack on the *Caroline* and had killed an American, both of which he denied. He was arrested in New York and charged with murder. The state would not release him and ignored pleas from the federal government. The British government held that a soldier in the armed forces, in action in defense of his country, could not be tried in a foreign court. It went further; it made clear that if McLeod were executed, the British minister would withdraw from Washington. Normal relations were further endangered by a series of incidents connected with British efforts to put an end to the slave trade. Ships suspected of falsely flying the American flag were stopped for search. Then came the *Creole* incident. The ship carrying slaves from Virginia to New Orleans entered a British port after a slave mutiny on board. To the dismay of southerners the British freed the slaves. All of these incidents added up to a crisis in American-British relations.

However, the Maine boundary issue surpassed all of these in importance. The territory in dispute was of no great commercial or agricultural significance, but the valuable timber lands and the strategic importance of the area, as well as the bold spirits of Maine land speculators, made it a dangerous tinderbox.

At the time Webster became secretary of state—March 1841—both the British and Americans were engaged in making plans for a war they did not want but that they expected. The British, deeply concerned about Canada's vulnerability, were engaged in strengthening border fortifications. By September the new ministry in London issued precautionary orders for four battleships to go to Bermuda.[1] At the same time the new Harrison administration was examining the nation's defenses. The president promptly increased the number of military officers, and Congress authorized the construction of three new warships. However, the United States was poorly prepared. The secretary of the navy warned that an enemy would be able to "harrass our whole seaboard, and to carry out all the horrors of war into the securest retreats of our people." The effect, he wrote, "would be terrible everywhere."[2] In New England these considerations carried great weight. The vulnerability of its large merchant fleet made war, to all but the extremists in Maine, a sobering prospect.

The Maine boundary controversy had its birth in the peace treaty of 1783. The peacemakers acknowledged that the lines they drew were based on incomplete information and that final determination of the Maine boundary line would have to be made after peace had been restored. Repeated efforts failed to bring about agreement, and with the passage of time self-interest and national honor widened the difference in treaty interpretations. Which of the several rivers was the St. Croix referred to in the treaty? Did the highlands spoken of have reference to mountains or simply to a watershed? The remoteness of the area permitted decision makers to procrastinate, but by 1838 time had run out. By then the United States and Great Britain confronted each other across a barrier of thorny disputes. In both countries the public held unfriendly images of the other; the Americans viewed the British as haughty, greedy, and untrustworthy, while the British thought the Americans crude, swashbuckling, and unlimited in ambition. The leadership in both countries wished to maintain peace, but both had to contend with irrational public feelings that could easily be aroused by the rivalry of political parties.

In 1826 President John Quincy Adams sent Albert Gallatin to London to settle a long list of disputes. Adams hoped to win the right to use the St. Lawrence River, settle the boundary dispute, and at the same time not yield any ground. Gallatin, a more realistic statesman, pointed out the difficulty of winning concessions unless he could offer something in return. He wrote to Secretary of State Henry Clay that "it was extremely improbable that this Government [the British] should agree with us, not on compromise, but on the true construction of the treaty." He added, "Even if they were satisfied that ours is correct, the pretensions of New Brunswick, the importance of obtaining a boundary that will connect that province with Canada, and public opinion, would prevent them from acceding to it, and induce them to try the chance of arbitration. . . ." Moreover, Gallatin acknowledged, there were "some real difficulties in the true construction of the treaty."[3]

Maine Governor Enoch Lincoln set out to make the federal government aware of its duties. He fixed on a sentence Gallatin had written to

Clay, stating: "An umpire, whether a king or a farmer, rarely decides on strict principles of law; he always has a bias to try, if possible to split the difference."[4] Gallatin's genial and wise observation concerning the nature of statecraft was interpreted by Lincoln as nothing less than unprincipled willingness to betray Maine. When word reached Lincoln that a convention had been entered into providing for arbitration by the king of the Netherlands, he expressed disgust. He notified the secretary of state that he could not "contemplate in cold blood submitting the destiny of Maine to an irresponsible arbiter," a European monarch with a bias against republics.[5] If a cession of territory was made, then, said Lincoln, in a spirit of defiance, Maine would "withdraw her deference and submission."

In January 1831 the king of the Netherlands informed London and Washington of his decision. Both governments agreed that he had gone beyond the terms of his assignment; and rather than drawing a line on the basis of the treaty, he had submitted a compromise. The British accepted the award but the United States declined. The award was far from unfavorable to Maine in terms of the division of land. Of the estimated 12,072 square miles in dispute the United States would receive 7,908 square miles and Great Britain 4,119 square miles.[6] William Pitt Preble, the United States minister at the Hague, an important personage in Maine, former state supreme court justice, and best known for his irascibility and defiant spirit, immediately denounced the award. The Maine legislature, with equal resoluteness, rejected the award on the grounds that the arbiter had not based his decision on an interpretation of the treaty.

The availability of fine stands of timber that could lure lumber companies into the area and the presence of settlers from both Maine and New Brunswick raised the question of British exercise of jurisdiction. In 1837 Governor Kent of Maine sent a land surveyor to the area. The authorities of New Brunswick arrested him and placed him in jail in Fredrickton, an act that outraged the people of Maine.

The following year the new governor, John Fairfield, received a report of extensive lumber operations in the valley of the Aroostook. Fairfield, with the approval of the legislature, sent a posse of 200 armed men to investigate and to drive out the alleged trespassers. On their arrival they arrested some of the trespassers, including James MacLauchlan, the British warden. Before long the Canadians retaliated and arrested Rufus McIntire, leader of the Maine posse. Governor Fairfield, in turn, called on the legislature to take defense measures. The legislature appropriated $800,000, and Fairfield called for volunteers. As 1838 came to a close there were 10,000 armed men from Maine in the disputed territory ready to take possession and do battle. The New Brunswick authorities called out troops. This action was promptly labeled the Aroostook War. No blood was shed but this harum-scarum venture could easily have resulted in war with England had not calmer and more judicious minds presided in Washington and London.

President Van Buren's message to Congress on 26 February 1839 reflected his anxiety over the possibility of war. He cited the happenings in Maine—and upheld the state's right to drive out the trespassers— and the informal understanding that neither side would interfere with the settlements of the other in the disputed territory. At the same time he informed Congress that Maine had been told that, while the federal government recognized its obligation to do all in its power to effect a settlement, it had "no other means to accomplish that object amicably, than by another arbitration, or by a commission with an umpire in the nature of an arbitration, and that in the event of all other measures failing the President would feel it his duty to submit another proposition to the Government of Great Britain, to refer the decision to a third Power." He would not, he said, recommend that the military force of the federal government be brought to the aid of Maine. An appeal to arms, he said, would not only prove fatal to Maine's present interests "but would postpone, if not defeat, the attainment of the main objects which they have in view."[7]

The question came before the House of Representatives where two representatives of Massachusetts took opposing sides. Caleb Cushing twisted the lion's tail, claiming that Great Britain was guilty of perfidy, and warned the British that the United States would no longer tolerate past practices—"No more delays, no more procrastinations, no more of the diplomatic chicanery by which Great Britain has so long sought to obtain from the United States by maneuver what is not hers by any just right, and what she cannot extort by force." As Webster was to say of

Cushing, he "always likes to ride a charger." Cushing firmly believed that the British, by virtue of their possessions, meant to hold the United States hostage and to prevent her from achieving world power status.[8]

Leverett Saltonstall of Salem, a man of quite a different type and more representative of New England, had no inclination to engage in bravado. He challenged the assertion of his more belligerent colleagues who contended that the United States had never before been confronted with the British claim of their right to exercise jurisdiction in the disputed territory. Those who held this view, he said, argued that if the British did not rescind the claim war was inevitable. Saltonstall showed that the British had made this claim for many years, that this was well known in both Washington and Massachusetts, and that Massachusetts had protested but the federal government never had.[9] Saltonstall deplored the decision of the Maine legislature to send militia into the disputed area, a move he called "indiscreet—unfortunate to say the least."[10] In conclusion he observed:

A great and new question is now presented, whether an indiscreet State shall involve this nation in a great and tremendous war? War between these two nations will be no child's play; all say that once begun, it will be long, that it may be of ten years duration; ten years of strife, of suffering, and of bloodshed.[11]

Edward Everett, now governor of Massachusetts, shared Saltonstall's views. He expressed apprehension of Maine's conduct.[12] In his annual message to the legislature Everett manifested no sympathy with the drastic steps taken by Maine, and he left the ardent Maine leaders feeling that they could not count on his support. Daniel Webster, too, wished to avoid extreme measures and favored a conciliatory course. During the debates in Congress in March 1839 he wrote a memo expressing favor for negotiation and a compromise line.[13] The moderation of the most influential leaders in Massachusetts counterbalanced the extremism in Maine where, as Everett said, politicians exploited the issue for political purposes. The posture of Massachusetts owed much to strong opposition to war with England, a war that would destroy that state's close commercial ties with the British. Equally important in shaping the views of men like Everett and Saltonstall was their personal aversion toward emotional harangues that obscured the relevant facts. Everett acknowledged that there were, as he said, several public acts and documents "which go to admit the jurisdiction of Great Britain over the disputed territory." [14]

Maine's desperate decision to resort to force and her failure to call on the national government to protect her interests left her standing alone. She was not without a few defenders in Massachusetts, but the extreme measures of Governor Fairfield and the Maine legislature alienated her friends. The editor of the influential *Boston Daily Advertiser* hoped that Maine would not repel a British offer made in a conciliatory spirit. [15] The question, he wrote some days later, was one for the national government. [16] He upheld Great Britain's right to exercise jurisdiction in the disputed territory and held Governor Fairfield's order to send in troops to be "a direct violation of the understanding." [17] A plea from Fairfield that Massachusetts should share the expenses of the military venture was treated with coolness. By early March the editor was calling Maine's action "a usurpation of authority." [18] When Secretary of State John Forsyth went to Maine to discuss matters, the editor again seized the opportunity to declare that the question must be settled by the federal government. Again he warned that the controversy would lead to war if "our Government is determined to follow the lead of Maine on this subject." The whole controversy, he held, was contemptible. [19]

The editor of the *Springfield Republican* hoped for a speedy settlement. He ascribed the high state of feeling in Maine to the "race for popularity between the two political parties." "It is this zeal of the two parties, which gives at this time such a threatening aspect to the controversy." [20]

Not only the press but the most influential leaders of the Whig party in Massachusetts viewed Maine's actions as unwarranted and dangerous. Edward Everett, on receiving Governor Fairfield's plea for help, advised the legislature that the question was one for the national government. [21] Maine had long rested her position on the constitutional provision that the federal government could not cede part of a state's territory to a foreign government or another state. Well before the violence of late 1838, Everett held that this constitutional provision was irrelevant to the dispute. [22] The question was not one of ceding territory but rather of locating a boundary. Everett held to this position throughout the controversy.

George Ashmun of Springfield, prominent Whig and speaker in the Massachusetts House of Representatives, sided with Maine and devoted his energy to proving Great Britain responsible.[23] He, unlike both Robert C. Winthrop and Leverett Saltonstall, held that the British had no right to exercise jurisdiction in the disputed territory and therefore Maine was justified in her actions. In the debate on a set of resolutions in the legislature, state Senator Wolcott of Middlesex took the opposing view.[24] The state senate adopted a series of resolutions, several of which upheld the treaty of 1783 and Maine's rights to the territory, but also a resolution stating that if Great Britain should show a conciliatory spirit and Maine persist in the use of force, she would bear a heavy responsibility. Maine should leave it to the general government to vindicate her rights.[25]

In the crucial months of March and April 1839 Everett, governor of Massachusetts, wrote a series of informative letters, first to Secretary of War Joel Poinsett and then to President Van Buren. Everett assembled all the available papers on the controversy, studied these with care, and then sought to educate the administration. He deplored the federal administration's failure to take up the problem earlier and at the same time believed that the British leadership was also poorly informed. In his letters to Poinsett he contended that the British had been guided by the inhabitants of New Brunswick. Some of them welcomed the prospect of war for "it would send a shower of gold upon them without exposing them to any injury." "The leading portion of the population," wrote Everett, "consists of the descendants of the refugee loyalists of the revolution." "They draw hatred of the U.S.," he observed, "with their mothers' milk." "The preposterous claim of the British Government to a territory south of the St. Johns," he charged, "originated with these men. . . ."[26]

Everett confided that he had been privy to documents of the negotiations made available by a friend who, however, was committed to secrecy. The British had published almost nothing whereas the United States had put everything into print. The information in the secret documents in the possession of Jared Sparks, Everett affirmed, supported the American claim and it would be well to pressure the British into taking it into account. Everett argued that the United States was entitled to the territory east of the St. John, and he ridiculed the British contention that this river did not flow into the Atlantic. He elaborated at length his own interpretation of the treaty, and he criticized in severe tones Palmerston's instructions to the commissioners making the survey because the British foreign minister, in ruling out any survey of that river, had rendered the survey useless; the United States would gain nothing by joining hands in it.

Everett wrote lengthy letters to President Van Buren stressing the same point and called Palmerston's assertion shameless. He advised Van Buren that topographical studies did not get to the heart of the problem. "The point of honor on both sides is a much more serious obstacle to amicable adjustment than the point of interest," Everett contended.[27] He outlined a possible settlement. His first point, and one he gave up well before negotiations began, was that the United States relinquish Oregon north of the Columbia River and, in turn, that Great Britain "acknowledge the N.E. boundary as claimed by the U.S." He acknowledged this to be liberal. The Oregon question was becoming increasingly important, he wrote, and the differences between the two countries would remain difficult to resolve unless both boundary questions were settled. He professed he could see no other way to restore good relations.

In a second letter to the president Everett summed up the difficulties. The rivalry of the two political parties in Maine, he said, "has been the great source of difficulty and embarrassment." Party rivalry in England was in the same way an obstacle to settlement. And now Maine had asked Massachusetts to share the cost of building military roads through the disputed territory. This, Everett believed, was nothing less than an attempt to exercise jurisdiction there. Everett would give no countenance to this.[28]

Daniel Webster, in the Senate, pondered long on how best to resolve the dangerous situation. On 9 March 1839 he drafted a lengthy memorandum for his own use, one that exhibited his great statesmanlike qualities. Webster lived with a frank and realistic appraisal of the centrifugal forces that made the Union so fragile. As early as 1839 he foresaw dangerous divisions on the Texas question and when asked about the desirability of acquiring California, he advocated caution. Adding too large a territory would not only raise divisions within the country, it posed the danger of creating a republic so extensive that outlying regions would feel remote and develop no loyalty to the central political unit. The northeastern boundary controversy could, if not properly managed, lead to danger should it become exploited by the national parties.

Webster's draft called for compromise and careful preliminary discussions with the British so that they would have a better understanding of the complexities from an American political point of view. He noted that it would be difficult to maintain peace in the area if the question were not soon settled. He also gave thought to winning the cooperation of Maine and Massachusetts. He clearly perceived the danger of negotiating a treaty and then having it disapproved by the Senate where Maine might find support. When the time arrived for negotiations three years later, Webster adhered to this early memo.[29] In the meantime he exercised caution, carefully avoiding contention with Maine and expressing in a restrained manner an understanding of Maine's point of view, yet not surrendering to the Maine position.

The crisis of early 1839 came to a close without violence, and the boundary controversy was placed on hold. President Van Buren sent General Winfield Scott to arrange for forces to be recalled. On his way to Maine Scott stopped in Boston and visited at length with Governor Everett who was well informed both on Maine politics and the pros and cons of the controversy. Massachusetts had much at stake for it held joint claim with Maine to the public lands in the disputed territory, but Massachusetts would not exercise jurisdiction in the area. Scott then went to Maine where he sought to have political parties agree to a truce. From there he went to Fredrickton where he met with Sir John Harvey, a friend of long standing. Harvey agreed he would not send troops into the disputed area unless he received new orders from his government. In turn Governor Fairfield agreed to withdraw Maine troops. During the truce both sides accused the other of violations, but there were no clashes.

During the anxious months of early 1839 Charles Sumner, who was in London, furnished Everett with detailed accounts of the British response. Sumner enjoyed access to both political leaders and newspaper editors. In England Sumner wrote, ". . . nobody knows anything about it." "A few newspapers cry aloud, whenever it is referred to, but I doubt if the editors have ever looked into it; the most remarkable editor of London . . . Faublanque of the *Examiner*, told me that he knew nothing of it." Sumner, after interviews with political leaders, concluded that the "Cabinet literally knows nothing about it." Sumner recommended that it would be well to send a "large collection of reports, articles, and documents relating to the question to London for distribution." Of the political leaders to whom he spoke only two were informed, and both thought the United States was in the right. Sumner defended the American position but he was distressed with "the illiterate, blustering papers of Governor Fairfield." Fairfield's proceedings, he wrote, were rash and vulgar. He believed that if the British would study the question, they would see the American side and the question would be settled amicably.[30]

On 12 April 1839 Everett, in a lengthy, unprovocative exposition of the issues, expressed the hope that the British would study the question, search the archives for the copy of the Mitchell map used in 1783, and make public, as the United States had done, all relevant material. Everett, like Albert Gallatin, had studied the question with care. Both agreed that Maine had a reasonable case, but both were prepared to compromise.

However, the British gave no signs of a willingness to compromise. A team of commissioners from England gave their findings in 1840. Gallatin found their report so obviously distorted that he published a strongly worded critique and protested the fact that the British government had approved their report.[31] A committee of the Massachusetts legislature, chaired by Charles Francis Adams, issued a report showing the incompleteness of the investigation made by the Britishers.

Massachusetts was not prepared to uphold Maine's claim, and it became increasingly clear that Maine stood alone. As early as March 1839 a Bostonian confided to Hannibal Hamlin of Maine that the people of his city were greatly alarmed by the prospect of war with England. He observed: "Property is scattered over every ocean and the enemy would make bankrupts of thousands in a few weeks, 5 per cent premium is demanded at the insurance offices against war risks only."[32]

In the spring of 1840 Boston's leading newspaper, the *Daily Advertiser and Patriot*, ran a series of editorials denouncing Maine's unwillingness to compromise. On March 31 the editor pronounced it "a senseless controversy." National honor, he wrote, was not at stake.[33] The award of the king of the Netherlands, he maintained, should have been accepted, and the editor proposed an adjustment on the basis of that award. The following day the editor held Governor Fairfield guilty of misrepresentation of the existing situation.[34] Again on April 18 the editor praised the Senate Committee on Foreign Relations for its pacific views.[35] The editor accurately reflected the opinions of political and business leaders in Boston who believed that Maine's obstinacy was foolish.

A year later, in 1841, Charles Francis Adams wrote a lengthy attack on the report of the British commissioners, G. W. Featherstonbaugh and Richard C. Mudge, a report submitted and accepted by the government in London. These agents, Adams charged, wanted to embroil the two countries in war. Their findings rested on a mere two months expedition in which they had traversed only a fraction of the territory. Adams, while critical of the report, had high hopes of peace because Governor Kent of Maine and Sir John Harvey of New Brunswick "are inclined to do everything within their power to maintain those friendly relations between the two countries, which are vitally important to the happiness and prosperity of both."[36] Maine's recalcitrance was being eroded by the cost of the military efforts of 1839 and by admission, however reluctantly acknowledged, that the state stood alone, that she could not expect support from Massachusetts, and that the federal government was not about to engage in a dangerous war over the boundary question.

In 1839 Webster visited England where he made friends readily, won respect, and appeared as the man with whom the British could deal on a reasonable basis. While in England he spent considerable time with Lord Ashburton whose banking interests he had represented in a legal capacity. They became friends. In 1841 with the accession of Tyler to the presidency, Webster, now secretary of state, sounded out his good friend Edward Everett as to whether he would be interested in assuming the post of minister to England. Webster wrote that he himself would very much like the post but that he could not afford it. Everett accepted, and it appeared that he would be the one to negotiate on the troublesome questions between the two countries. The appointment encountered resistance in the Senate from southerners who respected Everett but were uncertain that he could be trusted on the difficult slave trade question that was, at the moment, uppermost in their minds.

By this time the Conservatives were in power in England, and the conciliatory Lord Aberdeen had replaced Palmerston as minister of foreign affairs. Both Webster and Aberdeen were anxious for a settlement. In January 1842 Aberdeen appointed Lord Ashburton special envoy to the United States. A better appointment could not have been made, for Ashburton enjoyed great prestige at home and was known in the United States as a friendly person. A special mission in itself was flattering to Americans. Prior to leaving England, Ashburton spent much time with Everett who was well prepared to discuss the treaty of 1783, the political side of the issue in the United States, and what the United States could and could not agree to.

Webster was elated with Ashburton's appointment and made careful preparations for his arrival. After his first meeting with Ashburton Webster wrote to Everett in glowing terms of the pleasure in dealing with a man who was no less determined to achieve a satisfactory solution than himself. He wrote: "For my own part, no selection of a Minister could be more agreeable to me than that of Lord Ashburton, as I entertain towards him sentiments of great kindness and regard." [37] On his arrival Ashburton soon won the respect and admiration of those he met, and his presence did much to mitigate suspicion of England. As Charles Sumner wrote to a British friend: "Lord Ashburton and his suite spread a social charm over Washington, and filled everybody with friendly feelings toward England. Even John Quincy Adams relaxed in his opposition to all things English. . . ." [38]

The issues confronting the two countries did not lend themselves to easy solution. The recent *Creole* case, the yet unsettled case of the *Caroline*, the issue of search on the high seas, and the northeast boundary dispute were not insurmountable, but, as Webster wrote to Everett, there were men in Congress who stirred up a warlike spirit not because they wanted war but because they wished to embarrass the administration. Had the British been able to come to terms on the old impressment issue, it would have removed a cause of much distrust and opened the door to an agreement on the slave trade. Everett discussed the question at great length with Aberdeen and, with great skill and in a friendly manner, showed that yielding on this question could not possibly endanger Britain's ability to man her ships of war. Aberdeen appeared to have agreed, but he feared that public opinion would not accept it.

The *Creole* case was likewise a very real difficulty. Webster wanted compensation for those slaves who were taken and set free but who had not participated in the mutiny. He saw this as important in order to gain the support of southerners for the treaty he hoped to negotiate. Aberdeen's hands were tied when the law officers of the crown ruled that compensation would be illegal. Webster still had to be concerned about Maine's stance. As late as April a congressman from Maine advised him that it was unlikely that the state legislature would agree to sending commissioners to participate in the negotiations.

Not long after Ashburton's arrival, Webster indicated he was prepared to negotiate in a generous spirit. He told Everett he would not be extreme in the *Creole* case, that he would push immediately for a habeas corpus act that would bring any future McLeods before a federal court, and that he would "forgive the *Caroline* outrage" subject to the British making minor amends; he added, "I want to stipulate for such a limited and reciprocal right of inquiry on the coast of Africa as should save our flag from being prostituted to the uses of the slave traders." [39]

Another letter Webster wrote only two days later told of the fine reception given Ashburton but then spoke of the difficulties. The public, he wrote, had made up its mind that the American interpretation of the treaty of 1783 was the only one, while the British insisted on some points that the American public chose not to understand. Webster recognized that there were inconsistencies in the treaty, but he also held the view that where the treaty was specific and clear it should be honored. The greatest obstacle to compromise was determining equivalents for what Maine must yield. Webster considered the British view that she must maintain communication between Fredrickton and Quebec wholly reasonable. Maine, he proposed, should be compensated by having the boundary follow the St. John after the line running due north reached a certain distance. Here England had a clearly rightful claim and, recognizing this, Maine should be pleased. The second gain for

Maine would be to grant her the right to convey timber down the St. John to its mouth.[40]

Again on May 16 Webster praised Ashburton's approach, but Ashburton had now referred specific points to the government in London. Webster worried about the tenacity of both Maine and the British government "on points not important to either."[41] At this same time Aberdeen told Everett that the instructions to the British negotiators in 1779 clearly established British interpretation of the treaty. Everett promptly wrote a letter taking issue. A few days later Aberdeen acknowledged he had been mistaken. Everett then pressed him to search for the original map. Everett had in mind the map he had seen in the volume Sparks had shown him but that Sparks had missed seeing. Webster soon urged Everett not to press for maps, probably fearing that one would be found that would strengthen the British case.

On the American side of the Atlantic Daniel Webster faced the challenge of how he was to win Maine's acceptance of a compromise. Massachusetts posed much less of a problem, for opinion there favored compromise. He informed the governor of Maine that the federal government would agree to a conventional line. He also assured both states that no agreement would be reached without their consent, and he recommended that both states be represented by commissioners in the negotiations. The Maine legislature gave its approval on 18 May 1842.[42]

Maine's consent owed much to a plan carried out by Francis O. J. Smith, former member of Congress and prominent citizen, and Webster. While in Washington in May 1841, Smith met with Webster and proposed that, given the $800,000 expense to Maine of the military expedition of 1839 and the feeling of hopelessness among her people, opinion in Maine could be turned around to accept a compromise. Smith offered to undertake the task, but he explained that he would need financial assistance. Webster, with the approval of Tyler, allotted the necessary money from the secret fund, and Smith and his assistants worked to win the support of editors and some of the state's leaders. Webster also sent Peleg Sprague and Albert Smith to Maine to persuade members of the state legislature. Sprague, a federal judge, and Smith, a former member of Congress from Maine and a Democrat, were both convinced of the necessity of compromise.

Francis O. J. Smith was a man of ability, and he played a constructive role in the negotiations. He was not simply a propagandist. Smith saw clearly that Maine had become entrapped in the appeal to her honor and, over the many years of controversy, had lost her capacity to face the question realistically. He held that Maine had much to gain by settlement. Not to make any move toward a compromise might well mean another ten years before a settlement was reached. Maine, he thought, should take the initiative in forwarding an agreement. He took it upon himself to advise Webster how it should be done. First, the public lands in Maine should be taken over by the federal government under an arrangement whereby Maine and Massachusetts should receive compensation. This, he hoped, would enable Maine and New Brunswick to reach an agreement. Semiofficial intercourse between these two could then procede.

Second, he proposed to prepare public sentiment in Maine for a compromise by offering the prospect of an exchange of territory coupled with a pecuniary indemnity. This would suffice, he thought, as a recognition of Maine's rights and satisfy her honor and pride. Maine's "pecuniary condition will," he wrote, predispose her people toward it "if it can be made to seem to have its origin with themselves."

Third, public sentiment could "be brought into right shape in Maine by enlisting certain leading men of both parties and through them, at a proper time hereafter, guiding aright the public press." This was to be achieved by a few months of steady and well-directed correspondence. Smith, at this stage, proposed that the same should be done in the British province and then at the right time the two would get together. He noted that the mercantile interests in Maine would provide support, for they dreaded war.[43]

The leaders in Maine were to be drawn in silently and systematically in order to prevent the compromise from becoming a party question. The persons to be approached should be made to feel that it was "a subject worthy of their whole time and effort" both from a personal, political, and national point of view. It would be necessary to hold out promises of compensation. He, too, would require compensation. He estimated his own recompense would amount to $3500 per annum.

Smith launched his program of correspondence and soon received responses that were encouraging. All was done in secret, and the letters to Smith were unsigned. One of these correspondents, after sounding out the loco focos [Democrats] in Aroostook and elsewhere, reported they would be ready to give their support in the state legislature, feeling there was honor to be gained in restoring peace. He also found many anxious to open the Penobscot area.[44] The state's honor would be preserved by making a cession to the American government, and an indemnity, plus an agreement to open the St. John River for sending timber to the coast, would gain strong support.

In the summer of 1841 Smith visited different parts of the state and discussed the question with local leaders. He concluded that the way was now open to a satisfactory compromise. He then prepared an article that he published in a neutral church periodical. He made arrangements with newspapers of both parties to reprint it.

Smith was not lacking in ingenuity. In November 1841 he wrote to Webster explaining that he hoped to have two men in each county devote two months to gathering signatures for a memorial calling on the legislature to take the proper steps. This would serve to divert the question from one of party interest and party excitement. He concluded his letter stating, "If two or three thousand dollars could be rightfully employed in forwarding this matter at this juncture, it will accomplish more than armies can do after the subject shall be revived in a belligerent spirit."

In April 1842 Smith reported to Webster that the state senate would approve a compromise but it might be defeated in the House of Representatives. However, he believed that if Ashburton was found to have the authority to make an adjustment, the opposition could probably be overcome by calling a special session of the state assembly.[45] This special session, when it met in May, approved of the cession to the federal government and authority granted state commissioners to reach a settlement.

In reality changes were taking place in Maine before Smith met Webster in Washington. The Whigs came to power in January 1841. Not long before, Governor Fairfield had protested the establishment of a military post at Madawaska but the new Whig governor, Edward Kent and the legislature, wrote a Maine observer, "seemed altogether indifferent about it." The same writer noted that the state boundary committee did not meet until March and then passed some lukewarm resolves. The legislature did not take up the resolves until the very close of the session and then did so without giving them much attention.[46] The dispute, owing to its long history, had lost some of its inflammable quality, and some Whig leaders in Maine saw that continuing the controversy would be costly and futile.

In the spring of 1842 Webster sent Jared Sparks, professor of history at Harvard, to Augusta, the state capital, with a copy of the map he had found in Paris. Sparks had copied the red line, supposedly drawn by Benjamin Franklin, marking the boundary. Both Webster and Sparks had doubts as to the map's authenticity, but Webster used it to show that in the event the dispute went to arbitration, the British side had more weight. As Sparks' map showed a boundary highly favorable to the British, Webster hoped it would arouse fears among the Maine commissioners. Sparks' map was also shown to various Maine legislators in Augusta and later to the Maine commissioners in Washington. It bore no signatures of the peace negotiators, and the commissioners were certainly well aware that only a signed Mitchell map would serve as authoritative evidence. Scores of maps were in existence. Gallatin had submitted no fewer than nineteen to the king of the Netherlands when that monarch was asked to arbitrate.[47]

The optimism that prevailed in May 1842 was dissipated by delay as Ashburton received new instructions. In mid-June Ashburton was so discouraged that he was ready to return to England and declare the mission a failure. At this point President Tyler, who gave Webster his full support throughout the negotiations, met with Ashburton and persuaded him that it was absolutely necessary for him to stay and continue the exhausting negotiations. However, as late as 3 July 1842 Abbott Lawrence, Massachusetts commissioner in the negotiations, told John Quincy Adams that the commissioners from Maine "were tenacious upon trifles—Lord Ashburton was tenacious upon trifles—much more so than he had appeared to be when he first came."[48] Ashburton's new instructions were part of the problem. Another difficulty arose when he took up the cudgels for the New Brunswick agents who demanded Madawaska.

When Webster and Ashburton neared completion of their negotiations, the secretary of state presented the terms to the commissioners of Massachusetts and Maine. The commissioners of Massachusetts gave their approval first. The Maine commissioners delayed for a few days. Once Massachusetts approved, Maine would have been left in an awkward position had her commissioners not done the same.

On 11 August 1842 President Tyler submitted the treaty to the Senate. Four days later the Senate Committee on Foreign Relations gave a favorable report. Party considerations gave rise to some opposition. Thomas Hart Benton and James Buchanan opposed approval and used the opportunity to denounce Great Britain. Reuel Williams of Maine, a Democrat, defended the treaty of 1783 and held the new treaty to be a product of shady diplomacy. He introduced a resolution calling for resubmission of the treaty to the Foreign Relations Committee "with instructions to report a resolution directing the President of the United States to take immediate possession of the disputed territory."[49] This was defeated and the treaty approved by a vote of 39 to 9. Only Williams of Maine and Perry Smith of Connecticut, among the New England senators, voted in the negative. Reflecting on his success, Webster confided to his good friend, Jared Sparks: "The grand stroke was to get the previous consent of Maine and Massachusetts. Nobody else had attempted this; it occurred to nobody else; it was a movement of great delicacy, and of very doubtful result."[50]

When Everett, who had been so closely involved in the controversy since 1839, heard that the treaty had been signed, he wrote a lengthy letter reviewing the negotiations. He gave great credit to Ashburton. No one, he said, was as well qualified for the mission. "But then all this would not have prevailed," he wrote, "had not the control of the negotiations on our side been precisely what it is." A little more leaning either way, he thought, would have been fatal. Then he noted: "The calling in of the commissioners from Maine and Massachusetts was a masterly stroke." Aberdeen had questioned the strategy, but this move by Webster, Everett maintained, transplanted to Washington, "in the person of the four commissioners, the entire extent and power of local interest." "There," as he told Aberdeen, "it would be removed from popular excitement," would be "accessible to argument, and under responsibility."[51]

Since that time historians have debated the propriety of some of the methods used in pushing the treaty forward. Frederick Merk considered the granting of secret funds to Smith improper but excused the impropriety because it had been done in a good cause. Samuel Flagg Bemis censured Webster and made much of the record showing that Ashburton expended some $14,500. To whom he paid it is not a matter of record, but Bemis reached the conclusion on the basis of circumstantial evidence that it was Webster. Howard Jones, after an exhaustive study, concluded that Webster did not receive the money. The Maine historian, Henry Burrage, who wrote the first full account of the controversy, remained convinced that Maine had been cheated out of the territory that was yielded by the treaty.

Maine did have a strong case, but the determination of a boundary in a wilderness territory could not settle the dispute entirely. There was a larger question at stake than mere territory, one that was never stated explicitly, but one that was nevertheless very much on the minds of contemporaries. The negotiations took place in the midst of a great controversy over states rights. Maine's unyielding opposition to a compromise, her willingness to prolong the controversy, even in the face of war, and her attempt to override the national government on a dispute in the area of foreign affairs, presented a bold challenge to national sovereignty. In pursuing this course Maine received little sympathy. Maine's obstinacy had delayed a settlement ever since Jackson's presidency, but some degree of blame may be placed on the administration in Washington for its failure to act before the crisis of 1839.

Maine's boundary dispute offers a classic example of the difficulty of carrying on foreign relations under a federal form of government. In this instance the difficulty was doubled, because Maine could contend that the Constitution provided that the national government could not cede the territory of a state to a foreign power. Secretary of State Webster accepted this limitation and worked within it, but a settlement could have been achieved earlier had not Maine been free to stand in the way.

Maine's doggedness was understandable. The Maine controversy evoked further fear, for if the central government was so weak it could not override a single state on a question of foreign policy, then it was weaker than suspected. Everett saw this in 1837 and feared a breakup. Charles Sumner saw it while he was in England in 1839. He held Maine responsible for weakening liberal government throughout the world. He feared for the unity of the Republic and in a moment of despair hoped that President Van Buren would use military force in order to show the world "that our government is as ready to resist disorganization from within as invasion from without." [52] Lord Ashburton on his return to England expressed the view that a breakup of the United States was most likely.

However, the issue points out the difficulties of conducting foreign relations nationally when one state is free to stand in the way of the nation as a whole. The British were perplexed by the need for the American government to secure Maine's approval before entering negotiations and, later, in moving forward with these negotiations. The weakness of the Union was clear for all to see. This particular foreign relations issue was only one demonstration of that weakness. The ever increasing struggle between sections caused the future of the Union to seem precarious.

9

# New England and the Opening of Relations with China

The 1830s and 1840s were the golden age of the American shipping industry. New England and her chief port, Boston, prospered accordingly. The city increased in population from 43,000 to 61,000 in the 1820s and by 1842 reached 100,000. The growth owed much to the increase in shipping. In the years from 1835 to 1841, some 1,473 vessels entered from foreign ports, and in 1844 some 4,406 engaged in coastal trade entered Boston. Coastal trade surpassed total foreign trade and trade with Europe surpassed trade with any other area; however, New England's foreign trade was worldwide. The trade in hides from Brazil and California was of great importance. In return for hides the New Englanders exported cotton cloth and lumber. The New England shoe industry demanded large supplies of hides. In 1843, 311,000 hides were entered at the Boston customshouse: 100,000 came from Brazil and Uruguay; 46,000 from Chile; 33,000 from California. The remainder, some 48,000, came from New Orleans. Coffee was another important import from South America.

Trade with China was important. Tea accounted for eighty percent of imports from China. In 1840 imports of Chinese tea were valued at $5,417,589.[1] The value of all imports from that country stood at $6,640,829. Cotton goods, both from English factories and the new mills in New England increasingly became the major export to China. Opium, too, made up a considerable portion of most cargos. The importance of the China trade measured in terms of total foreign trade or compared with trade with western Europe or all of Latin America does not appear great. On the other hand, imports from China exceeded in value those from any one country with the exception of Great Britain and

France. In public estimates the element of its future importance was more significant than the bare statistics. Virtually all were agreed that trade across the Pacific would eventually surpass all other trade.

New England was at its heyday in commerce. Although Boston was the major port in the section, it was not the only port. Maine, with Portland and Bath, Connecticut with New Haven, New Hampshire with Portsmouth, and Rhode Island with Providence, all looked to foreign trade as an important factor in determining their economic well-being. The related industry of ship building also focused attention on world trade. The two states, Maine and Massachusetts, in 1840, built nearly half of the ship tonnage constructed that year, 56,747 tons out of a total of 118,309.[2]

Fascination with China owed almost as much to imagination stirred by stories of success and of American experiences at Canton as it did to the fortunes that were made there. Tales surrounding the great Chinese merchant, Houqua, made him a legend, and the story of how he had torn up a $72,000 promissory note from a Boston merchant went the rounds. Merchants spoke highly of the skill of the Chinese as traders and their fairness in dealings. Russell Sturgis, who carried on at least half of the China trade between 1820 and 1840 and who ranked among the first of the citizens of Boston, testified that "he never knew better gentlemen than the Hong merchants." John P. Cushing also held the Chinese in high regard, and, in turn, advised his successor, of the "advantages that are derived in business concerns by pursuing on all occasions an upright & honourable conduct & cultivating, & with all persons with whom you have transactions the good will of all. . . ."[3]

Of the several Americans who went to China and resided there as representatives of Boston firms, John Perkins Cushing achieved the greatest success and reputation. He first went to China at age sixteen, took over the management of Thomas Handsyd Perkins' office in Canton after a few months, and, with the exception of two brief visits home, he remained for thirty years. He returned a fabulously rich man. In Boston he erected a mansion, built around it a wall of Chinese porcelain, and employed several Chinese servants. His standing is reflected in a letter written by John Murray Forbes who was to go to China as the representative of Bryant and Sturgis. After meeting Cushing he wrote: "I have of course seen Mr. Cushing and liked him better than I expected, for you know that we have always looked upon him as many degrees higher than the pope in all his glory. . . ."[4]

China provided New Englanders with profits, pleasant discourse, and the fine porcelains and innumerable beautiful knicknacks for home decoration plus tea. In turn, New England supplied cheap cotton goods and opium to China. With the exception of the D. W. C. Olyphant firm of New York, all American merchants carried opium, usually from Turkey. His flamboyant name aside, David Washington Cincinnatus Olyphant earned distinction as a dedicated Presbyterian, member of the American Board of Commissioners for Foreign Missions, the Presbyterian Board of Foreign Missions, and the philanthropist who provided free transportation for missionaries. Among the latter were Elijah Bridgman, Samuel Wells Williams, and Peter Parker. Olyphant's moral principles forbade him to participate in the opium trade.

Opium filled the need for acquiring the exchange to pay for what the merchants carried home. Opium had not been widely used in China, but with the rise of foreign trade and the drug's increasing availability, consumption increased at least fourfold in the early decades of the nineteenth century. And as the market increased the balance of trade shifted in the foreigner's favor. As a result China's silver currency flowed out of the country, seriously weakening her currency system.

From time to time imperial decrees outlawed the use of opium. The decree issued in 1821 was forceful enough to cause foreign ships to deposit their opium at Lintin island many miles down the Pearl River where Chinese dealers bought it and smuggled it in. Hong merchants in Canton, always mindful that Peking was far away, distributed the drug among small shopkeepers. The British East India Company was by far the biggest supplier. The British government had a monopoly of the supply in India that allowed both government and the company to profit. In 1835 rumor spread that the imperial government was about to substitute a system of import duties on opium to replace prohibition. The foreign ships then moved their opium cargos closer to Canton.

Then, in 1839, with uncharacteristic energy, the imperial authorities issued a rescript drawn in both moral and economic terms. This new effort to abolish opium was aimed at both foreigners and the Hong merchants. Commissioner Lin, on March 26, issued an order to the foreigners to surrender their opium. His order was phrased in eloquent language. They should do so "because the dictates of heavenly reason so require it." In firm words he observed:

I have examined and found, that, during the last several tens of years, by means of your destructive opium poison, ye have duped our people out of I know not how many myriads of money. While ye, scheming after private advantage, have directed your minds to the sole object of gain, our people have been losing their properties and compromising their lives. . . . dread ye not the judgment of high heaven?

Second, Lin called on the merchants to observe the laws of the land. They had amassed great wealth thanks to the goodness of the emperor in permitting trade. ". . . how, then, shall it be supposed for a moment that ye alone, of all men, are not to stand in awe of the supreme majesty of our laws?" Third, they should respect the common feelings of mankind. In their home countries opium was outlawed. Finally, he warned that "the common people cherish a feeling anything but friendly" and the "rage of the multitude is a thing difficult to be repressed; and this is a circumstance that you ought to look forward to with the deepest respect."[5] The language of the rescript with its moral and incisive argument would have done justice to a New England divine blessed with literary talents.

The foreigners at first found it difficult to take the new order seriously, for they were well aware that Chinese officials and merchants rewarded imperial decrees with politeness and evasion. Then, with suddenness, they learned that the high commissioner at Canton, Lin, meant to spare no efforts in applying the decree. On 5 March 1839, the authorities marched a Chinese charged with violating the rescript to the front of the foreign factories and executed the man by strangulation. When British and American sailors, that same day, "by impudence and folly" aroused a mob of seven to eight thousand who attacked the factories with clubs and battering rams, it became clear that the foreigners faced a crisis. The execution in front of the factories was aimed at intimidating both the foreigners and the Hong merchants. The angry mob, it also became clear, could serve the empire as Commissioner Lin warned when he threatened to employ the militia.

Lin ordered the surrender of all chests of opium; they were to be burned. To assure delivery he also commanded that foreign merchants must sign bonds not to engage in the trade and that violators would be turned over to the Chinese. The penalty was death by strangulation. To give force to this order two Hong merchants in chains were placed before the factories, along with instruments for strangulation, and the two accused were to make clear to the foreigners that unless they agreed to comply the two merchants would meet death. A temporary agreement, subject to further discussion, allowed time for the British to refuse and the Americans to defuse the issue by substituting certificates for bonds. However, finally the British surrendered 1,000 chests of opium, a kind of down payment on the 20,000 they would soon deliver after Lin, on March 22, forbade all foreign trade.

These events and further developments in the months ahead were faithfully reported to Secretary of State John Forsyth by Consul P. W. Snow. Charles William King, associated with Olyphant and a keen analyst of Sino-British relations, and Snow kept Caleb Cushing, member of the House of Representatives, informed, and Cushing shortly became a spokesman in favor of government representation at Canton. Snow favored the abolition of the opium trade. China's millions, he wrote, will need clothing; it would be better to supply clothing than opium.[6]

Consul Snow and Commodore George C. Read were the only official observers of these scenes. Snow remained both calm and judicious in the face of these trials, but in a report to Secretary of State Forsyth, in the summer of 1839, he warned of further trouble, spoke of the unprotected state of the American community, and the need for a naval force. He also proposed that consideration be given to appointing a government representative, for the powers of a consul did not enable him to be "of any essential service to his countrymen in times of difficulty."[7]

The presence of two American naval ships off the coast of Macao was believed to have discouraged an attack there. By May only one of the ships, under Commodore Reid, remained. The merchants pleaded that he remain, but Reid decided against them. One hundred and ten in his force of six hundred were ill. Nine had died and the ship was without bread. Reid left.[8]

On 9 January 1840 eight merchants forwarded a memorial to Congress. Hoping to influence Congress, they wisely acknowledged the evils of opium and testified that they would willingly give up the trade in that item—which they never did. They acknowledged the difficulty faced by China as a result of the drainage of specie. They estimated that the British had drained off from 30 to 35 millions of dollars worth of gold and silver in the last few years. They cited the increase in the opium trade—from 3,210 chests between 1816 and 1817 to 23,670 between 1832 and 1833—and estimated an increase to a probable 40,000 in 1839 had there been no interference.[9]

However, these merchants could not "perceive the slightest ground for the justification of the robbery of the British subjects here" nor for other Chinese merchants. They justified the opium trade on the grounds that Chinese officials had connived and participated. The merchants were fearful of the consequences of a prospective British blockade of China. The use of force, they confidently expected, would cause the Chinese to change their ways, and they recommended that their own government should act in concert with the governments of Great Britain, France, and Holland should war come.

The memorial of 1840 included six recommendations closely approximating the future treaty. These included a treaty tariff, a system of bond warehouses, the opening of China's other ports, compensation for losses suffered, and, then, the origin of extraterritoriality in the recommendation that the treaty should rule out punishments greater than those provided for by English or American laws.[10] During the preceding ten months no demand made by Commissioner Lin had aroused greater opposition than the one calling for the surrender to the Chinese of all involved in any way with the opium trade. The Chinese concept of group responsibility for the evildoing of one man and the fear that Chinese witnesses from the lower orders of society would fit their testimony to the Chinese prosecution's preference made it appear that any concession on this point would make residing in China precarious.

At the close of that year, as the Opium War got underway and both newspaper editors and politicians decried the British assaults, John

Quincy Adams declared that opium was not the cause of the war, that Chinese trade restrictions were the cause, and that China had no right to follow a policy of seclusion.[11] He looked forward to a firm American policy.

In December of 1840 Peter Parker, the missionary doctor whose magnificent eye surgery was saving hundreds of Chinese from blindness, returned to the United States. Upon the suggestion of old friends at Yale, where he had studied medicine, he went to Washington to inform influential leaders of what ought to be done. There he not only conferred at length with Webster, who was about to become secretary of state, but he preached in the hall of the House of Representatives. In his talks with Webster he contended that it was advisable to send a minister plenipotentiary to China. Parker was to have a future role in this capacity.[12]

The Opium War in China in 1841 and 1842 postponed action by the United States, though Commodore Kearny was sent to provide protection. The commodore sought to stop American ships from participating in the opium trade but soon discovered there was no law on which to base his efforts.

The British Treaty of Nanking of 1842 left unsettled the question of claims and the rates to be set for import duties. American merchants found the Chinese giving no attention to their claims for losses suffered and as unwilling as ever to deal with foreigners as equals. William P. Pierce in Canton wrote to Caleb Cushing early in 1843 complaining that the Chinese were treating "the Americans with the real old fashioned contempt & [this] should be remedied now or never." "We want an envoy from home especially sent out with a respectable force to back him up to bring the Chinese to their senses," wrote Pierce, "and to tell them that America is not the insignificant country they suppose it to be."[13]

C. W. King wrote to Cushing in April 1843 that the British treaty added to the need for an American envoy. American merchants were receiving no hearing on their claims, and it appeared that British claims were being met. He cited other concerns. Americans might be excluded from the new ports because the United States was unable to offer a guarantee for the personal conduct of its citizens—something British consuls could do. British subjects also enjoyed the advantage of the safeguards of a British tribunal. The United States should move to provide for both and this required an envoy to be sent to negotiate a treaty. King saw benefits for China in the new arrangements. She could control her territory and "put a check on colonial aggrandizement." [14]

In March 1843 President Tyler and Secretary of State Webster made the first moves to send a mission. Webster informed Cushing that from the beginning he had "Mr. Everett in my eye." Webster wrote: "I consider it a more important mission than ever proceeded from this country, & more important than any other, likely to succeed in our day." He was convinced that Everett was the man for this job. [15]

Speculation was already abroad, and Everett learned of it before hearing from Webster. [16] Everett became distrustful at once and told Cushing that he had just become settled in London, that the president appeared pleased with his work and that he did not wish to be used to suit another's convenience. When Everett received word of his appointment from Webster he mentioned it to Foreign Minister Aberdeen who thought Everett might as well be sent to the moon. Everett declined the appointment on the grounds of family considerations. It appeared to many that Webster was making room for himself to take over the London post, but this he denied. [17] Ashburton, who had worked closely with Webster in Washington during the summer of 1842, freely stated that he expected to see Webster in London in the near future. Webster anticipated a deal whereby Great Britain would induce Mexico to sell upper California to the United States and, in return, the United States would agree to a settlement of the Oregon question along British demands. [18]

The question of who was to be appointed was reopened, and now Caleb Cushing had the support of his friend, Secretary of State Daniel Webster. At this time Cushing was in deep political trouble along with Webster. Both had defended President Tyler at a time when a large part of the Whig party was denouncing him. The reaction was so severe that Cushing found that he could not be reelected by his home district. Tyler, at this stage, nominated him for the post of secretary of the treasury. The Senate rejected the nomination. Webster was furious. He called the action scandalous and denounced the New England Whigs "for their anger, spleen, and violence."[19] The Whig senators from Vermont, Rhode Island, and Connecticut had voted against the approval of Cushing.

Cushing was at the center of the heated controversy. That he was an extremely able man few denied, but he was also very independent in his views and given to taking highly provocative positions. He was also, by the spring of 1843, flirting with the Democrats and involved with some of his admirers in plans for a new political party combining conservative Whigs and Democrats. Cushing was interested in foreign affairs, an exponent of expansion, and firmly committed to the view that the British possessions to the north, constantly being strengthened, posed a menace.[20]

For all his ability and independent spirit Cushing was abrasive. A loyal supporter from Worcester advised him to be more circumspect. He had written: "I regret exceedingly that you think it necessary to come out at this time with a manifesto." This individual had persuaded his friends in the press to be more forebearing toward Cushing, and they had followed this advice, but now Cushing was once again pursuing his own course at the expense of the party and wounding "the feelings of former personal as well as political friends."[21]

There were also loyal supporters who praised Cushing for courageously defending Tyler's vetoes of a tariff bill and a national bank bill. Given historical perspective, moreover, the so-called Ultra Whigs in their lampooning of Tyler and denunciation of his vetoes were as indiscreet as Cushing was in his attacks.[22] He need not have been so strenuous in his defense of the president, but Cushing was undoubtedly convinced, and with reason, that sheer political obstructionism led by Henry Clay was both unfair and unreasonable. Cushing, a studious and extremely serious personality, examined major measures recommended by Tyler and bills vetoed by the president without regard for party considerations.

On Webster's recommendation President Tyler appointed Cushing as his envoy to China. Webster was deeply indebted to Cushing who had loaned him money on several occasions without specifying an interest rate or a date for repayment. As Congress was not in session the question of approval by the Senate did not arise until the mission was completed.

Cushing was not, in terms of personality, an ideal choice, but he plunged into preparing himself with a vigor that was admirable. He read whatever books he could obtain and took pages of notes on Walter Henry Medhurst's *China: its State and its Prospects*; he talked to merchants familiar with China and embarked on a study of the language. The mission included Fletcher Webster, Daniel Webster's oldest son, as secretary, two missionaries in China to serve as interpreters, Peter Parker and Elijah Bridgman, four young attachés who volunteered their services, and a medical doctor.

Cushing departed against a backdrop of naval armament. The squadron included four ships, among them the new steam frigate *Missouri*. These ships mounted more than 200 guns. As the merchants with whom Webster had consulted advised, Cushing's instructions combined an emphasis on fair play with firmness. He was to act on the basis that his mission was "entirely pacific." His task was to open the way to "friendly intercourse." The laws of China, Webster wrote, "ought to be respected by all ships and all persons visiting its ports, and if citizens of the United States, under these circumstances are found violating well known laws of trade, their Government will not interfere to protect them from the consequences of their own illegal conduct." At the same time Webster emphasized that Cushing must be constantly alert to any treatment signifying that the United States was an inferior bearing tribute. Cushing was to seek the establishment of regular diplomatic relations with Peking and had orders to proceed there if the situation permitted.[23] Almost as important as his official instructions was the informal advice from Boston merchants that it would be fatal to show any sign of weakness for the Chinese would be quick to take advantage. Significantly, his outfit was to include a major general's uniform.

On his way to China he stopped at the Azores and then went to Gibraltar. Here the frigate *Missouri* caught fire and was destroyed. Cushing managed to rescue his papers and then proceeded on a British ship. He reached Macao on 25 February 1844. His early weeks, indeed months, proved to be a trial of patience, for the governor of the province was not authorized to negotiate, and he learned that he must await the arrival of the commissioner from Peking. In the meantime Cushing and the governor of the two southern provinces sparred. Cushing announced his determination to go to Peking and was put off with an explanation that this would be impossible because there were no officials or interpreters free to escort him from the coast to the capital. The real reason for the denial was, of course, that given the deep humiliation recently suffered at the hands of the British, the dynasty could not afford to admit a foreigner to the capital, for the populace would see it as a sign of great weakness. Cushing merely reaffirmed his determination and then, after having been told that no foreign warship was permitted to go up the Pearl River, he ordered the frigate *Brandywine* to proceed as far up the river as Whampoa. Several of his notes to Governor Ching had an overbearing tone.

The commissioner appointed to carry on the negotiations, Ch'i-ying, who negotiated the Treaty of Nanking, arrived at a village bordering on Macao on June 16. After the preliminary festivities, including a Chinese feast, the negotiations got underway in a nearby temple. Cushing, in his general's uniform and with a sheathed sword, impressed at least one American merchant as so imperial in his behavior that he was doing injury to the good relations that the merchants by then enjoyed with the Chinese.[24]

At the second meeting Cushing and Ch'i-ying agreed that the subordinates should draft the proposed treaty; Peter Parker played a major part in the drafting. Parker was well versed in what was desired. During the course of this work Cushing and Ch'i-ying engaged in a heated discussion over the former's insistence that he be received in Peking. The Chinese commissioner finally announced that if Parker continued to insist on this, he would break off the negotiations. Cushing then yielded and discussions proceeded smoothly. On 3 July 1844 the treaty was signed on a stone table in a shaded bower adjoining the temple.

The importance of the treaty did not lie in its provisions, for the rights provided for in that document were spelled out in the Treaty of Nanking, and these rights had already been extended to the United States and other countries by China. Cushing learned of this in a letter from Edward Everett, United States minister to Great Britain. The Cushing Treaty did go beyond the Treaty of Nanking in providing foreigners with the right to establish hospitals, cemeteries, and temples of worship in the five port cities; however, even in this respect, it should be noted that British missionaries had already moved into the new treaty ports and established hospitals. The treaty also set out specifically the right of extraterritoriality that the British treaty had only implied.

The Cushing Treaty is significant because it provided further evidence of a change in relations between the celestial empire and the western world. Months prior to Cushing's negotiations Americans in China had noted the change underway. Trade was flourishing, the authorities were friendly and reasonable, and it appeared that the hostility to foreigners had been laid aside.[25] The editor of the *Chinese Repository*, some days after the signing of the treaty but before he knew what it provided, hailed the change in Chinese policy and then observed: "We rejoice at these things, not so much indeed on account of what has been effected already, as because of what is coming." The editor saw in the developments the direction of "an Almighty hand" and the carrying out of divine purposes.[26]

However, even during the immediate glow of the new treaties, merchants recognized that acceptance by the Chinese of the foreigners as equals would take years. The Chinese concept of their country as the middle kingdom and the deeply rooted values and customs of Confucian society would not easily erode.

The Westerners, including the Americans, were to perpetrate Chinese distrust. The coolie system, the opium trade, and the abuse of extraterritorial rights promoted even greater distrust of the foreigner. Unfortunately neither the British nor the American treaty contained any provisions relating to the opium trade.

The focus on trade in these early years was not accompanied by any increase in the understanding of China. Since the days of the Revolution Americans had assumed that the growth of commerce would bring with it modernization of backward areas and that the benefits of trading partners would be mutual. China was commonly dismissed as a despotism, even by such an intelligent man as Edward Everett. The complexities of the Chinese political system wholly escaped contemporary observers in the 1840s. Not until the late 1850s did William Reid, minister to China, express serious doubts about the beneficent effects of foreign commerce on China.

Samuel Wells Williams, missionary-diplomat, was aware that commerce was accompanied by evils of exploitation, abuse, and the undermining of China's ancient civilization. New England spearheaded both the missionary movement and commerce with China. The American Board of Commissioners of Foreign Missions of the Congregational Churches, with its headquarters in Boston, created another important tie to China. The missionary movement within the United States aroused great popular interest in China, but it was characterized by a sense of superiority and paternalism. Quite understandably the complexities were not foreseen when Cushing signed, in 1844, the famous treaty on a stone table in the shady bower at Macao.

The Cushing Treaty placed relations between the two countries on an official level. It was approved by the Senate without a dissenting vote, evidence that the treaty was not a sectional question. Yet, it is also true that it came about through the commercial ties between New England and China, and that New Englanders were its architects and its negotiators.

# New England and Expansionism: The Crisis over Texas and Oregon

One of the enigmas of New England is her dedication to nationalism on the one hand and her readiness to defy national authority on the other. In domestic affairs she was nationalistic. In the two great crises in foreign affairs in 1812 and 1846, New Englanders boldly challenged the central government. This seeming paradox owed much to New England's interest in shipping and to her close ties with England. Opposition to a degree approaching defiance did not spring full-blown until the outbreak of the war with Mexico in May 1846, but New England's stance when Texas was annexed in 1845, and again during the war crisis over the Oregon question in early 1846, portended what lay ahead.

Expansionism was a broad national movement not limited to any one section. New Englanders from time to time looked with dismay upon territorial acquisitions seeing that their own political influence would diminish, and their dedication to protectionism and other conservative financial policies caused them to fear that an ever sprawling agricultural nation would sacrifice their interests. However, this train of thought existed side by side with a republicanism that included dreams of a nation as broad as the continent. John Quincy Adams suffered no rebukes as a result of his role in the annexation of Florida and the far-flung boundaries provided in the Transcontinental Treaty of 1819. New England, like the rest of the nation, accepted westward expansion as inevitable, for the rapidly growing population pressing forward would extend the domain. And New England, with her interest in trade with Asia, naturally looked upon both Oregon and California as important.

Indeed, New Englanders often led the way to settlement of these remote areas. The interest in Oregon began with the development of the China trade dominated by New Englanders, and in the 1830s it was the home missionary movement of the New England churches that added to the interest in Oregon and helped give rise to the first settlements. In 1834 the Boston schoolteacher, Hall Kelley, explored Oregon and then publicized the region, calling on political leaders to give him support in establishing a colony there. By 1840 a society in Maine developed a plan for settlement and approached Caleb Cushing of Salem for support. The previous year Cushing had given a stirring address in Congress calling for action and warning that the British had a broad overall plan for hemming in the United States and holding her hostage. The title to Oregon, Cushing contended, was sufficient "to be justly maintained, if necessary, by force." He charged that the Hudson Bay Company and the Northwest Company were sworn enemies and "most injurious and hostile" to the people of the United States. Their methods were sinister. The Indians in Oregon, won over by gifts from British traders, did their bidding and made war on American settlers. Oregon, said Cushing, "is a country ours by right; ours by necessities of geographical position; ours by every consideration of national safety. . . ." [1]

The aggressive congressman from Salem introduced a bill providing for the protection of American settlers. A report written by Cushing accompanied the bill. Cushing's interest in Oregon was tied to his interest in trade with China. Here, too, he led the way, and in 1840 wrote to Secretary of State Forsyth stating that the time had come to enter into diplomatic relations with China. [2] From this time on Cushing was looked to by numbers of prospective settlers as their best friend. [3] He persisted in pushing forward the Oregon question and in 1840 published an article in the *North American Review* extolling its advantages and its strategic importance. [4]

New England shipping reached California at an early date and the wonders of California's climate, scenery, and fine harbors were soon well known. In 1822 William Sturgis wrote a series of letters for the Boston *Daily Advertiser* on the importance of the Pacific coast. Nathan Spear of Boston established a store at Monterey in the 1830s. Spear corresponded with his brother in Boston who wrote at length of California's future importance. He described California in detail and referred to its rich mineral resources.[5] The trade in hides provided another link between New England and California. One estimate placed the number of hides exported from California in the years 1823 to 1847 at 5 million.[6] The Bryant and Sturgis Company, in 1822, sent ships to collect hides and tallow. In the course of the next twenty years the company sent sixteen ships. In 1841 three other groups of Boston merchants entered this trade.[7] And in 1840 Richard Henry Dana's *Two Years before the Mast* gave New Englanders a firsthand account not only of the hardships of life at sea but of California. As the readers read of the charm of this Mexican province, merchants discoursed on the fine harbors of San Francisco and San Diego.

New Englanders, prior to Texas independence, showed slight interest in Texas, but a Connecticut Yankee, Moses Austin, led the first settlement. As president, John Quincy Adams sought to buy the Texas territory. However, New England was largely indifferent until the question of annexation arose in 1837. The Texas question then became embroiled in the slavery question.

The interest of the New England Whigs in expansion ranked low on their scale of objectives. Protectionism, financial conservatism, opposition to the extension of slavery, and good relations with England had first priority among the dominant Whigs and their business allies.

Texas' war for independence and the possible annexation of Texas changed New England's views on slavery. William Ellery Channing's famous letter to Henry Clay in 1837 denouncing the war in Texas and the annexation proposal marked the turning point. Hitherto, except for a small group of abolitionists, New Englanders, while uniformly holding slavery to be an evil, refrained from making public attacks and accepted southern slavery as a question reserved to the states. The Constitution had so stated, and they were committed to it. They saw slavery as an evil imposed by the British on the colonies. It was not an evil for which they had to bear responsibility.

The question of annexing Texas brought a complete turnabout. To be party to extending slavery and assuring its continued growth was to assume moral responsibility for slavery. As this train of thought took control, the New England conscience came face to face with the fact that slavery was so intertwined with the federal government that not to free the Union from this tie was tantamount to endorsement. New Englanders came to see themselves as accomplices in the perpetuation of a barbaric institution. The federal government protected slavery on the high seas when slaves were transported from Virginia and the border states to the deep South. The federal government protected both slavery and the slave trade in the national capital and sanctioned slavery by the three-fifths provision for determining representation in Congress.

The moral impulse coincided with the ardent protectionist's belief that the South's attacks on the tariff were likely to cause their own ruination. Ever since 1828 the tariff question towered above all other political issues. As Charles Francis Adams put it, the tariff policy ruled the state of Massachusetts.[8] It ruled in Connecticut and Rhode Island as well. Southerners, with few exceptions, denounced protectionism with vehemence and sought at every opportunity to undermine it. From 1833 to 1842, tariff rates under Clay's compromise tariff slid downward. The North won a victory with the tariff of 1842, but with the election of Polk came a new assault on protectionism.

The full measure of distrust of the South came forth in John Quincy Adams' address to his constituents on 17 September 1842. The South, said Adams, "is as intent now to wreck the system [of protectionism] as it was at the time of the nullification crisis." Nullification principles, said Adams, "were never more inflexibly maintained, never more inexorably pursued than they have been, by all that portion of the South, which *ever* gave them countenance, from the day of the death of William Henry Harrison to the present." Adams then turned to the question of Texas and slavery. "The Texas Land and Liberty jobbers had spread their contagion of their land-jobbing traffic all over the free States throughout the Union." Banks had financed land speculation in Texas and then "furnished vociferous declaimers for the recognition of Texas independence." And now the Tyler administration was ready to carry forward the plot of Jackson and the land jobbers.[9]

New England saw the South not only as a slave power but as an aggressive oligarchy determined to subordinate the federal government to its own interests. Everett and Winthrop were convinced by the late 1830s that the South was ruthless in its determination to impose its control. They feared that the aggressiveness of the South was unlimited.

As the tension increased New Englanders arrived at the view that southern society was hostile to the basic value system of the Republic. New England prized freedom of speech, respect for orderly political procedures, and a reverence for law. Theirs was a society that maintained a delicate balance between law and order.

John Quincy Adams' fight for the right to petition against slavery centered attention on freedom of speech. The annexation of Texas by joint resolution and the enactment of a new tariff law in 1846 (during which all debate in the Senate was cut off), a strategy denounced by Webster as unprecedented, took on special significance given the tempestuous political climate of the mid-1840s. Leaders of such widely divergent views as Daniel Webster and Charles Francis Adams gave much publicity to what they saw as gross violations of the Constitution. The conservative leadership in New England revered these political principles with the devotion of a Bible-reading puritan.

Of course it was easier to see the mote in the rival's eye than to look at their own political behavior realistically. Only an Adams could do that. The behavior of the Whigs in the Massachusetts legislature so dismayed Charles Francis Adams that, at the close of the legislative session in 1842, he concluded that the party was beyond redemption. It was, he said, "A party held together by no principles and led on by political gamblers. . . ."[10] And even while New Englanders condemend slavery, many of them were racist. A bill to permit intermarriage was defeated five times before it passed in 1843. That same year a bill that would have permitted blacks to ride in railway cars was defeated.

The antislavery forces in Massachusetts did not lack sincerity. However, some of the force behind the antislavery movement had their sources in such key questions as the protective tariff, the question of centralized banking, and foreign policy issues.

In the winter of 1844 the first signs of crisis appeared. John C. Calhoun, by now secretary of state, tied the Texas question to slavery in a letter to the British minister in Washington. Texas must be annexed to provide a safety valve for slavery, and slavery, he contended, was a superior and beneficent institution. Shortly afterwards the Senate received a treaty negotiated with Texas providing for annexation. Petitions flowed in from every New England state opposing the treaty. Only

Levi Woodbury of New Hampshire voted for the treaty in the Senate. Every other New England senator opposed it.

From 1844 to 1848 the nation lived in repeated crises. The defeat of the treaty of annexation led the Tyler administration to circumvent the required two-thirds vote on treaties. The Democratic Convention at Baltimore, in 1844, launched a crusade for the reannexation of Texas and the annexation of Oregon all the way north to 54° and 40'. Reason and calm deliberation gave way to a wave of blustering cries for conquest. The British and French sat back in astonishment, wondering what this new giant would do in the future.

This daring, reckless adventurism had several roots. Americans assumed that the country would eventually extend to the Pacific and not a few saw it enveloping all of North America. An aggressive spirit, unchecked by powerful neighbors and fed by ethnocentrism, thrived. Ambitious politicians exploited these feelings in garnering votes.

Just below this stratum of public emotion lay a deep distrust of Europe, especially Great Britain. European powers were on the march for empire, and Great Britain manifested an interest in Texas and in California. Americans feared that Great Britain and France aimed at achieving a balance of power in North America; this fear was not fanciful, for leading statesmen in both countries did entertain such hopes.

Expansion also owed much to land hunger. No nation was so rich in territory and in fertile land. Although great portions of it were still unsettled, the westward flow of population was as relentless as an ocean tide. In a country where agriculture surpassed all other pursuits, the dream of most young men was to own land. No place was too far distant to attract settlers. Oregon had five thousand settlers by 1844 when the vast expanses of the trans-Missouri West were still unoccupied. The antislavery leaders who organized a new political party in 1848 and named it the Free-Soil party, shrewdly appealed to this love of land. The party appealed to a widespread interest when they portrayed the slave labor system as excluding free labor from new territory, for everywhere were sons who expected to move into new areas where land was cheap.

New Englanders shared in the idea of mission and recognized the importance of both Oregon and California, but rejected the reckless expanionism that marched under the banner of manifest destiny. To the New England Whigs what mattered was their economic program, including protective tariffs and financial stability. Territorial aggrandizement posed greater dangers than rewards, dangers of ever increasing southern control and conflict with Great Britain. However, those outside the pale of Whiggery in New England, who shared the political views of the Jacksonians, favored expansion and supported the annexation of Texas and the Oregon territory. These were lone voices that counted for less and less as the antislavery movement made headway.

New England convictions on adding slave territory were already strong by January 1844, and in March both houses of the Massachusetts legislature unanimously passed resolutions against the annexation of Texas. Tyler's proposed annexation of Texas by joint resolution set the stage. This question had scarcely been settled when Polk's call for termination of the treaty of joint occupation of Oregon led to a war crisis, and this question was only approaching settlement in May 1846 when Polk declared that war existed by act of Mexico. These momentous issues were divisive in the South and West, but in both of these sections Polk's course had majority support. New England, on the contrary, resisted national policy with such vigor that it became temporarily isolated from the country at large. The war not only failed to rally New England support, it led to such bold opposition that in the eyes of the ruling party, New England appeared to be bordering on treason.

New England's pursuit of an independent course was already well under way before the spirit of manifest destiny seized the country. Failure of the federal government to provide defenses for Boston Harbor in 1839 almost caused the Massachusetts legislature to appropriate money for the purpose, hoping to be reimbursed later.[11] In 1841 the revenue bill passed by Congress placed duties on raw materials necessary for manufactures, thereby arousing a storm of protest in Boston.[12] Not only were sectional issues threatening to tear the union apart but the Whig party was divided. In 1842 Edward Everett, Daniel Webster, and Robert C. Winthrop were in despair over sharp divisions in the party. Winthrop wrote to a political associate: "It is an open, unconcealed, unpalliated case of party dissolution and decay, without all hope, I fear of resurrection." [13] The party and the Union appeared more and more fragile. When Lord Ashburton met Everett in London upon his return from his mission in the United States, he confided that the Union was on the point of breaking up. [14]

President Tyler's program deepened sectional divisions. The Virginia Whig pursued a course at odds with the basic tenets of the New England Whigs. His stand on the tariff and the national bank question split the party in New England. When Daniel Webster and Caleb Cushing remained loyal to Tyler, the former suffered sharp criticism and the latter lost his standing in the Whig party. When Tyler moved to annex Texas and Polk was elected with a mandate to carry out a program of expansion, a low tariff, and a currency system adverse to New England's interests, what had been a crack in national unity took on the dimensions of a gulf. These sharp divisions strengthened the disposition of New England leaders to oppose Polk's foreign policy.

At the same time these developments coincided with the rise of a younger generation of Whigs in Massachusetts. Among them was Charles Francis Adams, who was distinguishing himself in the Massachusetts legislature. The dominance of Daniel Webster, a politician constantly in debt to the manufacturing interests, offended the younger generation of Whigs. Charles Francis Adams could never forgive Webster for his high-handed manipulations preventing his father's election to the Senate in 1834. Nor could Adams respect a man who sold himself to the wealthy. On Webster's departure for England in 1839 he wrote: "Mr. Webster is going to Europe and his friends again come forward to pay his debts and set him up. His career is entirely unexampled in our history. And it is much to be desired that it should never be emulated." [15] Late in 1842 he wrote that Webster "with his infamous morals must be a dreadful deadweight to any party." [16]

Adams, once described by Marcus Morton as the greatest iceberg in the northern hemisphere, was both an ardent nationalist and an impeccably moral man, as well as a devout churchman. He was first of all a student of history who wrote with a reverence for reality. He climbed to prominence as a writer on financial questions. His conservative views were matched by a hatred of racism and slavery. In late March 1844 Adams contributed nine articles on the Texas question to the Boston

*Courier*, and he noted in his diary that the wealthy classes cared little for abstract principle "and not much for any agitation whatsoever." On March 25 he added a note concerning his own role: "Must I, ought I to continue to throw myself more and more in the gap? Perhaps this is the purpose of my life."

Charles Sumner, another young Whig, rose to prominence as a literary figure and orator. He practiced law without enthusiasm, hoped to be named professor of law at Harvard, and was deeply hurt when rejected. During the late 1830s, while still a young man, he became a friend of William Ellery Channing. The restless young Sumner, in search of a gospel, soon immersed himself in prison reform and the peace movement. His rhetorical skill made him welcome among reformers. Like many of them he saw issues in black and white, ruled out complexities, and permitted the big idea to completely dominate him.[17] On 4 July 1846 he delivered an oration in Boston entitled "The True Grandeur of Nations." In print it was 125 pages long. Sumner enriched it with historical and literary allusions, marshaled virtually every argument in condemnation of war, and argued that the law of nations must be revised and war outlawed. We must determine, he said, how we may best secure the welfare of the people so that the Republic "may perform its part in the world's history, so that it may fulfill the aspirations of generous hearts, and practicing that righteousness which exalteth a nation, attain to the elevation of True Grandeur."[18]

By 1846 Adams and Sumner together with John G. Palfrey and Henry Wilson sent shocks through the Whig party. They had one cause, the cause of antislavery. Their link to the abolitionists was Wendell Phillips, but they were anxious not to permit the much more radical abolitionists to dictate their course. The zest of these Conscience Whigs, as they came to be called, challenged traditional Whigs such as Webster, Everett, and Winthrop, whom they viewed as morally scarred. They saw Everett and Winthrop quite unfairly, as mere hangers-on of Webster.[19]

Adams and Sumner sought to lift politics out of the tawdry rut into which they had fallen. The traditional Whig absorption in defending the interests of manufacturers and the political game of compromise seemed to them unworthy. Public leaders should have more noble purposes. The most urgent cause at hand and most deserving of support was the antislavery cause. The young Whigs had found the political arena as dull as a millpond, and they meant to inject it with new life.

Tyler's proposal to annex Texas by joint resolution served as the catalyst for an outpouring of New England feelings on both sides of the question. Petitions opposing the proposal streamed into Congress, but in both New Hampshire and Maine Tyler's proposal had support. In New Hampshire the legislature passed resolutions in favor of annexation. However, Senator John P. Hale, a Democrat, broke with his party and opposed annexation. His break with the state Democratic organization was dramatic and occasioned a heated public controversy.[20] In Maine, too, the prominent Democrat, Hannibal Hamlin, rebelled. The fiercely independent Hamlin had long been an ardent Jacksonian and a bellicose critic of the Whigs and their program; however, the fight over the right to petition, beginning in 1836 and led by John Quincy Adams, spurred him on in a fight for the right to petition in spite of the position of the Democratic party.[21] Again, in 1845 in the debate over the joint resoluton, Hamlin pursued an independent course. He favored, he said, the annexation of Texas if it were to be done in a manner that would benefit the nation as a whole, but he could not support a measure designed to serve the slave interests of the South.[22] Hamlin voted against the resolution. These two turnabouts in Maine and New Hampshire heralded the later split in the Democratic party.

The majority of New Englanders opposed the resolution. New England representatives declared the whole scheme unconstitutional and charged that the Committee on Foreign Relations had considered it for less than an hour. The resolution passed in the House of Representatives on January 28 by a vote of 120 to 98. All nine of the Massachusetts representatives voted against it; every Connecticut representative voted against it; three of the four representatives from Vermont voted against it; both representatives from Rhode Island did the same. One representative from Maine and three from New Hampshire voted for it.[23]

The debate in the Senate was prolonged until the closing days of the session. Upham of Vermont presented resolutions adopted by the state legislature that unanimously condemned the Senate resolution. Rufus

Choate of Massachusetts spoke for three hours, denied the resolution's constitutionality, and held "that we have no need at all of this vast foreign domain—no more need than we have of Java, or the islands of the Mediterranean."[24] George P. Marsh of Vermont was more blunt concerning a major cause of New Englanders' apprehension. He contended that annexation was aimed at destroying the protective policy. The heart of the struggle, said Marsh, was to create five or six new states enabling the South to exercise control.[25] A representative from Ohio turned this around and charged that the only reason northern Whigs were opposed was that annexation would end the protective policy.[26]

To some the most important issue was economic, particularly, the tariff. To others the slavery question was paramount. The great number of petitions sent to Congress objecting to the extension of slavery suggests that with the public at large the issue was slavery. A simple stereotyped picture of the South had emerged that emphasized the worst aspects of slavery. Most important, once slavery became an issue, the entire conflict between the sections was transformed into a moral question making compromise difficult.

Strong feelings erupted. At Fanueil Hall in Boston a great meeting took place on the question of annexation. The crowd applauded wildly when the speaker said "that the dissolution of the Union was a great evil, but the annexation of Texas would be a greater." At this meeting, on January 29, William Lloyd Garrison presented a resolution in favor of the dissolution of the Union. This was defeated much to the relief of Charles Francis Adams who described it as "one of the most anxious scenes in my public life."[27] Moral fervor took hold of the state legislature, and on February 18 the state senate adopted a resolution stating that annexation of Texas would have no binding force on Massachusetts.

On February 27 the United States Senate passed the resolution annexing Texas by a vote of 27 to 25. New England senators voted along party lines. Senators from Massachusetts, Rhode Island, and Vermont and Huntington of Connecticut and Evans of Maine voted against the resolution. Four voted affirmatively: Niles of Connecticut, Fairfield of Maine, and Atherton and Woodbury of New Hampshire.

The young Whigs in Massachusetts resolved to continue the struggle. They hoped that Congress would reject Texas as an applicant for admission. These Conscience Whigs included John G. Palfrey, a former professor of theology at Harvard, Charles Francis Adams, Charles Sumner, Henry Wilson, and George Hilliard. Theirs was to prove a futile fight.

The Conscience Whigs seemed to act as if they alone were opposed to slavery. The fact was that men like Webster, Winthrop, and Everett were serious in their opposition to slavery. However, the so-called Cotton Whigs committed themselves to a broad program in which antislavery was only one of several goals.

As the antislavery impulse reached a crisis point in lower New England, the Oregon question thrust itself upon the scene. The existing treaty of joint occupation left that vast territory open to trade to both England and the United States but denied to each the exercise of sovereignty. This limitation placed no handicap on the British for British traders in the area were effectively governed by the British Northwest Fur Company. The swelling stream of American settlers, beginning in 1839, were left with no government to provide a judicial system, to establish schools, and to protect them from the Indians. Accordingly, they sought to have Congress create a territorial government.

A settlement of the Oregon question was long overdue. The British recognized this in 1842 and instructed Lord Ashburton, special envoy to the United States, to seek a satisfactory division. Much to the disappointment of Lord Aberdeen, British foreign minister, the negotiators bypassed the question. Everett and Aberdeen discussed the question and reached an agreement that was almost identical with that finally accepted some years later after a war crisis.

Then, at the Democratic Convention in Baltimore in June 1844, the excitement of popular expansionism tossed the question into the political arena. The platform wanted to claim all of Oregon up to 54° 40'. Polk, a long time champion of expansion, was nominated, and he helped make the call for all of Oregon the battle cry of the election campaign. No more popular cause could have rallied the voters of the Midwest.

Once in office Polk concluded that because his predecessors had offered to settle for the forty-ninth parallel he must do so. Bungling diplomacy by both sides wrecked the chance for a settlement. Richard Pakenham, British minister in Washington, recklessly rejected the offer, and Polk, rather than making further inquiries in London, withdrew the offer and laid claim to all of Oregon. Polk had learned from his hero, Andrew Jackson, that the first rule of diplomacy was to be bold and firm. He added a second strategy, namely, to remain silent and let your diplomatic rival wallow in anxiety. He told his secretary of state, James Buchanan, to tell the British minister nothing. Polk was equally secretive with his own cabinet and members of Congress. In his annual message in December he boldly laid claim to all of Oregon and recommended termination of the treaty of joint occupation.

Having thrown the question into the lap of Congress without giving any indication of a willingness to compromise, thoughtful members of that body had reason to ask if Polk meant to make war. In New England the prospect of a war with England provoked fear, but Democrats in Maine and New Hampshire supported the president. Hannibal Hamlin of Maine entered the fight for all of Oregon with fiery enthusiasm. He denounced British "usurpation and aggression," called the Webster-Ashburton Treaty a British land grab, and contended that a firm and bold stand would bring peace.[28] Cullen Sawtelle, Hamlin's colleague in the Senate, a Democrat, ridiculed the notion that termination of the treaty would lead to war. Those who so argued he held guilty of vaporizing, gasconading, and mock heroics.[29] New Hampshire Democrats in Congress followed the same line. It was a dangerous course, for England was by no means prepared to surrender all of Oregon and sacrifice what she deemed to be her national honor.

The New England Whigs shunned heroics and called for sober realism. Winthrop saw no reason for abandoning negotiations simply because the British minister had rejected the president's offer. Winthrop thought that if negotiations failed, they should resort to arbitration. To reject arbitration in favor of war would be a "fearful responsibility"; to terminate the treaty and occupy Oregon "must lead to war." He warned: "And what would be the consequences of a war under such circumstances—the consequences not upon cotton or upon commerce—not upon Boston or Charleston or New York, but what would be the consequences so far merely as Oregon itself is concerned? The cry is now, 'The whole of Oregon or none,' and echo would answer under such circumstances, 'none!'" [30]

Early in the Senate debates Webster held that the resolution that had been introduced relating to Oregon had created unnecessary alarm. He said it "disturbed the calculations of men; it deranged the pursuits of life, and even, to a greater extent, changed the circumstances of the whole business of the country." "This truth," he said, "will be felt more especially by every gentleman acquainted or connected with the seaboard." [31] In a later speech Webster asked "after termination, then what?" If the president would treat for nothing less than all of Oregon, he should say so. "Compromise," said Webster, "I can understand— arbitration I can comprehend; but negotiation, with a resolution not to settle unless we obtain the whole, is what I do not comprehend in diplomacy on matters of government." [32]

New England Whigs viewed Polk's moves as sheer folly. As they saw it, the claim to all of Oregon was wildly exaggerated. It had been formulated in a large political convention by men who had no knowledge of the background of the question. These men had been mesmerized by the notion that North America was by right an exclusive American province. Those same men made light of a war with England. New Englanders could not see it this way, for should war come it would be disastrous to shipping, probably result in bombardment of coastal cities, and disrupt the economy.

In January 1845 William Sturgis, prominent merchant, had delivered a lecture pointing out that a boundary satisfactory to both parties could be drawn through Puget Sound ceding Vancouver to Great Britain while assuring the United States of the waterway she needed for trade. The lecture was printed and widely circulated. [33] The argument he presented became the basis for Whig protests.

Sturgis' connections with leading Britishers and with George Bancroft, Polk's secretary of the navy, suggest at the very least that Polk knew in the late summer of 1845 that the British would settle for the boundary Sturgis proposed. Sturgis' unnamed British friend persisted in the opinion that this was so. Sturgis also informed Bancroft that an article in the *Edinburgh Review*, written by a Mr. Senior, author of another article in the *London Examiner*, supported the proposal of Mr. Sturgis. He also informed Bancroft that both articles were submitted to Lord Aberdeen before publication and were approved by him.[34]

The leading Whig newspaper in Boston, the *Daily Advertiser*, repeatedly supported the line proposed by Sturgis and showed that many in England favored this proposal. In January 1846, at the peak of the heated debates in Congress, the *Daily Advertiser* reprinted lengthy articles from the *London Times* suggesting the line proposed by Sturgis.[35] The editor took issue with Polk's enunciation of the Monroe Doctrine, which he saw as a demand for exclusive control of colonization in North America. Again the editor endorsed the settlement that had been proposed. That settlement would protect British interests and yet leave the Americans masters of Oregon. This, the editor stated, would be a surrender of "a naked right for an undeniable good." He noted that the *London Times* was very close to the British government.

The *Daily Advertiser* repeatedly supported the proposed line throughout the winter and spring of 1846. This, too, was the position of Webster who made the point that the forty-ninth parallel had long been supported as the boundary by the United States. For good reasons the United States could accept no less but he added, "As to all straits, and sounds, and islands, in the neighboring area, all these are fair subjects for treaty stipulation."[36]

In late March the *London Quarterly Review* published a lengthy article arguing that the forty-ninth parallel, subject to adjustments in the Fuca Straits, would constitute such a reasonable offer that the United States could not reject it except "by throwing aside all idea of common rights and equitable partition, and setting up an exclusive claim to the possession of the whole. . . ." The *Daily Advertiser* republished this article and the editor endorsed its point of view.[37]

In the end, many factors contributed to the settlement of the Oregon controversy.[38] Britain's readiness to agree to a compromise owed much to the importance of the American market, dislike of a war with the United States at a time when relations with France were disintegrating, the declining importance of the area between the Columbia River and the forty-ninth parallel, and the peaceful disposition of the British foreign secretary, Lord Aberdeen. America's willingness to compromise owed much to economic considerations. In addition, the stance of Polk and the extreme expansionists such as William Allen of Ohio, Edward Hannigan of Indiana, and Lewis Cass of Michigan, placed the United States in an untenable position. Their blustering anglophobia and flamboyant assertions of an indisputable American claim to all of Oregon rested on no foundations. Their repetitious arguments in defense of the claim were so vulnerable that critics reduced them to nullity. Their blindness to the legitimate interests and honor of England were more embarrassing than useful in maintaining the legitimate interests of the United States.

The recklessness of the expansionists blinded them to the cost and horrors of war, the economic interests of the Northeast in foreign trade, the importance of British credit, and the importance of the British market to southern cotton. Whig leaders had the best of the argument in Congress and in the press and gradually nullified the cries of a "clear and unquestionable" claim to 54° 40'.

Although New England did not fight the campaign for a peaceful settlement alone, she did play an important role. The persuasive arguments of Winthrop in the House of Representatives and Webster in the Senate were aligned with the equally strong speeches of John C. Calhoun and John J. Crittenden of Kentucky. Their support rescued the question from being a purely sectional alignment. And behind the scenes, Edward Everett's extensive correspondence with influential British leaders not only warned them of the limited concessions the United States would accept but served to assure the British there was a strong strain of good judgment ready to combat the extremists in the United States. Everett's correspondence and the presence of Webster in the Senate, together with the strong opposition to Polk's strategy, strengthened Aberdeen's hands in London. Joshua Bates and Thomas Wren Ward, New Englanders in the employ of Baring Brothers, had direct access to British leaders and contributed to quieting the alarm promoted by Polk and the expansionists.

New England's opposition to the termination of the treaty of joint occupation did not mean opposition to the annexation of Oregon south of the forty-ninth parallel. A bill to organize a territorial government south of that line had passed the House on 27 January 1845. All eighteen New England representatives voted for it.

# New England and the Mexican War

Relations with Mexico in the winter and early spring of 1846 gained few and only brief notices in the press. The negotiations of John Slidell in Mexico, owing to the internal convulsion there, ended in failure. When word reached Polk of Mexico's refusal to recognize Slidell, Polk made his decision in favor of war. Slidell's instructions were to present Mexico with three options: first, cession of California and New Mexico to the United States and an award of $25 million to Mexico; second, a boundary giving the United States northern California, including San Francisco but not Monterey, and Mexico $20 million; third, a boundary at the Rio Grande and cession of New Mexico in return for which Mexico was to receive $5 million. In no case would the United States settle for less than the Rio Grande. Polk dawdled briefly between peace and war—he would have preferred peace—but his desire for California overruled the preference. Slidell carried out negotiations with American naval squadrons located off both shores of Mexico and General Zachary Taylor and an army of almost four thousand men in the disputed territory between the Nueces and the Rio Grande; as a result, Polk's efforts at negotiations were looked upon with distrust both in Mexico and by his critics at home.

Polk's eyes were fixed on a railroad to California and on the fine port of San Francisco. General Taylor and the Pacific naval squadron had orders as early as June 1845 to occupy the desired territory should war come. Polk's orders to Taylor early in 1846 to move his troops from Corpus Cristi to the Rio Grande left Polk open to charges of having started the war, for Texas had not exercised jurisdiction in this territory, and even General Taylor considered it to be disputed territory subject to negotiation. It was in this disputed territory, near the Rio Grande, where Taylor first encountered hostility.

On April 24 a party of Taylor's dragoons became engaged with an enemy force. Sixteen Americans were killed or wounded; the others were taken prisoner. Polk received a report of the incident in the evening of May 6. Earlier that day, with the concurrence of his cabinet, he had decided to send a special message to Congress calling for a declaration of war. Polk declared that American blood had been shed on American soil and war existed by act of Mexico.

Although under the Constitution Congress alone could declare war, the actions of the president created a situation wherein Congress was not entirely free to make the decision. Opposition was inevitable. A few weeks earlier Polk had entertained the notion of asking Congress for a special appropriation of $1 million for a down payment on a cession of Mexican territory, and he was told Congress would not approve.

The president's declaration that war already existed opened the door to vigorous assertions that only Congress could declare war and that the skirmish in the disputed territory did not automatically create war. To circumvent the opposition the administration tied the bill declaring war to an appropriation of funds for the support of General Taylor who was supposedly beleaguered by Mexican forces. To vote against the war was to vote against support for Taylor and his troops.

Garrett Davis of Kentucky called for further information and Robert C. Winthrop sought to delay action by calling for a reading of the correspondence submitted by the president. Both failed. The House of Representatives passed the bill by a vote of 174 to 14. Seven of the fourteen votes against a declaration of war were cast by New Englanders. In the Senate only two negative votes were cast—one of them by John Davis of Massachusetts—but Luther Severance of Maine raised questions concerning the disputed territory west of the Nueces River and the presence of American troops there. Charles Hudson of Massachusetts declared the preamble false. War, he said, did not exist by act of Mexico, and the United States was the aggressor.[1]

The vote was misleading: many of the strong opponents only voted for the declaration of war because they felt they could not refuse to vote support for Taylor. Among them was Robert C. Winthrop. A few days after the vote Winthrop explained his vote to his close friend, J. H. Clifford: "I confess I could not bear to have the whole Massachusetts delegation mixed up with a few third party men, or ultra abolitionists, in opposing supplies. My Whig friends from East and West & South all begged me not to forfeit all my influence for good on other questions by a fruitless opposition to this. . . . Heavens knows my heart is sickened at the idea of a war with any country, & at a war with Mexico especially. I fear it will lead to mischief of every kind."[2]

The prospect of war with Mexico confronted the New England Whigs with frightening political problems. Western expansionist appetites appeared insatiable. The nation seemed hell-bent on recklessly propelling the Republic into a continental empire. This raised the prospect of foreign war. Caution and careful calculation would not be served by headlong territorial aggrandizement. War with England or Mexico would upset the best-laid plans of merchants, manufacturers, and Whig politicians.

To add to the apprehension, the explosive slavery question, carefully avoided for the sake of party harmony up to now, could no longer be ignored. Antislavery sentiment grew rapidly after 1840, and by 1845 a group of young Whigs, disillusioned with the decorum of counting-house politicians, were demanding that the Whig party embrace ennobling principles of freedom. Whigs championed philanthropy but not wild-eyed political reformers who would use the powers of the state to erase evil from the world.

The double-pronged danger of expansionism and antislavery challenged the most basic of traditional Whig attitudes and beliefs. The party, dedicated to protectionism and conservative financial policy, relied on southern Whigs for support in return for avoiding the sensitive slave question. This was the immediate concern, but by no means the only one, for the nation appeared ready to defy the most sacred beliefs of the Whigs. The highest Whig values were law and order, stability, orderly change, and the love of the Union. Now they faced what appeared to them to be a tumultuous society. Improvement, the Whigs believed, was to be achieved by economic growth, education, and preservation of the Union. They did not approve of slavery, but its remedy lay in preventing its extension and patiently waiting for the modern age to obliterate this relic of barbarism. The Union must be preserved. From

William Ellery Channing, the genteel reformer, who wrote of the Union in a spirit of pious reverence, to Daniel Webster, Robert C. Winthrop, and Rufus Choate, to whom preservation of the Union surpassed all other aims in importance, the New England Whigs were committed nationalists who looked to the Union as the alternative to anarchy.

Daniel Webster, who spoke authoritatively for the Whigs, expressed the party's views in a letter he wrote to Anthony Colby, when Colby was elected the first Whig governor of New Hampshire. This confidential letter of advice from the shrewdest of politicians reveals more about the typical Whig approach than scores of party platforms and resolutions adopted at party conventions. He advised Colby to tread a cautious course: "Nine-tenths of all the electors who voted for you are strictly *conservative*; they fear all change, in fundamental things; and wish to hold on, steadily, to what has been tried and found useful. I should therefore recommend no fundamental changes." Webster continued: "No state in the Union is more interested in internal improvements and the operation of an effective tariff than New Hampshire." There was a crying need for roads and railroads, and because "New Hampshire is a state composed principally of farmers the more demand there is for agricultural products, and the nearer that demand is to the place of production, the better." He concluded by advocating a protective tariff to stimulate industry. As to the war with Mexico that had been declared one week before, Webster advised: "Whatever we may think of its necessity, or the course of policy which has led to it, we must join in all proper efforts to defend the country and maintain its rights." Finally, Webster, in regard to the slavery issue, thought it best for Colby to let his own discretion be his guide. Slavery, Webster said, is "a great blot on our system" and the hope of all good and wise men is "that the providence of humanity, religion, moral improvement, and better notions of what the good of society actually requires, will hasten on the day, without bloodshed or violence, when the whole system will be abolished."[3]

The slavery issue defied hopes for a peaceful solution. As early as 1837 Rufus Choate warned, "We sail amid ten thousand shoals and beyond them all is that vast lee-shore, the slavery question, on which we are at last to go to pieces."[4] The annexation of Texas was foreboding. Polk's decision to go to war with Mexico for the sake of extending the Republic still further meant that the time had come when the Union would face its greatest trials.

The rise of the antislavery movement in New England was reflected in the writings of John Greenleaf Whittier, James Russell Lowell, Henry Wadsworth Longfellow, and of individual clergymen. William Ellery Channing's writings helped make antislavery views respectable. The earlier abolitionists took such a radical stance on a whole series of issues that they won few followers. When Richard Dana attended an abolitionist meeting in 1843 he was horrified to hear the churches denounced and a call made for their destruction so that slavery might be abolished.[5] Abolitionist attacks on the Union further alienated the great majority. Channing spoke of the Union with reverence and in his attacks on slavery deplored violence and hatred of southerners. Channing spelled out in calm tones the evils of slavery;[6] his disciples, however, showed no such restraint.

Charles Sumner attended Channing's church and also sat in on Channing's weekly discussion groups. He contended that Christian morality was no less binding on the state and statesmen than it was on the individual. Sumner spoke in blunt terms: slavery was a sin and whoever gave it any support was a sinner. Sumner had two allies among the Unitarian clergy, John G. Palfrey and Theodore Parker. Palfrey wrote effectively, denouncing what he called the slave power. Parker, a gadfly of the highest order, who had upset his fellow clergymen by espousing German biblical criticism and ruling out divine revelation as a transient opinion no longer worthy of notice, was unsparing in his attacks on political leaders who failed to attack slavery with a vengeance. He loved confrontation, was a brilliant speaker who swayed large audiences every Sunday at the Melodeon, and joyfully took the lead in mass meetings.

Other denominations also had antislavery spokesmen. The Methodists in New England made their views known in *Zion's Herald*, a strong critic of slavery. The Congregationalist *Boston Recorder* likewise espoused antislavery views. However, it should also be said that local churches and denominational organizations were extremely cautious. They objected to slavery on moral and religious grounds but refrained from political action. They much preferred to believe that southerners would eventually see the error of their ways and rid themselves of slavery.[7]

New Englanders could agree that slavery was an evil, but they differed sharply on what to do about it; likewise, they differed on expansion and the Mexican war. This was partly a result of sectionalism within New England and of party lines. Maine and New Hampshire constituted a section within a larger section. Democrats controlled both states. Their leaders endorsed the annexation of Texas and applauded Polk's war and its expansionist goals. In both states the more remote rural areas dominated the state governments. Democratic leaders profited from control of patronage during the 1830s. And in these two states, where industrialization came much later and on a smaller scale, the Whig ideals of protectionism, a sound currency, stability, and friendship and economic ties to England had little appeal compared to the robust demands of frontiersmen for low-priced public lands, cheap currency, territorial aggrandizement, and the trumpeting of the virtues of the common man. Rural Vermont was an exception and there the Whigs, thanks to strong leadership and popular devotion to protectionism, retained control.

Beginning in 1844, the outburst of antislavery feelings that came with the controversy over Texas tore old party loyalties with the violence of a New England northeaster. In New Hampshire the Liberty Party, an antislavery party that had roots in more than forty towns, polled 4,000 votes in the 1844 elections. In January of that year John P. Hale, United States senator, and a leading Democrat, parted ways with his party on the Texas question, made direct appeal to the public by letter explaining his stand, and then, in spite of the opposition of party leaders, won the election.[8] On February 22, 1845 a segment of the party, taking the name Independent Democrats, sponsored a mass meeting in Exeter and resolved that "any direct or indirect advocacy of slavery was wrong and would have evil consequences for the entire civilized world."[9] The meeting supported Hale's candidacy for the Senate, and the state legislature later elected him to that post. In 1846 the Whigs, for the first time, won the governorship and control of the legislature, and the following year Anthony Colby, a Whig, was elected governor of New Hampshire with the help of the newly formed Independent Democrats. Colby began his administration by denouncing the war with Mexico as nothing less than "wholesale duelling." [10] In Maine, another leading Democrat, Hannibal Hamlin, broke with the party on the Texas question. Maine Democrats divided into Wildcats and Free-Soil Democrats. [11]

In Massachusetts, too, the Democrats split. The Henshaw and Morton factions divided on basic principles and engaged in a bitter struggle for control of the party. Henshaw, the conservative, looked to John C. Calhoun for leadership on the national level. Morton was an enemy of corporate privilege and held antislavery views. As director of the Boston Customshouse he expected to control federal patronage but soon found that Henshaw enjoyed the favor of the Polk administration. Morton looked to Martin Van Buren and the New York barnburners as his allies. Well before Polk's administration came to a close Morton's sympathies were with the new Free-Soil party, and he privately supported that party in the election of 1848. [12]

Nowhere did political tempers reach a higher pitch than in Massachusetts where unbending Conscience Whigs did battle with unbending Cotton Whigs, both of whom opposed the Polk administration and the war with unparalleled obstinacy. The Cotton Whigs stood for stability and protectionism and, much to the disgust of the Conscience Whigs, were more ardent on the tariff issue in the months after war began than they were on the war question.

To the Conscience Whigs there was one primary fact that served as the catalyst for all their thinking: slavery was a sin. Charles Francis Adams bluntly pronounced slavery the greatest wrong existing in the world. [13] Sumner, whose political vision was more tunneled, took no interest in orthodox Whig measures. Sumner, the disciple of Channing, declared slavery to be a sin. [14] Before he went to Washington as senator some years later, he promised Theodore Parker that he would be "in morals, not in politics." [15] John G. Palfrey, clergyman and professor of theology, was a stranger to compromise and dogged in his hatred of slavery. The Mexican war appalled these three leaders.

The most able of this coterie, Charles Francis Adams, together with Palfrey, Sumner, and other Conscience Whigs, purchased the nearly bankrupt newspaper, *The Whig*, in May 1846. Adams served as editor.

The purchase coincided with Polk's declaration of war and offered the editor a new opportunity to attack the Whig leaders. The paper's chief targets were Robert C. Winthrop and Nathan Appleton. Adams wrote of the "manifest degeneracy which prevails among our politicians, a tone which blusters about the rights of sheep and falls into the softest whisper when dealing with the rights of man." [16]

Winthrop lent himself to attack when he voted in support of Polk's declaration of war. In the judgment of the Conscience Whigs Winthrop was a weak man, bound to the wealthy merchants and manufacturers, men like Nathan Appleton and Abbott Lawrence. Sumner eagerly took on the assignment of censuring Winthrop. He had not forgotten that at the close of his speech against war Winthrop had offered the toast "Our Country, whether bounded by Sabine or Del Norte—still our country—to be cherished in all our hearts—to be defended by all our hands." Sumner took it as an insult and chose to interpret the toast as the equivalent of "Our Country Right or Wrong."

Sumner, never a man of moderation and readily given to carrying the virtue of integrity to such lengths that it became self-righteousness, accused Winthrop in voting for the war bill of disloyalty to truth and freedom. In a follow-up attack he held Winthrop guilty of voting for an unjust war in the cause of slavery. [17]

Winthrop was appalled. In a long letter to John C. Gray he poured out his heart. The major point he made was that the Whigs had put up a strong fight on the bill's preamble, had shown their disapproval, and felt it necessary to vote supplies. [18] In another letter to his friend, J. F. Clifford, Winthrop wrote: "Instead of tracing that war to its true source—annexation and the election of Mr. Polk—they are bent on making their own friends responsible for it. This is for their own purposes, & they are welcome to all the good they can get out of it." The editors of the *Daily Advertiser* and the *Atlas* rose to Winthrop's defense. William Hayden, of the *Atlas*, wrote a personal letter calling the attacks outrageous: "There is a certain class of theorists about here, who are quite excited upon this subject—and find no terms too harsh to use towards anyone who speaks with the least calmness about or gives the least countenance to the Mexican War. They have abused *us*, and our paper most violently—accused us of being bought up by the Lawrences, the Appletons, and the money interests generally, to be quiet to the Slave Interests of the South." [19]

The incident was significant. Winthrop was an outspoken critic of Polk and the Mexican War, and he voted for the Wilmot Proviso nine times though he declared early in the war that he would vote for support of the war. Winthrop's fault, more calmly stated, was not that he was not strongly antislavery, for he was. His fault lay in the fact that he represented the old school of New England sectionalism, fought for the whole gamut of the section's interests, and gave to the party, to protectionism, and to the Union a high priority.

Nathan Appleton, wealthy merchant and manufacturer, was soon under attack. He disapproved of slavery but felt no compulsion to subordinate all other interests to antislavery. Appleton had a distinguished record on financial questions, promoted sound financial practices, and was an authority on central banking. In this area he had distinguished himself as being above seeking personal or party advantage. At the same time he was a devout churchman, attended Channing's Federal Street Church, supported foreign missions, and was a generous philanthropist. In politics and in business he was guided by a strong sense of public responsibility, but he saw slavery as a local problem and as one that would decline in importance as the larger part of the country was developing without it.

Palfrey devoted a considerable portion of a series of articles in *The Whig* to attacking Appleton. Appleton's crime lay in not supporting the Texas committee when it continued its fight against admitting Texas after Congress had passed the joint resolution in early March 1845. He considered further agitation a waste and refused to give the committee additional support. This led Palfrey to hold Appleton responsible for the Mexican War, charging that if Texas had been denied admission there would not have been war. This assumed that if Appleton had supported the Texas committee Texas would not have been admitted. Appleton retorted: "Heaven bless us! Is this a joke or in earnest?" [20] Appleton dismissed Palfrey's charges as nonsense, but the real issue was not Appleton's refusal to support the Texas committee. He had opposed the annexation of Texas, but as Palfrey, Adams and Sumner knew, Appleton despised the abolitionists and preferred not to engulf the country in a controversy over slavery. This the Conscience Whigs could not tolerate.

Appleton explained his position in a letter to Sumner who had also attacked him. As Appleton saw it the war was begun by Mexico. Polk's statement that "war exists by the act of Mexico," wrote Appleton, was "no national lie." Polk, he believed, was not justified in ordering Taylor's army into the disputed territory, but Polk "had been placed in command by the American people and it was his party that should be called into account for the wrong." "In the meantime," wrote Appleton, "I suppose every good citizen is bound to contribute of his means in defense of his country in the war in which she is actively engaged." He held that it was the obligation of Congress to give support to the army's efforts to do its duty. Finally, Appleton believed that it was not a war to extend slavery. The annexation of Texas did that. In conclusion he informed his correspondent, Sumner, that the question was "a case in which patriotic and conscientious men might differ and did differ—as they will in their judgments upon it—but the assumption that any one opinion is the only right one, 'appears to me,' to be simply wrong." [21]

Sumner replied to this letter stating he "read it with grief," as indeed was inevitable in view of his strongly fortified convictions on the evil of slavery. Sumner did not believe that Appleton's letter refuted any one of his charges holding Winthrop guilty of "wrong doing." The war was evil and he could not see how a representative of Boston, "a place of conscience and morality," "the city of Channing," could support injustice. [22]

Appleton, in a letter to a clergyman in Pittsfield, the Reverend I. W. Danforth, presented his analysis of the slavery question. Slavery, he wrote, "is a curse which has been entailed upon us." He labeled it "a tremendous social and political evil"; but because New Englanders are free from it, he argued, we "ought to be able to look at it calmly and coolly." The South, he thought, was wrong in claiming the right to introduce slavery into territory now free and as a matter of principle ought to be resisted by the free states. "At the same time as a practical question it is probably unimportant since there is apparently no inducement to introduce slave labor in either Oregon, California, or New Mexico." "As to the existence of slavery in the slave states, secured by the

Constitution, I see no reason why we of the free states should make ourselves very unhappy about it. Why not leave it to the party immediately concerned. It is a matter sufficiently troublesome." In conclusion he observed, "There is little doubt that slavery will gradually be abolished in the most northern of the slave states. It may be abolished in all of them when slave labor ceases to be profitable." [23]

The Conscience Whigs had little interest in protectionism or in financial questions and did not prize the Whig party as an end in itself. They prized principles. Economic interests gave them little concern. Unlike men such as Everett and Winthrop, they saw antislavery as the paramount issue. On that issue they had strong allies in the northern areas of New York, Ohio, and Illinois. They fought not for New England interests but for a cause that transcended any one section.

As the Massachusetts Whigs gathered for the annual state convention in Boston in September 1846, the test of supremacy was at hand. The Conscience Whigs dominated the proceedings in a meeting in Faneuil Hall. Charles Sumner, Wendell Phillips, and Theodore Parker spoke. Nathan Hale, of the *Daily Advertiser*, reported: "They dealt however in no sparing terms with the members of existing parties—that is to say, nearly all the voters of the Commonwealth—as being negligent in their duty, and false to their consciences." [24] The sharp split in the party led the Whig editor to express the hope "that in any resolution which the Convention may pass as containing an expression of the sentiments and purposes of the party, they will not undertake to pledge the Whigs of Massachusetts to a creed which will cut them off from full communion with the Whigs of other states, and deprive them of their just influence in the councils of the nation, . . . ." [25] The Conscience Whigs lost the battle at the convention to adopt their resolutions, several of which would have offended the south. The editor of the *Daily Advertiser* now felt assured that the party possessed an element of stability amid the scenes of turbulence sufficient "to preserve its own integrity, and with it the safety of the State." [26]

The conservatives did not lose their hold in Massachusetts, and they continued to oppose the war. However, in Congress they voted financial support for the war but only because, for political reasons, they could not be in the position of denying troops and supplies. An incident in

January 1847 exhibited the full extent of their feelings. Caleb Cushing, now a Democrat and a member of the state legislature, supported the war. He was convinced that the annexation of Texas was necessary and desirable, both to prevent the British from hemming in the Republic and because annexation was no more than the natural course of empire. He was also influenced by his brief visit to Mexico upon his return from China. His experience led him to hold that country in contempt.

Cushing volunteered to raise a regiment to go to Mexico. His recruiting efforts garnered slightly more than a thousand men. He asked the state legislature for assistance in the amount of $20,000. The committee he chaired gave its approval. The proposal immediately became the target of the Whigs who saw in it an opportunity to denounce the war. The editor of the *Daily Advertiser* contended that the legislature could not with propriety give away public money for such an object.[27] One ardent opponent said that if the federal government did not provide adequate support and the volunteers were in need, it was also true that many other people were in need and were equally deserving of assistance.[28] By a vote of 4 to 1, the state house of representatives voted down the appropriation.[29]

# The Press and Congress

An examination of New England newspapers reveals a press split along three lines: those who shared the views of the Conscience Whigs; those who took the Whig party line, condemning Polk and the war; and finally, the Democratic party papers who defended Polk, held the war to be just, and approved of the acquisition of territory. All three were present in each of the six states. The newspapers of the day made no pretense of being neutral. They followed party lines without deviation and often resorted to violent pronouncements. New Englanders had the opportunity to hear both sides. Not only editorials but the published speeches of leaders in state government provided the public with opposing views.

Those opposed to the war held the upper hand in New England, but there were also those who supported the war, and this side was not lacking in able spokesmen. The aggressive and sharp criticisms of Polk and the war set forth by the Whigs usually put the Democrats on the defensive. They spent much time repudiating Whig charges that Polk, by ordering Taylor's army into the disputed territory, had provoked the war, and that it was a war of conquest intended to add slave territory.

The *Boston Statesman* took sharp issue with the Whig argument. A speech by a member of the Massachusetts House of Representatives, printed in full, challenged the Whig case. The speaker, Mr. Branning, declared, "When we annexed Texas we were bound by every consideration of duty to defend her limits as we found them." The United States, in annexing Texas, acknowledged her "with a well-known and well-settled boundary—fixed and defined by her organic law and acknowledged by Santa Anna himself in his public acts." Mexico, he contended, commenced war because of the annexation of Texas and not because of Taylor's presence in the disputed territory. Texas had existed as an independent nation for ten years. "Whatever may have been suffered by the Mexicans, upon them rests the responsibility. . . . We had manifested the utmost forbearance. From the first, we had sent the olive branch of peace in advance of our armies, but time and again it had been contemptuously, insolently rejected by that infatuated nation."[1]

The deep conviction that the United States was in the right came forth in a speech of George Boutwell, state representative from Groton, Massachusetts. The special significance of his remarks lies in the fact that he had antislavery leanings, was elected governor in 1850 by a coalition of Democrats and Free-Soilers, helped draft the Fourteenth Amendment, and capped his career in 1900 by serving as president of the Anti-Imperialist League. Boutwell held that Polk had the duty to defend Texas within the boundaries she had established by her victory over Mexico in her war for independence. Taylor was attacked in American territory. After war began Polk sought to negotiate but Mexico declined. Moreover, Mexico was guilty of spoliations on American commerce, and had put American citizens to death. Mexico had signed a treaty in 1839 agreeing to pay claims arising out of spoliations and then "used every means in her power to prevent the fulfilment of that treaty."

Boutwell then dealt with the question of indemnity. Mexico could only pay in land. "What probability," he asked, "is there that she will ever be able to redeem that land?" Previous to the war, some Mexican states were in revolt against the central government. Moreover, there were moral advantages to an extension of territory. Great Britain was suffering "for want of territory for her cramped and bowed down millions, whose energies cannot find room for development. And but for the outlet to the west, the condition of the people of New England would not have been very dissimilar now. . . ." He portrayed the new opportunities that would soon be available: "The commerce of a vast empire is open to them. They will secure the control of the commerce with China and the East Indies. By the aid of proper communication between the harbor of San Francisco—the best in the world—and the Atlantic coast, Boston and New York will become the successful rivals of London for the commercial rule of the world." And mining, too, would increase, for California possessed precious metals.[2]

The Boston *Daily Times* denounced the Whigs of Boston as the descendants of the Federalists who betrayed the nation in 1812. The editor dismissed Whig charges against Polk as being full of misrepresentations and absurdities.[3] Texas, wrote the editor, was not annexed because of an alleged "grasping spirit of this republic." Texas had turned to the United States for support after winning independence. "Is it grasping to protect the weak from the strong? Is sympathy with brethren an evidence of rapacity?" Polk was now carrying out the wishes of the people. Given this position at the outbreak of the war, the *Daily Times* continued to staunchly defend Polk, the war, and the annexation of new territory throughout the conflict. Mexico, it was affirmed, commenced hostilities and "on her head rests all the responsibility for the consequences."[4]

The *Eastern Argus* of Portland, Maine, and *The Age* of Augusta, Maine, upheld Polk and defended the war. "In such an emergency it becomes the men of all parties to cooperate with the national authorities in maintaining the rights and honor of the country," declared the Portland editor of the *Eastern Argus*. When the Whigs, during the first months of war, held that the United States was the aggressor, the editor called this preposterous. Mexico went to war not because American troops had crossed the Nueces River but because of the annexation of Texas. And the United States had every right to annex Texas. The *Eastern Argus* went well beyond other Democratic papers in denouncing Mexico. That country, wrote the editor, was "only half civilized" and "her institutions are but a step in advance of barbarism."[5] In a bold pronouncement he declared, "Whenever such a government exists, annoying neighboring powers, itself subject to constant civil revolutions, these adjoining States have the admitted right to conquer the offender, and appropriate them as they may choose." California, he wrote, had long been thought to become a part of the United States, and now it appeared that this was to become a fact in the near future. This, he wrote, was inevitable for "it is the actual destiny of the Anglo-Saxon race not only to occupy what they now possess, but to extend the cause of freedom to the limit of the North American continent."

The *Argus* denounced the Whigs for catering to the abolitionists. Raising the slavery question was the work of "red hot anti-Texas madcaps" who condemned all those determined to maintain the Union.[6] The vital issue as seen by Maine Democrats, aside from the war, was to free laboring men from the taxes they paid under the protective tariff. Webster's defense of protectionism in December 1846 was rendered in service to the capitalists of Massachusetts who "settled a fortune upon him for that very purpose." As regards Webster's statement that "We are all laboring men" the editor commented, "How the champagne loving dons must have chuckled."[7]

The prospect of a large increase in territory delighted Maine Democrats. John Winchester Dana, in his gubernatorial message to the legislature in 1847, looked forward to securing "an extent of coast on the Pacific, almost equal to that on the Atlantic, with a practical line of communication between the two oceans" placing "ourselves in a condition to command the commerce of the world." Dana, however, unlike many Maine Democrats, held strong antislavery views and supported the Wilmot Proviso.[8]

Dana's views were shared by *The Age* of Augusta. Mexico had perversely launched a war leading to her ruin. Now she should be made to pay and the territory she must cede should be opened to freemen. With such a population on her borders Mexico would be made to keep the peace among themselves and break the chains of oppression.[9] *The Age* firmly opposed the extension of slavery but promised to regard southern rights as sacred and not interfere with slavery where it already existed. The editor regretted that the war had been prolonged and blamed this on the Whigs whose opposition to the war had induced the Mexicans to believe that the war could not be prosecuted against them.[10]

In the other New England states Democratic newspapers also defended Polk, the war, and expansion. The Providence *Republican Herald*, spurred on by a hatred of the Whigs for their actions during the Dorr Rebellion, supported Polk enthusiastically, held Mexico responsible for the war, and labeled Whig opposition as "alike anti-American in feeling, blind and blundering in counsel, and tyrannical in power."[11] The *Transcript*, of the same city, held Mexico responsible for the war and called for Americans to give their full support to it. *The Weekly Connecticut Review* called for a low tariff and criticized those who failed to support the war on the grounds that it was unjust. "We are sure that our country, however many stains that from time to time soil her garments, will one day achieve a glorious destiny; and that with her, for the present at least, sinks or swims the hopes of the world." [12] *The Hartford Times* held that Mexico's conduct had been such "that the U.S. government, so long as it had any respect for itself, or regard for its citizens, could not avoid a collision with it." [13]

Although Democrat editors supported Polk, their loyalty to him does not wholly explain why they adopted the position indicated in their columns. There were deeper reasons both for the stance they took and for why they perceived the war so differently from the Whigs. Years of bitter party rivalry had created hostility toward the Whigs whose policy of protectionism seemed to employ government in the service of capitalists. Unlike the Whigs, who feared that expansion would add strength to their political rivals, the Democrats had no such fears. Their bias caused them to look at Polk's course with sympathy and to overlook any errors. Why be concerned about minor legal questions or tactical details? As the war promptly became a war for new territory they saw only the new opportunities and wealth that a victory would bestow on the nation. The extension of the slavery issue did not greatly concern most Democrats. They did not believe the war was a plot of the slavocracy, and they questioned the sincerity of Whigs on the slave question. How could the Whig party, led by Henry Clay, who had so often sided with slave interests, suddenly become antislavery? Men like George Boutwell of Massachusetts and John Winchester Dana of Maine had arrived at antislavery convictions, but they could support the war because they did not see the war as involving the slave question.

The Whig newspapers outnumbered the Democratic ones, giving the party an advantage. This advantage was compromised to some degree by the split in the Whig ranks and the newspapers supported by the Liberty party. Whereas many of the leading Whig papers played down the slavery issue, *The Whig* of Boston, the *Worcester County Gazette*, and the *Massachusetts Spy* of Worcester focused their attention on the slave issue and the South's determination to dominate the federal government. Each of the three newspapers chided the dominant Whig group for bending their knees to the South. [14] *The Gazette* was supported by the Liberty party. The paper had no sympathy with protectionism and ridiculed the Whig cry that the country faced ruin if tariff duties were lowered. "Was ever a people more humbugged by their rulers than is this by their political demagogues!" [15] The *Gazette* supported the Anti-Texas Committee, led by Charles Sumner, Charles Francis Adams, and John G. Palfrey.

The *Massachusetts Spy* of Worcester set the tone for the war period during the debate on the resolution to annex Texas. At that time it was declared that if the resolution passed, the Union would be virtually annulled. In May 1845 the editor announced that the same operators who had pushed through the annexation of Texas were "proclaiming their intentions in regard to a vast and fertile territory, to which they have no shadow of claim, and which is and has been for years in quiet possession of a neighboring friendly Power." [16] Where would this wild expansionism lead? According to the editor, it would mean war and all the evils connected with war. And, wrote the editor, it was a war "entered upon and carried out, for the purpose of sustaining the institution of human slavery." The editor referred to the decline of New England's influence. Texas, with 9,000 voters, would have 2 senators, the same number as Pennsylvania with 400,000 voters. The outlook was frightening. "If the tariff be repealed, it will be by Texas votes." [17] The eventual outcome of further annexation would be that the vast majority of American people "will be subjugated by the intrigues and boldness of a feeble minority of slaveholders, warring against industry as if it were dishonor." [18]

Whig newspapers hammered on a series of points in an effort to whip up an antiwar spirit. They focused on Polk's decision to launch a war of aggression. He was responsible for having ordered Taylor's army into the disputed territory where Texas had never exercised jurisdiction. Therefore Polk's declaration that war existed by act of Mexico was a lie.

The Pittsfield *Massachusetts Eagle*, like the *Massachusetts Spy*, both representing the strong antislavery sentiments in the central part of the state, followed the Whig line but went a step further and supported the position of the Conscience Whigs in Boston. In Vermont, where Whig ascendancy was higher than in any other New England state, the *Bellows Falls Gazette* pronounced Polk a liar and a man of unholy purposes. The annexation of Texas was attributed to Polk, and the fact that it had been admitted to the Union brought "hot blood of shame mantling to the cheek." [19] It evoked "honest indignation, shame, disgust and humiliation." The editor, at the outbreak of war, held that Polk's course was one of "impropriety, or at least impolicy." However, the editor called for full support of the war. [20] This sudden burst of patriotism gave way to dismay and bitterness as the war dragged on. The government of Mexico, to be sure, was "miserable, unprincipled, a perfidious cabal" but this furnished "no justification for such a contest as this." "Can any man assign one justifiable reason for the war; or suggest one single possible advantage to be derived from it. . . ." [21] It was, in the eyes of the editor, an unjust and unnecessary war.

The *Burlington Free Press* condemned Polk on the grounds that he was guilty of ill-considered and lawless acts. [22] Polk had "needlessly, and by unconstitutional exercise of power, involved the nation in the dreadful calamities and the enormous expense of war." [23] Some months later the editor called on the people to demand, "in tones of thunder," the immediate recall of the armies from Mexico.

The major Whig newspaper in New England, the Boston *Daily Advertiser*, made its opposition clear but employed more restrained language than others. One striking aspect of the pages of the *Daily Advertiser* is the relative little editorial space it gave to the war. However, reports from the war front were complete; great joy was expressed as victories were won; victorious generals were acclaimed for their valor; and soldiers were praised for their bravery. The *Daily Advertiser* took the Whig's position, supporting the war with adequate appropriations while at the same time condemning Polk and the war.

However, the Whigs were fearful of appearing unpatriotic in a time of national crisis. The fate of the Federalist party at the close of the War of 1812 was still too much alive in Whig memories to permit total opposition. When the Democratic *Salem Advertiser* charged the Whigs with a lack of patriotism and asserted that half the people of Massachusetts were traitors, the editor of the Boston *Daily Advertiser* affirmed that the newspaper had never stooped to failing to support the war. The war, the Whigs held, was unnecessary, but once entered into, they had no choice but to support it. The editor of the *Daily Advertiser* on another occasion denied undermining the war effort and held that the newspaper simply asked what the war was for, its reasons, its objects, its probable results, "and for information as to the manners, means, and time in which these results are expected."[24] The orthodox Whigs were anxious to present an image of restraint and of thoughtfulness combined with loyalty to the nation.

This strategy still allowed for persistent and strong editorial opposition to the war. Immediately after the declaration of war the Boston *Daily Advertiser* stated: "The panic under which the administration and Congress have acted, from the sudden menace of a military force which has hitherto been regarded as contemptible, is almost ludicrous."[25] In June 1846 the editor declared: "This is Mr. Polk's war. Congress has passed an act declaring that it exists, but Mr. Polk caused it to exist."[26] This opinion, frequently repeated throughout the war, constituted the editorial policy of the Boston *Daily Advertiser*.

This policy, of course, accorded with party politics. Polk and his party were to be held accountable. This is not to say all Whig denunciation of Polk was wholly politically motivated. Whigs were sincere in their condemnation of Polk's high-handed course and the extension of slavery.

The Whig political net was broad enough to contain supporters of disparate views. To have placed greater emphasis on the slavery aspect and given priority to limiting or abolishing slavery would have run counter to the strongly conservative feelings of the party. Not to have focused on Polk, who declared war on the protective tariff and the proposed national bank, would have been to miss the opportunity to gain political effectiveness by personalizing the evil. Consequently Polk became the embodiment of all evil for the Whigs.

The Mexican War evoked sincere argument at the time, but it also created a political war between the two major political parties, both of whom had much at stake. Editors were servants of the parties, readily engaged in selective perception of actions taken and, with equal readiness, to avoid what was damaging to their cause. There were momentous questions to be faced: the question of executive domination in the area of foreign relations; of war for the sake of conquest; the question of extending slavery. No one of these lent itself to ready solution. In the heat of party rivalry and in the course of a foreign war, it could scarcely be expected that these questions could be analyzed in an atmosphere free of either rancor or of party interests.

The debates in Congress from the first weeks of the war were vigorous. Polk had expected the war to be of short duration but found that Mexico, though weak, was persistent. American armies won battles and took over vast stretches of territory, but no government in Mexico would make peace even after the occupation of Mexico City. Once it became clear that Polk planned to take over large parts of Mexico, anger mounted. The war's prolongation further increased the bitterness of its opponents who vented their spleen by denouncing the war and the president.

Critics at home were as tenacious in obstructing Polk's plans as the Mexicans. Party rivalry, distrust of Polk, and opposition to the extension of slavery promoted the sharpest internal dissensions since the War of 1812. As in the instance of the War of 1812, New England, more than any other section, offered the stiffest resistance, but the resistance was far less uniform than previously.

In Congress opposition to the war rode in tandem with a bitter fight against Polk's tariff program. The Walker tariff bill was before the House of Representatives as the war began. The bill came to the fore in July and promoted a storm as great as the declaration of war. At this time Polk called for a special appropration to be used in negotiating with Mexico. Representatives from Massachusetts, Connecticut and Rhode Island led the fight against the lowering of the tariff. Robert C. Winthrop delivered a lengthy speech attacking the tariff bill and won high praise from Nathan Appleton and the Whig protectionists.[27]

Webster led the fight in the Senate. He declared that the bill was "so novel, so dangerous, so vicious in its general principles; so ill considered, so rash, and I must say so intemperate in many of its provisions, [it] cannot but produce in the country the most serious and permanent mischief should it become law."[28] The major fault of the bill, Webster declared, was that it provided for *ad valorem* duties, that is, the evaluation of the goods by the importer. He cited a petition from Boston dry goods merchants protesting that adoption of the *ad valorem* system would result in the abandonment of their business to unscrupulous foreigners who would declare values that were lower than the actual cost on their imports. Senator Davis of Massachusetts added that the low duties "were designed to produce revolution in the affairs and business of the country." It was said that these low duties aimed at putting into effect the Democrats' theory of free trade.[29] Senator Niles of Connecticut joined the fight, charging that the low duties were based on abstractions rather than realities. "The principle of this bill," said Niles, "has a strong southern squint—a squint towards cotton and tobacco." The New England protectionists convinced no one. Webster was shouted down, and McDuffie, the veteran opponent of protection, pointed out that the reductions were on manufactures "owned by capitalists, now realizing 20 to 40 percent on their capital."[30] The bill met a tie vote in the Senate and only passed by the favorable vote of the vice-president. The Walker Tariff lowered duties more than enough to raise the wrath of old line New England Whigs.

This was the prelude to the heated debate over Polk's request for a sum of $2 million for possible advance payment to Mexico to facilitate settlement of the boundary question. Winthrop, who usually spoke in a calm and reasoned fashion, denounced the request in angry tones: "Not a word about peace, Not a word about Mexico, Not a syllable about the disputed boundaries on the Rio Grande. . . . They might employ this money towards buying California, or buying Cuba, or buying Yucatan, or buying the Sandwich Islands, or buying any other territory they might fancy in either hemisphere."[31] In the Senate John Davis led the fight against the appropriation and killed the bill by filibustering during the closing hours of the session.

In the course of the debates in the House a new and incendiary amendment, the Wilmot Proviso, was introduced. Hannibal Hamlin of Maine, who helped draft it, was disposed to support Polk on the war question, but he was also a conscientious critic of slavery and determined to oppose its extension. Hamlin shared this view with a group of antislavery Democrats led by Preston King of New York. These Democrats were motivated in part by their disillusion with Polk who seemed to them to favor the southern wing of the party. They were also influenced by the growing antislavery sentiment among their constituents.[32]

The Wilmot Proviso would have outlawed slavery in any territory acquired from Mexico.

The Wilmot Proviso passed the house, but the Senate adjourned without voting on it. It shortly became the rallying point of antislavery people, from the most radical to the most conservative. As Frederick Merk has written: "The Northern public clung to the proviso as a warning to expansionists in both sections of the Union that if Manifest Destiny was ever to be fulfilled, at least slavery was to have no part in it, and that slavery was, in any case, never to be spread by the sword."[33] Daniel Webster, the most notable exception, objected to the proviso on the grounds that it implied annexation of territory. Webster saw all annexation at this time as the source of dangerous sectional divisions and preferred postponement.

In his annual message of December 1846 Polk did his best to defuse the attacks made upon him. In an extremely lengthy message he set forth his case. The message impressed his New England critics as nothing less than blasphemy. Polk not only failed to appease his opponents, he ignited further passions. John Davis promptly asked, "What right had General Kearny to proclaim New Mexico to constitute a part of the United States? If the American people were prepared to fold their arms, and see such tricks perpetrated before high heaven and in their presence must make the angels weep, and yet do nothing, farewell to their rights—farewell, a long farewell to their liberties."[34]

Winthrop charged the president with equating opposition to the war with treason. Polk's message, he said, menaced the concept of freedom of debate. He concentrated his attack on the president's congratulatory message to the country in which he spoke of the vast extension of "our territorial limits." What did this mean, he asked.[35]

Charles Hudson, also of Massachusetts, accused the president of seeking to limit freedom of speech. Engaging in a war, "without cause" and then suppressing opposition, was an outrage. He added, "A doctrine more corrupt was never advanced; a sentiment more dastardly was never advocated in a deliberative assembly." The president himself, said Hudson, was the aggressor.[36]

Winthrop was slightly more moderate. He announced he would vote for financial support of the war on the basis of his belief that once a nation is at war, regardless of who was the aggressor, that war became in part a defensive war. This war, he held, was provoked by the president though Mexico was not without fault. Ordering troops into the disputed territory was an act of war, and the chief motive in going to war was to wrest territory from Mexico. He added that New England was resolved that there should be no extension of slavery.[37]

In his message Polk asked for $3 million to purchase Mexican territory. This set off heated argument among members of both parties. Their attack centered on denouncing the war as a war of conquest. In the Senate, Upham of Vermont introduced an amendment—essentially the same as the Wilmot Proviso—to the $3 million bill, prohibiting slavery in any new territory.[38] Foote of Connecticut, in the House, opposed all annexation with or without slavery. Hudson of Massachusetts supported the Wilmot Proviso, declaring that the new territory should be open to free labor.[39] Dillingham of Vermont took the same position.[40] Winthrop again denounced the war as unjust, urged peace, and warned that New England was resolved that there should be no extension of territory.[41] Hamlin of Maine spoke strongly against the extension of slavery in the new territories.

New England's representation in Congress reached virtual unanimity on the question of the extension of slavery but differed on other issues. Niles, a Democrat, who defended Polk and the war, did not wish to see Mexico despoiled but believed she should pay, if not with money, then with a small stretch of land.[42] Foote of Connecticut opposed all annexation with or without slavery.[43]

When Congress met in December 1847, condemnation of the war and of slavery reached a new peak. The most vigorous critic, John Hale of New Hampshire, a Democrat, announced he would vote "against the war in all its forms; against any measures for the supply of troops, either regulars or volunteers." He presented a number of petitions calling for an end to the war. One was thirty-six yards long, signed by 2,931 ministers and laymen of the Unitarian Church.[44] Smart of Maine presented the Senate with a series of resolutions passed by the state legislature condemning slavery and its introduction into the new territories.[45] The antislavery Democrats shortly gained control of the Maine legislature. George Perkins Marsh of Vermont declared that the "War had been the boldest experiment tried on the credulity of the American people."[46] There was no excuse for an indemnity—Texas was enough. Webster announced that, in his opinion, the entire new country to be annexed "was not worth a dollar," and noted that the addition of the three new states with less population than Vermont would send six senators to Congress.[47] The more conservative Whigs took refuge in attacking the costs of the war. Hudson of Massachusetts applauded the cost, for it would awaken the people to their true condition. In 1847 alone the expenditures rose from $3 million to $33 million, and Hudson calculated that they would reach $58 million.[48] Hudson moved a resolution calling for withdrawal of the army and setting the boundary between the Nueces and the Rio Grande. The resolution lost by a vote of 137 to 41. Of the ten representatives from Massachusetts, eight voted for it, and of the four from Connecticut, three voted for it.[49]

There were several complicated and interwoven issues confronting the American nation at this time: expansion, the slavery question, party rivalry, and the broader question as to which section was to control the Union. Men opposed the war because it appeared to extend slavery; or, because it would tip the scales in favor of southern control of the Union; or, because Polk had gone beyond the Constitution in provoking war; or, because the war was unjust to Mexico. New Englanders' old fear of losing influence in an ever expanding union also found occasional expression. More often, all of these considerations entered into shaping the opinions of the New England Whigs.

All the factors causing New England Whigs to oppose the war had a common origin in the basic political philosophy and the hopes and ideals of the Whigs. Few expressed the basic Whig outlook more accurately than George Perkins Marsh, one of Vermont's representatives in the House of Representatives. Marsh was a lawyer, an eminent scholar, who was master of eight European languages, a prolific writer on linguistics, and author of the book, *The Earth as Modified by Human Action*, which earned him acclaim as the father of human ecology. In February 1848, in a debate on Polk's request for ten new regiments, Marsh spelled out why the war was wrong.

Marsh began by asserting that the nation's moral responsibilities extended to her enemies and therefore Mexico should be justly treated. There could be no distinction between private and public morality. The war's primary cause was the annexation of Texas, its immediate cause the dispatch of troops into the disputed territory, but neither made war inevitable. The administration had then precipitated war by making no conciliatory effort to avoid it. Marsh held that the right role for the United States, given its rich resources, would have been to turn its efforts to cultivating the arts of peace: "To cultivate war, in preference, was an inversion of statesmanship. . . ." Marsh proceeded to state what was basic to the Whig view: "The policy of this people was to increase by natural growth and by accretion, not to spread by acquisition and conquest." The Polk administration, Marsh held, could not be expected to follow such a course, for it was hostile to the encouragement of the useful arts and the protection of domestic industry. Instead it turned to conquest and sought support of the people "by dazzling them with the prospect of admitting the East India trade into the ports of California."

A dedicated Whig, Marsh accused the administration of employing Machiavellian tactics in promoting the war, a war that brought shame. "The only remedy for the evils we endure was a just and honorable peace." The glory of a nation lay not in the size of the army or navy; on the contrary, they were means of executive patronage. Nor was size of territory a measure of national grandeur. All the territory that was necessary was what was needed to sustain human life by moderate industry. The United States had reached that point long ago.[50]

The major spokesman for the Whigs in the House of Representatives, Robert C. Winthrop, agreed with Marsh but did not condemn expansion if achieved by fair means. He condemned the morality of a foreign policy bent on conquest of territory and which set aside the code of behavior that nations had generally accepted. Winthrop was a moralist in foreign affairs; his judgments, however, were not based on religious teaching but on the secular tradition of the law of nations. Although other Whigs had condemned the war as unjust, Winthrop alone gave clear and explicit expression to this approach. As early as the debates on the Oregon question, this led him to ridicule the champions of the doctrine of manifest destiny. In one of his finest speeches Winthrop referred to it as "the new revelation of right which has been designated as *the right of our manifest destiny to spread over the continent.*" Here was a new "right" boldly asserted and a "right" possessed by the United States alone "for I suppose the right of a manifest destiny to spread, will not be admitted to exist in any nation except the universal Yankee nation!" Where was such a right to be found? "Perhaps it may be found," he said, "in that same Illinois cave in which the Mormon Testament has been discovered."

Winthrop saw that the doctrine of manifest destiny, now set forth by close friends of the Polk administration, challenged the concept of the law of nations, ruled out negotiation and arbitration, and was an "impeachment" of those who, like John Quincy Adams and Albert Gallatin, proceeded by negotiation to defend national interests. There was a moral obligation to rely on negotiation. Only in an extreme case was a nation justified in going to war, a case where a nation's rights, as defined by the law of nations, was threatened—a case such as impressment.[51]

The heated arguments for and against the war were an extension of the bitter party rivalry that existed before the war. Roy Nichols, one of the most distinguished historians of these years, observed that it was "not an age of calm and orderly development but of jangling nerves, poor health, uneasy conscience, and a wildly and widely ranging imagination." Above all, he wrote, that fear of losing power can stimulate even greater exertion than the desire to grasp it.[52] The papers of New England Whigs testify in support of this. Throughout the correspondence of Robert C. Winthrop and Edward Everett in these years are repeated references to the driving ambition of the South. Lesser figures, too, shared this feeling. New England Whigs, deeply troubled by the schisms within the party and disconsolate over the divisive effects of the rivalry between Clay and Webster, believed that the South controlled the Union and threatened to achieve permanent domination. Behind all the editorials and speeches in Congress was an anxiety that gave distortion the upper hand. Detached and cool judgment was in short supply.

The supreme irony, given the heated opposition to the war and the extension of slavery, was the nomination by the Whigs of Zachary Taylor for president. Taylor was named because he could win, not because of his qualifications. Long before the close of the war political leaders turned their attention to the next election. The Whigs were desperate. Should they fail to elect their candidate, many Whigs believed it would mean the end of the party. Prominent leaders in the party offered little hope of victory. Henry Clay, defeated so many times, inspired no hope of victory. Daniel Webster, identified with antislavery, would receive no support in the South. This situation opened the door to newcomers.

Zachary Taylor's early victories in the war, culminating in his victory at Buena Vista in February 1847, ascended from the lower depths of anonymity to the peak of popularity. The public cared little about his shortcomings as a general. He had won battles when his army was greatly outnumbered and this sufficed. A pro-Taylor enthusiasm swept the country and, in turn, swept the victorious general to the front as a presidential candidate.

Taylor's candidacy widened the split among the Massachusetts Whigs. The party was already divided into a Conscience Whig faction, a Cotton Whig faction led by such party stalwarts as Abbott Lawrence, Nathan Appleton, and Robert Winthrop, and a third group led by Daniel Webster. The Cotton Whigs fixed their energy on Taylor by late 1846 believing that he alone could be elected. Webster, who, as Winthrop put it, suffered from a persistent infirmity, ambition to be president, was still an influential figure with a considerable following.

Taylor's promotion by the Cotton Whigs confirmed the Conscience Whigs in their view that the cotton manufacturers and their hangers-on were sheer opportunists, in league with southern slaveholders. Sumner, in the summer of 1848, at a convention in Worcester, labeled it a conspiracy between the lords of the lash and the lords of the loom. Then followed a lengthy exchange of letters between Appleton and Sumner. In the course of the exchange Sumner told of a visit with Abbott Lawrence, who was then being prominently mentioned as the probable vice-presidential candidate. Sumner urged him to withdraw, believing him caught in an enterprise of evil meant to further the interests of slaveholders. Sumner recalled that at this point in his conversation with Lawrence he said, "You have recently given $50,000 to Harvard College—I honor you for your munificence; but I cannot forbear saying that the evil which will ensue from your participation in the movement for Taylor will counterbalance all the good which can arise from your munificence."[53]

Lawrence and Appleton felt that Sumner was no more than an errant boy who had gone over to the abolitionists, but others in that faction wrote of Sumner, Charles Francis Adams, and their allies as "damned philanthropists." The editor of the *Daily Advertiser* lost all patience and in a letter to Winthrop referred to them as a "pack of aspiring, canting, & malignant humanitarians."

Webster and his close friend, George Ashmun of Springfield, viewed the rise of Taylor with despair. Ashmun described Taylor's popularity as a "high state of inflammation." He expressed concern because "the great mass of Whigs seem only bent on killing Loco-focoism, indifferent by what means it shall be done, & hopeful, merely, as to the future."[54]

Webster was appalled by the enthusiasm for Taylor and his eventual nomination in June 1848. He pleaded with Ashmun to put together all the information about happenings in the convention so that it could be shown to the people of the free states that their delegates had been indifferent. The votes for Taylor from Vermont, Rhode Island, Connecticut, and Maine struck Webster as abominable. Massachusetts had stood alone in the fight against Taylor. Webster was at work preparing a pamphlet attacking the convention for nominating Taylor.[55]

Others in Massachusetts warned Webster that if Taylor were the candidate, they would organize an opposition party. Henry Wilson, a Conscience Whig, predicted that they would carry at least twenty thousand votes. Wilson hoped that Webster would agree to be their candidate.[56] Another Conscience Whig, E. Rockwood Hoar, wrote to Webster stating that the nomination of Taylor was "as great a political blunder as it was an abandonment of principle." He thought that if Webster were to come out against Taylor "it would blow out of existence this Taylor faction throughout New England, and throughout the North, in twenty-four hours."[57]

The Conscience Whigs, in despair, left the party and joined hands with the strong antislavery groups in New York and Ohio in organizing the Free-Soil Party. A convention of Free-Soilers met in Buffalo in August and nominated Martin Van Buren for president and Charles Francis Adams for vice-president.

As Taylor's foremost biographer has noted: "Taylor's military victories *alone* did not gain the Presidency for him." He had able supporters, led by Truman Smith of Connecticut, who organized a campaign with great skill while Taylor remained on his Louisiana plantation, professed to prefer private life, and, except for a few indiscreet slips in his correspondence, managed to give the appearance of having transcended party interests.[58]

Taylor was elected in November 1848. His greatest support came from the slave states, but he also won in Massachusetts, Connecticut, Rhode Island, and Vermont. Cass, the Democratic candidate, was no option for voters holding antislavery views. Van Buren, the Free-Soil candidate, did well in Massachusetts, Maine, and Vermont. A new party system was clearly in the offing.

The dramatic growth of the United States in the decades prior to 1860 brought with it an equally dramatic change in the position of the United States in world affairs. The nation reached its continental limits in 1848. It was now the dominant power in the western hemisphere. Sectional rivalries played a much lesser role in both domestic and foreign affairs. The Mexican War and the election of Zachary Taylor marked the close of an era. The three divisions that appeared in the New England press reflect, in part, the basic transition taking place in the life of the Republic. These divisions were not unique to New England, for they were present in the West and South. What is significant is that, with the exception of a few voices, the opposition to the war with Mexico was not based on opposition to westward expansion, so long a major position of New Englanders. The opposition to the war rested chiefly on three grounds: opposition to bold aggrandizement at the expense of a weak neighbor; opposition to the extension of slavery; and, equally important, a belief that the war would open the door to the breakup of the Union. The wrangle over the territorial question became central by 1850, and with it the Union faced breakup. This was clearly foreseen by men like Edward Everett and Robert C. Winthrop. Both were opposed to slavery, and both were ardent Unionists who were seeking a way to rid the country of slavery and at the same time preserve the federal government. The sobriquet "Cotton Whigs" did not accurately describe them, for they saw something much more important at stake than protectionism. The next decade revealed the futility of their hopes. As the newspapers reveal, the conflict was not simply one of Conscience Whigs versus Cotton Whigs.

# 13

# New England and the Making of Foreign Policy

Largely as a result of party rivalries, New England did not speak with one voice. The Whigs dominated Massachusetts, Connecticut, Rhode Island, and Vermont, but New Hampshire and Maine were controlled by the Democrats. The four Whig states surpassed New Hampshire and Maine in population, in wealth, and in influence in national affairs.

Together the New England states constituted an area with a common interest in shipping and later in manufacturing. They were exposed to the outside world and vulnerable to economic and political changes in the world at large. In event of war they were almost defenseless and their economies, if cut off from foreign markets, sources of materials, and British credit, faced disastrous disruption. Their vulnerability was even greater on the high seas where New England ships, laden with cargos worth many millions of dollars, would be seized by the enemy. This exposure to the outside world, close ties to the world economy, and dependence for credit on London, induced caution, a strong preference for peace, and opposition to western territorial expansion.

The conservatism of New England society strengthened this spirit of caution. The Federalists of the early decades admired Alexander Hamilton and, like him, firmly believed that economic realities must overrule theory and political ideology. Leaders, conditioned by the atmosphere of countinghouses, took greater interest in figures on assets and liabilities than in abstract ideas. The later generation of Whigs, no less averse to changes in institutions and equally distrustful of majorities and public passions, looked on law as the guardian against public distempers for assurance of order as well as liberty.

The dominance of the Congregational churches, particularly in the small towns, strengthened conservatism. Trained to think that they had a special responsibility to protect public morals, to instill a feeling of final accountability to God, and to promote the virtue of the state, the clergy placed a cap on both frivolity and radical thought. When Charles Dickens visited Boston in 1842 he took note of "the peculiar province of the pulpit" and "the denouncement of all innocent and rational amusements." "The church, the chapel, and the lecture room are," he wrote, "the only means of excitement excepted; and to the church, the chapel, and the lecture room the ladies resort in crowds." [1] The clergy served not only as the guardians of propriety but as symbols of learning and as the explicators of divine wisdom.

Those aspiring to political leadership found social approval in church-going, in exhibiting calmness and composure, in demonstrating a knowledge of law and skill in rhetoric. Given the meager salaries paid those holding public office, they had to have private means. The governor of Vermont received an annual salary of $750 in the years 1801 to 1857, and governors in Rhode Island were paid even less. Public officeholders, the great majority of whom were lawyers, frequently found it necessary to return to practicing their profession in order to recoup their fortunes. The more fortunate lived by means of inherited wealth or the benefits betowed by marriage into a wealthy family. Edward Everett, Charles Francis Adams, and Robert C. Winthrop were free to pursue political careers because each had private means. Daniel Webster only survived because he received large gratuities from Boston's wealthy. These requirements for political success almost assured a conservative leadership, and the well-ingrained social habit of deferring to the leaders in the community offered further assurance of conservatism.

Leaders of the Democrats came from the middle class. They were often successful lawyers or newspaper editors. From a twentieth-century point of view they were far from radical; they were friendly to humanitarian reforms and challenged the granting of special privileges to corporations in charters approved by the state legislatures. Their position on foreign relations issues reflected party ties and their heavy dependence on patronage bestowed by the national administrations.

The dominant Whig party in New England approached relations

with England with a conciliatory attitude. Democrats, on the other hand, shared the anglophobia so prominent in the West. Caleb Cushing, first a Whig and then a Democrat, took a wholly independent view. He was convinced that the British were determined to hem in the Republic and that, with the help of their Indian allies, were in a position to endanger national security and compromise American achievement of national goals. However, the great majority of New Englanders admired and trusted the British. This attitude was firmly rooted in both economic ties and in shared political attitudes. New Englanders shared the Burke tradition that change must come slowly, and they admired British reverence for law and representative government. Leading Whigs— Daniel Webster, Edward Everett, and Robert C. Winthrop—enjoyed lengthy visits in England and felt as much at home in the estates of the British aristocracy as they did in the spacious mansions on Boston's Beacon Hill.

The tie drew closer as a result of a common approach in foreign relations. Ideology was foreign to both the Whigs and the British. Both were committed to a pragmatic approach and energetic in advancing their own interests, whether they be the interests of shipping or manufacturers' interest in foreign markets.

From George Cabot to Daniel Webster, New England's business leaders and their political allies viewed foreign relations in much the same way as merchants engaged in foreign trade viewed their overseas correspondents. Advantageous transactions sufficed as a goal. Government had the obligation to protect foreign trade and to facilitate it by negotiation of favorable commercial treaties. The attitude of the Massachusetts Whigs during the Maine boundary controversy illustrated the approach. A concession of a stretch of territory enabling the British to achieve what appeared as reasonable, an overland military passage from the coast to Quebec, in return for which the British yielded Aroostook and Madawaska, plus the freedom for Americans to ship their timber down the St. John River; this was a mutually advantageous bargain and well worth the price of setting aside the ancient boundary claims sanctified by a treaty.

At the same time New England Yankees could be as stubborn at the diplomatic bargaining table as they could be in driving a bargain with foreign merchants. When New England interests were directly involved, as in the case of fishing rights off Newfoundland and freedom to trade with the British West Indies, tenacity overruled the spirit of give and take. John Quincy Adams, dedicated nationalist, overreached himself in the diplomatic negotiations and formulation of policy in 1823 when he inserted the principle of no further colonization by European powers in the western hemisphere into Monroe's message. He did so again in 1826 when his instructions to Albert Gallatin, who was to negotiate with the British, asked for much and offered little in return, a weakness the shrewd Gallatin was quick to protest on the grounds that his chances of success would be sharply limited.

Given the prominence of the church in New England life, religion and politics on two occasions became intertwined. Public policy, domestic and foreign, was discussed in moralistic terms and judged as Christian or unChristian when a sharp crisis occurred. This tendency reached its peak in the War of 1812 and again during the Mexican War. In the first instance the Congregational clergy, almost to a man, condemned the war against England, contending that it allied the United States with infidel France. The clergy took a much less active part during the Mexican War, but the arguments against the war rested on moral considerations. The war was condemned on the grounds that it was a war of conquest and unjust and that it was a war to extend slavery.

Moral opposition to the war raised the question as to whether Christian principles were applicable to public policy. Two influential leaders, Charles Sumner and George Perkins Marsh, who were not political allies, stated explicitly that Christian teaching applied to public measures in the same way that they applied to individual behavior. Neither chose to confront the problem of how a pluralistic society committed to different interpretations of Christian teaching was to arrive at a common judgment as to what was Christian teaching and what was not; nor did either ask how a state confronting the ruthless tensions of a world made up of sovereign states was to survive if it adhered to the principles enunciated in the sermon on the mount. However, they represented a point of view that had nothing but foreboding for political compromise. The antislavery movement at large assumed that slavery was a moral evil, and this conviction, when held with fervor, ruled out compromise and hastened the day when only war could resolve the issue. This is not to deny that slavery was a moral issue; it is only to suggest that clashes reduced to moral issues limited the probabilities that the conflict could be resolved within the democratic process. What is notable is that from 1789 to 1812 and from 1815 to 1845 the Whigs did not take a moralistic approach toward slavery in spite of their devotion to the church. This basic problem had not troubled New England Whigs in the previous decades. Yankee ingenuity was no less ingenious in reconciling Christian duty and self-interest than they were in convincing themselves that a high protective tariff served the laboring class quite as much as the manufacturer. Christian duty and practical considerations were kept in separate compartments. This in no way meant that religious convictions were limited to Sabbath meditations.

Secular newspapers overflowed with religious sentiments. Public leaders viewed their religious obligations with great seriousness. Their private letters abound in references to God, the final ruler of the universe, the arbiter of what was right and what was wrong. At the same time they leaned heavily toward the practical and were reluctant to develop a set of moralistic rules for everyday life. God was real but so was the world, the realities of human behavior, and the need for realism in a world that was often ruthless. The result was not a compromise offering easy composure but tension. Consequently, New Englanders, in the long run, did not intertwine piety and politics. However, they had as great respect for the law of nations as they did for law at home. The Cotton Whigs adhered to this tradition even throughout the crisis of the Mexican War and condemned the war on constitutional grounds and because Polk's actions did not accord with the dictates of international law.

New Englanders in general were deeply conscious of the fact that they did not share the same approach to foreign relations as did people in other sections, especially the people of the West. Less vulnerable in the event of war, more land hungry and proexpansionist, and less cautious, the West—both to the north and south—supported the Louisiana Purchase, called for a bold policy in West Florida in 1805, and demanded the annexation of both Texas and Oregon in 1845. The appetite for new lands consumed the Democrats in their 1844 convention at Baltimore. Expectations of taking all of Oregon and Texas became battle cries in the mouths of men like Allen of Ohio, Hannegan of Indiana, and Cass of Michigan. They ridiculed the danger of war with England and dismissed it with bravado. New Englanders were appalled, though some of the evidence suggests that the recent immigrants in eastern cities shared the western expansionist views.

The New England attitude toward the western frontier states had its origin in a stereotyped picture of the frontier as the land of lawlessness, heavy drinking, and pistol fire and in the fear that rapid development of the West would drain New England of its labor supply. Together these factors stood in the way of a political alliance of the two sections.

The home missionary society of the churches and the lyceum tours of New England's intellectual leaders aimed at raising the country's level of civilization. The lyceum program, organized by Josiah Holbrook in Massachusetts in 1826, aimed at promoting a cultured society. This institution, so typical of New England in the decades before the Civil War, soon extended its activities to the Northwest where the presence of a large New England migration furthered its growth. Conditions on the early frontier, the consuming labor required to clear the land, allowed little time for intellectual pursuits, but as towns and cities came into being, westerners hoped to develop a culture of their own. New Englanders, confident of their cultural superiority, eagerly set forth to establish colleges and promote New England Congregationalism in order to promote moral stability. The westerners were quick to resent suggestions that New England was superior, and lecturers found it necessary to hide their feelings, but underlying the movement was the effort to promote religion, education, and culture. This feeling found expression in the first meeting of the Society for the Promotion of Collegiate and Theological Education in the West where it was affirmed:

It is in its *nature* just as truly a missionary work to educate youth of the valley of the Mississippi for the Gospel ministry, or for teaching common schools, or to rescue children from ignorance and from Papal and other delusions, as it is to do the same work in the Sandwich Islands or on the banks of the Ganges.

Three years later a member of the same society put it even more bluntly when he said: "What more benign or blessed work could we project or accomplish, than to plant another New England, or raise up such a population as New England has furnished in some other portions of our country beyond the mountains?"[2] This attitude, combined with the awareness that New England's political clout grew weaker with the addition of each new state, dulled interest in expansion to such a degree that editors and politicians were supercilious. Refusal to accept the fact that the westward movement could not be halted led them to dream of a republic bounded by the Mississippi river. This stance alienated the West.

As late as the Mexican War editors and political leaders belittled the value of the new territory. The staid and sober George Perkins Marsh, as we have seen, professed to see no gain in the vast new area taken from Mexico. In the course of the debate on Oregon the editor of the *Boston Atlas* spoke of the territory as "these Siberian wilds."[3] Edward Everett wrote to Winthrop at one point in 1843 dismissing Oregon as of no vital importance and referred to the westerners as "wicked unprincipled factions."[4] Robert C. Winthrop was the first to demolish the doctrine of manifest destiny, called by Albert K. Weinberg, "this new theologico-legal doctrine."[5] Here was a doctrine that, if adopted by all nations, would completely destroy the existing law of nations.

The friction between New England and the West also had its source in the depletion of New England's labor supply. Westerners, such as Thomas Hart Benton, campaigned for ever lower prices on public lands so as to hasten settlement. The conflict came into the open in 1829. The drain on New England's labor supply ran counter to the interests of the new and growing manufacturing interests. Senator Samuel A. Foote of Connecticut introduced a resolution proposing that the Senate Committee on Public Lands consider the expediency of limiting the sales of public lands, a proposal that caused Benton to strike back in a speech denouncing New England. In domestic politics New England and the West parted ways on this question, with a few notable exceptions, including Webster, just as they did on foreign policy issues that involved expansion.

By 1850 forces were close to terminating the alignments that had submerged the political life of the nation in sectional conflict since the War of 1812. New England and the Northeast, thanks to the rapid growth of manufacturing, merged in their political interests, particularly in their support of high tariffs. As inland transportation, roads, canals, and steamboats improved, the Northeast and West were tied more closely. In the next decade came the East-West railroads, strengthening the ties further. These developments paralleled the growth of the antislavery movement throughout the North. As these developments took place, continental expansion came to a close, and an issue that had been so important to New England disappeared. This lessened any danger of war with England and thus, while anglophobia did not disappear, relations with England took a different turn, and the issues between the two nations in the future affected the country as a whole in much the same way.

New England as a region, with a separate political and economic identity, became merged with the larger section composed of the Northeast and the West. In the realm of foreign relations, too, New England was no longer a section whose views distinguished it from other areas north of the Mason-Dixon Line. The lines of battle on the great foreign policy questions were no longer drawn on sectional lines.

# Notes

## Chapter 1

1. Henry Lee, "The Magee Family and the Origins of the China Trade," *Massachusetts Historical Society Proceedings*, 1969, vol. 8, p. 108.

2. Samuel Eliot Morison, *Maritime History of Massachusetts, 1783–1860* (Boston: Houghton Mifflin, 1921), p. 91.

3. Percy Wells Bidwell, "Rural Economy in New England at the Beginning of the Nineteenth Century," *Transactions of the Connecticut Academy of Arts and Sciences*, 20 (1916): 304.

4. Timothy Pitkin, *Statistical View of the Commerce of the United States* (New York: August M. Kelley Publishers, 1967), pp. 76–77.

5. Kenneth Wiggins Porter, *The Jacksons and the Lees: Two Generations of Massachusetts Merchants* (Cambridge: Harvard University Press, 1937), p. 26.

6. Edward Gray, *William Gray of Salem, Merchant* (Boston: Houghton Mifflin, 1914), p. 35.

7. Ibid., p. 24, n. 1.

8. Carl Seaburg and Stanley Paterson, *Merchant Prince of Boston: Colonel T. H. Perkins, 1764–1854* (Cambridge: Harvard University Press, 1971), p. 418.

9. Porter, *The Jacksons and the Lees*, p. 26.

10. Thomas G. Cary, *Memoir of Thomas Handsyd Perkins: Containing Extracts from His Diaries and Letters* (Boston: Little, Brown, 1856), pp. 18–26.

11. Ibid., pp. 13–42.

12. Seaburg and Paterson, *Merchant Prince of Boston*, p. 55.

13. Porter, *The Jacksons and the Lees*, pp. 28–29.

14. Gerard W. Gawalt, *The Promise of Power: The Emergence of the Legal Profession in Massachusetts, 1760–1840* (Westport, Conn.: Greenwood Press, 1979), p. 13.

15. Bidwell, "Rural Economy," p. 319.

16. Ibid., pp. 320–21.

17. Timothy Dwight, *Travels in New England and New York*, ed. Barbara Miller Solomon, 4 vols. (Cambridge: Harvard University Press, 1969), 2:184.

18. Ibid., p. 373.

19. Carl Bridenbaugh, "The New England Town: A Way of Life," *Proceedings of the American Antiquarian Society* 4 (April 1946): 22.

20. Ibid., p. 24.

21. Ibid., p. 315.

22. This interpretation has been applied to the famous extreme Federalist clique

224 Notes to pages 11-19

known as the Essex Junto, by David H. Fischer. See his article, "The Myth of the Essex Junto," *William and Mary Quarterly*, April 1964.

## Chapter 2

1. *Annals of Congress*, 1st Cong., 1st sess., vol. 1, pp. 222–23.
2. Ibid., p. 212.
3. Ibid., p. 229.
4. Henry Cabot Lodge, *Life and Letters of George Cabot* (Boston: Little, Brown, 1878), p. 76.
5. Ibid., p. 589.
6. Ibid., p. 586.
7. Ibid., p. 589.
8. Ibid., 2:1628.
9. Ibid., p. 1646.
10. Ibid., p. 1771.
11. George Cabot to Benjamin Goodue, 5 May 1790, in *George Cabot*, Lodge, pp. 36–37.
12. The representatives from Pennsylvania held out against assumption, using it as a bargaining point to have the capital moved to Philadelphia. Ames noted that this was an issue between the grogshops in New York and the grogshops in Philadelphia. Once the removal to Philadelphia passed, the Pennsylvania delegation supported assumption of state debts.
13. *Annals of Congress*, 1st Cong., 2d. sess., p. 1753.
14. Ibid., p. 1153.
15. Seth Ames, ed., *Works of Fisher Ames with a Selection from His Speeches*, 2 vols. (Boston: Little, Brown, 1854), 1:21.
16. Ames to George Minor, 3 May 1789, ibid., p. 35.
17. Ames to Minor, 29 May 1789, ibid.
18. Ibid.
19. Ames to Minor, 3 September 1789, ibid.
20. Ames to Minor, 2 July 1789, ibid.
21. George Cabot to Rufus King, 2 August 1793, in *George Cabot*, Lodge, p. 74.
22. M. W. Patterson, *Sir Francis Burdett and His Times, 1770–1844* (London: Macmillan, 1931), vol. 1, pp. 48–52.
23. Philip S. Foner, ed., *The Democratic-Republican Societies, 1790–1800: A Documentary Sourcebook of Constitutions, Addresses, Resolutions, and Tracts* (Westport, Conn.: Greenwood Press, 1976), p. 42.
24. Ibid., p. 42.
25. Lodge, *George Cabot*, pp. 57–58.
26. Samuel E. Forman, *The Political Activities of Philip Freneau, Johns Hopkins University Studies in Historical and Political Science* (Baltimore: The Johns Hopkins Press, 1902), pp. 75–76.
27. Ibid., p. 77.
28. Ames, *Works of Fisher Ames*, p. 150.

29. Thomas Jefferson to William Short, 3 January 1793, in *Writings of Jefferson*, ed. Paul Leicester Ford, 10 vols. (New York: G. P. Putnam's Sons, 1895), 6:238.

30. *American State Papers: Foreign Relations*, 1:301.

31. *Annals of Congress*, 3d Cong, 1st sess., p. 215.

32. Ibid., p. 290.

33. Ibid., p. 272.

34. Ibid., pp. 329–30.

35. Ibid., p. 340.

36. Ibid., p. 350.

37. Ibid., p. 386.

38. Ibid., p. 498.

39. See Charles E. L. Wingate, *Life and Letters of Paine Wingate*, 2 vols. (Medford, Mass.: published by author, 1930), 2:427–29.

40. *Annals of Congress*, 3d Cong., 1st sess., p. 602.

41. Ibid., p. 582.

42. Ibid., p. 568.

43. Ibid., p. 587.

44. Alexander Hamilton to President George Washington, 8 March 1794, in *The Papers of Alexander Hamilton*, ed. Harold Syrett, 44 vols. (New York: Columbia University Press, 1972), 16:136.

45. Ibid., pp. 132–33.

46. Hamilton to Jay, 6 May 1794, ibid., pp. 381–85.

47. Jerald A. Combs, *The Jay Treaty: Political Battleground of the Founding Fathers* (Berkeley: University of California Press, 1970), p. 151.

48. Sedgwick to Williams, 6 March 1794, Sedgwick Papers, Massachusetts Historical Society.

49. Syrett, *Alexander Hamilton*, 18:404–54.

50. Combs, *The Jay Treaty*, p. 152.

51. *Annals of Congress*, 3d Cong., 2d sess., p. 862.

52. The British captured a French ship carrying dispatches from Fauchet who wrote of receiving valuable information from Randolph and implying that he had asked Fauchet for money. The British forwarded the information to Hammond, the British minister, who arranged for this information to be passed on to Washington. See Combs, *The Jay Treaty*, pp. 166–69.

53. Stephen Higginson to Timothy Pickering, 16 August 1795, in *Letters of Stephen Higginson*, ed. J. Franklin Jameson, Annual Report of the American Historical Association, 1896, p. 791.

54. Lodge, *George Cabot*, pp. 80–81.

55. Ibid., p. 86.

56. *Annals of Congress*, 4th Cong., 1st sess., p. 1275.

57. Ibid., p. 1244.

58. Ibid., p. 1245.

59. Ibid., p. 1291.

60. Ibid., p. 1247.

61. Ibid., p. 1190.

62. See Bradford Perkins, *The First Rapproachement: England and the United States, 1795–1805* (Berkeley: University of California Press, 1967). The author also owes a debt to Bradford Perkins for his excellent *Prologue to War: England and the United States* (Berkeley: University of California Press, 1961) in which he gives due attention to the position of the New England Federalists in the years 1805 to 1812.

63. Nathan O. Hatch, *The Sacred Cause of Liberty: Republican Thought and the Millenium in Revolutionary New England* (New Haven: Yale University Press, 1977), p. 130.

64. Fred C. Luebke, "The Origins of Thomas Jefferson's Anti-Clericalism," *Church History*, September 1963, p. 346.

65. *American State Papers: Foreign Relations*, 2:5, and ibid., 2:8–9.

66. E. Wilson Lyon, "The Directory and the United States," *American Historical Review*, April 1938, p. 515.

67. Ibid., p. 516.

68. F. J. Turner, ed., *Correspondence of French Ministers to the United States, 1791–1797*, Annual Report of the American Historical Association, 1903, 2:950–52.

69. Alex De Conde, *Entangling Alliance: Politics and Diplomacy under George Washington* (Durham, N.C.: Duke University Press, 1958), p. 446.

70. Lyon, "The Directory and the United States," p. 517.

71. Charles Francis Adams, ed., *The Works of John Adams*, 10 vols. (Boston: Little, Brown, 1856), 9:114.

72. *Annals of Congress*, 5th Cong., 1st sess., p. 72.

73. Ibid., 378–80.

74. Ibid., pp. 384–85.

75. Quoted in Ralph Adams Brown, *The Presidency of John Adams* (Lawrence: University Press of Kansas, 1975), p. 99.

76. Ibid., pp. 181, 183.

77. Lodge, *George Cabot*, p. 235.

78. Ibid., p. 234.

79. For a full and valuable description of Pickering, see Gerard H. Clarfield, *Timothy Pickering and the American Republic* (Pittsburgh: University of Pittsburgh Press, 1980).

80. *Annals of Congress*, 6th Cong, 2d sess., Appendix, pp. 1191–92.

81. Ibid., pp. 771–78.

## Chapter 3

1. Dumas Malone, *Jefferson and His Time: Jefferson the President, Second Term*, vol. 5 (Boston: Little, Brown, 1974), pp. 6–7.

2. Thomas Jefferson to Archibald Rowan, 26 September 1798, quoted in *Letters of Thomas Jefferson*, ed. Frank Irwin (Tilton, N.H.: The Sanbornton Bridge Press, 1975), pp. 92–93.

3. Ibid., p. 110.

4. Jefferson to Ceasar Rodney, 10 February 1810, ibid., p. 199.

5. Ibid., pp. 199–200.

6. Jefferson to William Wirt, 3 May 1811, ibid., p. 200.

7. Jefferson to Ceasar Rodney, 10 February 1810, ibid., p. 199.

8. *The Diary of William Bentley*, 4 vols. (Salem, Mass.: The Essex Institute, 1907), 2:102.

9. James Walker, "Memoir of Daniel Appleton White," *Massachusetts Historical Society Proceedings*, 1862–1863, p. 268.

10. John Pierce, "Memoir of President Kirkland," *Massachusetts Historical Society Proceedings*, June 1894, p. 149.

11. Nathan O. Hatch, *The Sacred Cause of Liberty: Republican Thought and the Millenium* (New Haven: Yale University Press, 1977), pp. 121–31.

12. Ibid., pp. 130–31.

13. In 1794 Fisher Ames wrote: "The Democratic Club met lately in Faneuil Hall. This is bold, and everything shows the fixed purpose of their leaders to go desperate lengths. It is not a pleasant thing for the yeomanry to see their own Government taken out of their hands and themselves ciphered by a rabble formed into a Club. Thus Boston may play Paris, and rule the State." Charles Warren, ed., *Jacobin Junto or Early American Politics as Viewed in the Diary of Dr. Nathaniel Ames, 1758–1822* (Cambridge: Harvard University Press, 1931), pp. 7, 57.

14. Henry Cabot Lodge, *Life and Letters of George Cabot* (Boston: Little, Brown, 1878), p. 337.

15. *Diary of Bentley*, p. 421.

16. Nathaniel Emmons, *Sermons on Various Important Subjects of Christian Doctrine and Practice* (Boston: Samuel T. Armstrong, 1812), p. 361.

17. Ibid., p. 423.

18. Quoted in *Jefferson the President*, Malone, vol. 4, p. 5.

19. David Hackett Fischer, *The Revolution of American Conservatism: The Federalist Party in the Era of Jeffersonian Democracy* (New York: Harper & Row, 1965), see particularly chap. 2.

20. Harrison Gray Otis to Woodbury Storer, 29 August 1804, quoted in ibid., p. 59.

21. Seth Ames, ed., *Works of Fisher Ames with a Selection from His Speeches*, 2 vols. (Boston: Little, Brown, 1854) 1:315.

22. Ibid., pp. 323–24.

23. Ibid., p. 329.

24. Lodge, *George Cabot*, pp. 333–34.

25. For a discussion of the debate in Congress on the reexport trade see Burton Spivak, *Jefferson's English Crisis: Commerce, Embargo, and the Republican Revolution* (Charlottesville: University Press of Virginia, 1979), p. 31. In late 1805 the representatives from New England were deeply concerned over the danger of losing the reexport trade. Southern members of Congress had almost no direct stake in this trade and were hesitant to make it a major issue.

26. Lodge, *George Cabot*, p. 239.

27. Ibid., p. 351.

28. Ames, *Works of Fisher Ames*, 2:356.

29. *Annals of Congress*, 9th Cong., 1st sess., p. 91.

30. Ibid., p. 684.

31. Ibid., p. 452. On February 25 Jefferson entertained John Quincy Adams and fourteen other Federalists at dinner. Adams recorded: "Conversing with the President on public affairs, he told me that he understood Mr Gregg's proposition was to be abandoned, and that the question would be between Mr Nicholson's resolutions or nothing. I said it seemed probable that *nothing* would eventually have the preference. He said that then we must abandon our carrying trade for that unless something were done in aid of negotiation Great Britain would never yield on the point. His own preference is manifestly for Nicholson's resolution. . . ." in *The Works of John Adams*, ed. Charles Francis Adams, 10 vols. (Boston: Little, Brown, 1856), 1:415.

32. *Annals of Congress*, 9th Cong., 1st sess., pp. 658–60.

33. Ibid., p. 842.

34. Ibid., pp. 877–78.

35. Irving Brant, *James Madison: Secretary of State, 1800–1809* (Indianapolis: Bobbs-Merrill, 1953), p. 371.

36. Burton Spivak shows that the British held the upper hand in the negotiations and meant to use their power in refusing to make any significant concessions. Monroe was well aware of this and had serious doubts about entering into negotiations at this time. Spivak, *Jefferson's English Crisis*, p. 55.

37. Harry Ammon, *James Monroe: The Quest for National Identity* (New York: McGraw-Hill, 1971), p. 259.

38. Samuel Flagg Bemis, *John Quincy Adams and the Foundations of American Foreign Policy* (New York: Alfred A. Knopf, 1950), p. 141.

39. Henry Adams, *New England Federalism* (Boston: Little, Brown, 1877), pp. 116–17, 181–83.

40. Henry Adams, ed., *Writings of Albert Gallatin*, 3 vols. (Philadelphia: J. B. Lippincott, 1879), 1:367.

41. Adams, *New England Federalism*, p. 188.

42. Jefferson fixed on the embargo as the only way to protect the merchant marine. Madison, from the beginning, looked upon it as a measure of economic coercion. Both men seriously overestimated the willingness of the public to pay the price of hardship over an extended period. See Spivak, *Jefferson's English Crisis*, pp. 106, 109–10.

## Chapter 4

1. George Henry Haynes, ed., "Letters of Samuel Taggart, Representative in Congress, 1803–1814," *Proceedings of the American Antiquarian Society*, vol. 33, p. 123.

2. Ibid., p. 222.

3. Ibid., pp. 223–24.

4. John Quincy Adams, *American Principles: A Review of the Works of Fisher Ames* (Boston: Everett and Munroe, 1809), p. 6.

5. Ibid.

6. Thorp Lanier Wolford, "Democratic-Republican Reaction in Massachusetts to the Embargo of 1807," *New England Quarterly*, March 1942, pp. 49, 53.

7. *The Diary of William Bentley*, 4 vols. (Salem, Mass.: The Essex Institute, 1907), 3:336.

8. *Warren–Adams Letters, Being Chiefly a Correspondence Among John Adams, Samuel Adams, and James Warren*, vol. 2 (Boston: Massachusetts Historical Society, 1925), p. 357.

9. Edward Gray, *William Gray of Salem, Merchant* (Boston: Houghton Mifflin, 1914), p. 48.

10. *Bentley Diary*, 3:350–51.

11. Worthington Chauncey Ford III, ed., *The Writings of John Quincy Adams*, 7 vols. (New York: The Macmillan Company, 1913–1917), 3:189–223.

12. Samuel Flagg Bemis, *John Quincy Adams and the Foundations of American Foreign Policy* (New York: Alfred A. Knopf, 1950), p. 148.

13. *Annals of Congress*, 10th Cong., 1st sess., pp. 1850–54.

14. Ibid., pp. 161–75.

15. Carl Seaburg and Stanley Paterson, *Merchant Prince of Boston: Colonel T. H. Perkins, 1764–1854* (Cambridge: Harvard University Press, 1971), p. 196.

16. *Annals of Congress*, 10th Cong., 2d sess., p. 1540.

17. Richard J. Purcell, *Connecticut in Transition: 1775–1818* (Middletown, Conn.: Wesleyan University Press, 1963), p. 178.

18. *Annals of Congress*, 10th Cong., 2d sess., pp. 175–191.

19. Ibid., p. 536.

20. Dumas Malone, *Jefferson and His Time: Jefferson the President, Second Term*, vol. 5 (Boston: Little, Brown, 1974), pp. 608–10, 613.

21. Ford, *The Writings of John Quincy Adams*, 1:248–53.

22. Henry Adams, ed., *The Writings of Albert Gallatin*, 9 vols. (New York: Antiquarian Press, 1960), 1:451–52.

23. Burton Spivak, *Jefferson's English Crisis: Commerce, Embargo, and the Republican Revolution* (Charlottesville: University of Virginia Press, 1979), pp. 186–89.

24. Ibid., p. 198.

25. J. C. A. Stagg, in an article on the causes of the War of 1812, emphasizes that Madison's decision in favor of war in the late summer of 1811 was largely a result of the threatened breakup of his party by a violent factionalism. Gallatin, secretary of the treasury, was highly unpopular with the Smith faction in Baltimore. The Clinton faction in New York attacked Madison on the grounds that he was weak in the face of British abuses. James Monroe and his supporters criticized Madison for taking too legalistic a stand in his negotiations with Great Britain; they favored compromise. Madison faced the possibility that he would not be renominated. This situation, in addition to the fact that when the new British minister, Augustus Foster, arrived, he made it clear to Madison that there was no prospect of British concessions, caused Madison to decide for war. J. C. A. Stagg, "James Madison and the 'Malcontents': The Political Origins of the War of 1812," *William and Mary Quarterly*, October 1976, pp. 557–85.

26. Samuel Eliot Morison, *Harrison Gray Otis, 1765–1848: The Urbane Federalist* (Boston: Houghton Mifflin, 1969), p. 313.

27. Roger H. Brown, *The Republic in Peril: 1812* (New York: Columbia University Press, 1964), p. 45.

28. Mercy Warren to James Winthrop, in *Warren–Adams Letters*, vol. 73 (Boston: Massachusetts Historical Society, 1925), p. 375.

29. James Winthrop to Mercy Warren, 28 February 1813, ibid., p. 375.

30. Elbridge Gerry to Mercy Warren, 28 February 1812, ibid., p. 374.

31. Abigail Adams to Mercy Warren, 29 June 1813, ibid., pp. 382–83.

32. Morison, *Harrison Gray Otis*, p. 326.

33. Ibid., p. 331.

34. *Bentley Diary*, 3:213.

35. Ibid., 2:329.

36. "The Charlestown Association for the Reformation of Morals: A Tract Containing A Discourse Delivered at the Organization of the Association by the Reverend Jedidiah Morse," *Early American Imprints* (Boston: Armstrong, 1813).

37. "Miscellaneous Remarks on the Police of Boston," *Early American Imprints* (Boston: Cummings and Hilliard, 1814), p. 5.

38. "Clergyman's Almanac," *Early American Imprints* (Boston: Lincoln and Edwards, 1814).

39. Carl Bridenbaugh, "The New England Town: A Way of Life," *Proceedings of the American Antiquarian Society*, April 1946, p. 36.

40. The Reverend Samuel Cary, *Fast Day Sermon in Kings Chapel, Sept. 9, 1813, Early American Imprints* (Boston: Isaiah Thomas, Jr., 1813), pp. 1–11.

41. "An Address to Members of the House of Representatives," *Early American Imprints* (Boston: Cutler, 1812), pp. 1–27.

42. "Odes Composed for the 174th Anniversary of the Ancient and Honorable Artillery," *Early American Imprints* (Boston, 1812).

43. William Alexander Robinson, "The Washington Benevolent Society in New England: A Phase of Politics During the War of 1812," *Massachusetts Historical Society Proceedings*, March 1916, pp. 275–77.

44. *Washington Benevolents: Second Book of Washington Benevolents otherwise called the Book of Knaves* (Boston: Nathaniel Coverly, Jr., 1813), pp. iii–vi.

45. William Sullivan, "An Oration Delivered Before the Washington Benevolent Society of Massachusetts April 30, 1812," *Early American Imprints* (Boston: John Eliot, Jr., 1812), p. 19.

46. Lewis Bigelow, "An Oration Pronounced at Templeton, July 5, 1813, in Commemoration of the Thirty Seventh Anniversary of American Independence before the Washington Benevolent Societies in the northern section of the County of Worcester," *Early American Imprints*, p. 12.

47. Richard Dana, "An Oration Delivered before the Washington Benevolent Society at Cambridge, July 4, 1814," *Early American Imprints* (Cambridge: Hilliard and Metcalf, 1814).

48. Josiah Dunham, "An Oration Delivered at Hanover in the Vicinity of Darmouth College before the several Washington Benevolent Societies of Hanover,

Lebanon, Lime, Norwich, and Hartford on the Twenty Eighth Anniversary of American Independence, and the Commemoration of the Great Events in Europe, which Have Terminated So to the Allied Arms, and So Triumphantly Glorious to the Cause of Humanity," *Early American Imprints* (Hanover: Charles Spear, 1814), p. 29.

49. Quoted by William Gribbin, *The Churches Militant: The War of 1812 and American Religion* (New Haven: Yale University Press, 1973), p. 25. This study is one of the most thoughtful analyses of the role of the clergy during the war.

50. Thomas Snell, "Sermon Preached in North Brookfield July 23, 1812, A Day of Prayer, Recommended by His Excellency the Governor," *Early American Imprints* (Brookfield, Mass.: E. Merriam, 1812), p. 19.

51. David Osgood, "A Solemn Protest Against the Late Declaration of War Delivered on Sunday after the Declaration of War by the Pastor of the Church in Medford," *Early American Imprints* (Boston: Hilliard and Metcalf, 1812), p. 12, 13.

52. Samuel Taggart, "God's Visitation of Sinful Nations: Two Sermons Delivered in Colrain, on the Public Fast, July 23, and Afterwards in Shelburne August 20, 1812," (Greenfield: Dennis and Phelps, 1812), pp. 58–60.

53. *Sketch of the Church Solemnities at the Stone Chapel and Festival at the Exchange, Thursday, March 25, 1813 in Honour of the Russian Achievements over the French Invaders* (Boston: Munroe and Francis, 1813), p. 22.

54. William Plumer, *"Address to the Clergy of New England on Their Opposition to the Rulers of the United States,"* *Early American Imprints* (Concord, Mass.: I. and W. Hill, 1814), pp. 5, 6.

55. Solomon Aiken, *"An Address to Federal Clergymen,"* *Early American Imprints* (published by the minister, 1813), p. 77.

56. Titus T. Barton, "Fast Sermon in Calvinistic Congregation Church in Fitchburg, July 23, 1812," *Early American Imprints* (Fitchburg, Mass.: Salmon Wilder, 1812), p. 12.

57. Stephen Bemis, *"Two Discourses Delivered at Harvard, Mass., August 20, 1813 and May 29, 1813,"* *Early American Imprints* (Harvard, Mass.: Sewall Parker, 1814), p. 27.

58. John R. Schutz and Douglas Adair, eds., *The Spur of Fame Dialogues of John Adams and Benjamin Rush, 1805–1813* (San Marino, Calif.: The Huntington Library, 1966).

59. For an excellent exposition on the Federalists' opposition, see Brown, *The Republic in Peril*, chap. 8.

## Chapter 5

1. Charles Francis Adams, ed., *Memoirs of John Quincy Adams comprising portions of His Diary from 1795 to 1848*, 12 vols. (Philadelphia: J. B. Lippincott, 1874–1878), 4:193. Hereafter cited as *Memoirs*.

2. Victor S. Clark, *History of Manufactures in the United States* (New York: McGraw-Hill Book Company, 1929), p. 546.

3. James Truslow Adams, *New England and the Republic, 1776–1850* (Boston: Little, Brown, 1926), p. 352.

4. Carl Russell Fish, *The Rise of the Common Man* (New York: The Macmillan Company, 1927), p. 252.

5. Samuel Flagg Bemis, *John Quincy Adams and the Foundations of American Foreign Policy* (New York: Alfred A. Knopf, 1949), p. 260.

6. Henry Cabot Lodge, "Letters of Hon. Elijah Mills," *Massachusetts Historical Society Proceedings*, September 1881.

7. Leverett Saltonstall to his wife, 24 February 1825, Saltonstall Papers, Massachusetts Historical Society. Dexter Perkins wrote of John Quincy Adams: "Aciduous, combative, suspicious, Adams was none the less a great personality, great in his unswerving and intense patriotism, great in his powerful and logical intelligence, great in his immense industry, great in his high integrity." Dexter Perkins, *A History of the Monroe Doctrine* (Boston: Little, Brown, 1955), p. 29.

8. Worthington Chauncey Ford III, ed., *The Writings of John Quincy Adams*, 7 vols. (New York: The Macmillan Company, 1913–1917), 3:207–208.

9. Allan Nevins, ed., *The Diary of John Quincy Adams, 1784–1845: American Diplomacy, and Political, Social, and Intellectual Life, from Washington to Polk* (N.Y.: Frederick Ungar, 1969), p. 467.

10. Lyman H. Butterfield and Marc Friedlander, eds., *The Diary of Charles Francis Adams*, vol. 6 (New York: Atheneum, 1967), p. 79.

11. Nevins, *Diary of John Quincy Adams*, p. 531.

12. *Annals of Congress*, 14th Cong., 2d sess., p. 806.

13. Ibid., pp. 774–87.

14. *American State Papers: Foreign Relations*, 4:380.

15. John Bartlett Brebner, *North Atlantic Triangle: The Interplay of Canada, the United States and Great Britain* (New Haven: Yale University Press, 1945), pp. 90–91.

16. Bemis, *John Quincy Adams*, p. 279, and Adams, *Memoirs*, 4:86.

17. Henry Adams, ed., *The Writings of Albert Gallatin*, vol. 2 (New York: Antiquarian Press, 1960), pp. 84–85, and Rush to Monroe, 10 November 1818, Monroe Papers, Library of Congress.

18. *Annals of Congress*, 15th Cong., 2d sess., Appendix, pp. 1581–86.

19. *Memoirs*, 4:148–49.

20. Adams observed: "The officers of the United States have been the principal causes, by connivance, or by something worse, of all the piracies which for these three or four years have issued from that city." *Memoirs*, 4:308.

21. Onis to the secretary of state, 19 October 1817, U.S., Department of State, National Archives, Washington, D.C.

22. *Memoirs*, 4:90.

23. Ibid., p. 79.

24. Ibid., p. 109.

25. *Annals of Congress*, 15th Cong., 2d sess., Appendix, pp. 1823–28.

26. Ford, *The Writings of John Quincy Adams*, 6:385.

27. *Annals of Congress*, 15th Cong., 2d sess., pp. 256–68.

28. Ibid., pp. 1135–36.

29. The debates in Congress were greatly influenced by political considerations. Adams discussed the maneuvering with Rufus King who was on the Senate committee. Adams wrote of King: "He is also well acquainted with all the caballing and electioneering passions and practices that are miingled up in this affair, . . . ." Adams, *Memoirs*, 4:245. Adams believed the sole object of the Senate report was to defame Jackson, ibid., p. 278.

30. William Eustis to James Monroe, 23 October 1819, Monroe Papers.

31. Rush to Monroe, 1 October 1818, ibid.

32. Rush to Monroe, 1 November 1818, ibid.

33. Gallatin to Monroe, 7 November 1818, ibid.

34. Bemis, *John Quincy Adams*, p. 340.

35. *American State Papers: Foreign Relations*, 4:539–45.

36. *Patriot and Daily Chronicle*, 9 January 1819.

37. *Columbian Centinel*, 3 March 1819.

38. Dearborn to Monroe, 31 December 1819, Monroe Papers.

39. Ford, *The Writings of John Quincy Adams*, 7:51.

40. *Memoirs*, 4:443.

41. Ibid., 5:152.

42. Ibid., 4:354.

43. Ibid., 4:438–39.

44. Ford, *The Writings of John Quincy Adams*, 7:113–18.

45. Ibid., p. 117.

46. Quoted in *John Quincy Adams: A Personal History of an Independent Man*, Marie B. Hecht (New York: Macmillan, 1972), p. 331.

47. Ford, *Writings of John Quincy Adams*, 7:201.

48. *Memoirs*, 5:164–65.

49. Ibid., p. 200.

50. Ibid., p. 325.

51. A particularly important article entitled, "The Principles of the Holy Alliance; Or Notes and Manifestoes of the Allied Powers," appeared in the *North American Review* in October 1823. The author expressed deep concern over the aims of the Holy Alliance but was equally critical of England, "a greater monopolist of the world than even Spain."

52. Worthington Chauncey Ford III, "The Genesis of the Monroe Doctrine," *Massachusetts Historical Society Proceedings*, June 1902; Dexter Perkins, *The Monroe Doctrine, 1823–1826* (Cambridge: Harvard Historical Studies, 1927); Harry Ammon, *James Monroe: The Quest for National Identity* (New York: McGraw-Hill, 1971).

53. *Memoirs*, 6:178.

54. Ford, "Genesis of Monroe Doctrine," p. 391.

55. Perkins, *History of the Monroe Doctrine*, p. 47.

56. *Boston Evening Gazette*, 6 December 1823.

57. Edward Everett, the eloquent orator, at a meeting at the Exchange Coffee House, said: ". . . there could be but one feeling on the subject, among the friends

of liberty and humanity throughout the civilized world—and that was a deep
sympathy for this brave and suffering people." *Columbian Centinel*, 24 December
1823.

58. Governor William Eustis praised the Greeks and said: ". . . to them we owe
our religion and concept of liberty." *Columbian Centinel*, 10 January 1824.

59. *American State Papers, Foreign Relations*, 4:261–62.

60. *Annals of Congress*, 17th Cong., 1st sess., vol. 2, pp. 1094–1100.

## Chapter 6

1. *The Boston Centinel*, 1 January 1820.

2. Ibid.

3. Ibid., 6 May 1820.

4. Memorial of Boston Merchants, *American State Papers: Finance*, 6:671–76.

5. Howard S. Russell, *A Long, Deep Furrow: Three Centuries of Farming in New
England* (Hanover, N.H.: University Press of New England, 1976), p. 352.

6. Ibid., p. 364.

7. Walter Hill Crockett, *Vermont: The Green Mountain State*, 5 vols. (New York:
The Century History Co., 1921), 3:192, 211.

8. Peter J. Coleman, *The Transformation of Rhode Island: 1790–1860* (Providence: Brown University Press, 1963), p. 257.

9. Jarvis Means Morse, *A Neglected Period of Connecticut's History* (New Haven:
Yale University Press, 1933), pp. 71–72.

10. *Register of Debates in Congress*, 20th Cong., 1st sess., p. 743.

11. Ibid., p. 2071.

12. Speech of Mr. Hill of New Hampshire on the subject of Mr. Clay's resolution
in relation to the tariff, *New Hampshire State Historical Library*.

13. *Boston Patriot*, 24 January 1827.

14. Ibid., 31 January 1827.

15. Papers of Edward Everett, Massachusetts Historical Society. The author was
privileged to use microfilm copies of these papers in the library of Michigan State
University.

16. *Register of Debates*, 19th Cong., 2d sess., p. 786.

17. Ibid., pp. 858–71.

18. Ibid., p. 750.

19. Ibid., pp. 997–1000.

20. Ibid., p. 1028.

21. Ibid., 20th Cong., 1st sess., p. 2326.

22. Ibid., pp. 750–70.

23. Quoted in *Diary of John Quincy Adams*, ed. Allan Nevins, (New York:
Frederick Ungar, 1969), p. 400. Ferdinand Mendez Pinto, a Portuguese adven-
turer who traveled in China in the sixteenth century wrote a colorful account of his
journey.

24. *Register of Debates*, 21st Cong., 1st sess., pp. 95–119.

25. Webster differed from the majority of New Englanders on the question of
public lands. He took the position that the sooner the western lands were settled

the better and consistently advocated low prices so as to hasten this settlement. On this question he differed sharply with John Quincy Adams and his colleague in the Senate, John Davis of Massachusetts. For a full exposition of Webster's stand on this issue see Peter J. Parish, "Daniel Webster, New England, and the West," *Journal of American History*, December 1967, pp. 524—49.

26. Ibid., p. 80.

27. Richard N. Current, *Daniel Webster and the Rise of National Conservatism* (Boston: Little, Brown, 1955), p. 62.

28. *Register of Debates*, 21st Cong., 1st sess., p. 883.

29. Ibid., p. 911.

30. Ibid., 22d Cong., 1st sess., pp. 3120—70.

31. Ibid., p. 3155.

32. Ibid., p. 3309.

33. Ibid., p. 3205.

34. Edward Everett to Alexander Everett, 4 February 1832, Everett Papers.

35. Ibid.

36. Robert C. Winthrop, "Memoir of Hon. Nathan Appleton," *Massachusetts Historical Society Proceedings*, vol. 5, p. 274. Appleton made the same assertion before the House of Representatives on 21 January 1832. *Register of Debates*, 22nd Cong., 1st sess., p. 1603.

37. Edward Everett to Alexander Everett, 17 January 1832, Everett Papers.

38. Everett to Everett, 17 March 1832, ibid.

39. *Register of Debates*, 22nd Cong., 1st sess., Appendix, pp. 79—93.

40. Ibid., pp. 3665—66.

41. Ibid., p. 3738.

42. Ibid., p. 3768.

43. Ibid., p. 3519.

44. Ibid., pp. 3523—26.

45. Abbott Lawrence to Nathan Appleton, 30 December 1831, Lawrence Papers, Massachusetts Historical Society.

46. For a discussion of the final moves in Congress on the bill, see Edward Stanwood, *American Tariff Controversies in the Nineteenth Century* (New York: Russell and Russell, 1903), vol. 1, pp. 380—86.

47. Edward Everett to Alexander Everett, 1 July 1832, Everett Papers.

48. John Quincy Adams and Lewis Condict, Report of the Minority of the Committee on Manufactures (Boston: John H. Eastburn, 1833). This thirty-nine-page pamphlet, located in the Massachusetts Historical Society, is a valuable source.

49. P. C. Brooks to Everett, 1 March 1833, Everett Papers.

50. Brooks to Everett, 13 February 1833, ibid.

51. Brooks to Edward Everett, 9 February 1833, ibid.

52. Charles M. Wiltse, ed., *The Papers of Daniel Webster: Correspondence*, vol. 3 (Hanover, N.H.: University Press of New England, 1973), p. 217.

## Chapter 7

1. Ronald Story, *The Forging of an Aristocracy: Harvard and the Boston Upper Class, 1800–1870* (Middletown, Conn.: Wesleyan University Press, 1980), p. 201, n. 42.

2. Ibid. In his excellent book, Story treats the changes at Harvard in detail.

3. "Public and Private Charities in Boston," *North American Review*, July 1845, p. 153.

4. William Pease and Jane H. Pease, "Paternal Dilemmas: Education, Property, and Patrician Persistence in Jacksonian Boston," *New England Quarterly*, June 1980, p. 148.

5. Kenneth Wiggins Porter, *The Jacksons and the Lees: Two Generations of Massachusetts Merchants, 1765–1844*, 2 vols. (Cambridge: Harvard University Press, 1937), 1:89.

6. Robert Sobel, *The Entrepreneurs: Explorations within the American Business Tradition* (New York: Weybright and Talley, 1974), p. 39.

7. *Boston Daily Advertiser*, 25 September 1838.

8. Diary of Charles Francis Adams, entry for 2 March 1839, Adams Papers, Massachusetts Historical Society.

9. For a discussion of the credit offered by the Baring Brothers, see Ralph W. Hidy, *The House of Baring in American Trade and Finance: English Merchant Bankers at Work, 1763–1861* (Cambridge: Harvard University Press, 1949), pp. 261, 249. Of course the Barings dealt with states outside of New England and especially with merchants in New York.

10. *Columbian Centinel*, 15 June 1822.

11. Charles McCarthy, *The Anti-Masonic Party: A Study of Political Anti-Masonry in the United States, 1827–1840*, Annual Report of the American Historical Association, 1902, pp. 504–514.

12. Everett explained the situation in a letter to Henry Clay, 22 April 1823, Everett Papers.

13. Joseph Slater, ed., *The Correspondence of Emerson and Carlyle* (New York: Columbia University Press, 1964), p. 122.

14. Ibid., pp. 283–84.

15. Diary of Charles Francis Adams, entry for 12 April 1840, Adams Papers.

16. Ibid.

17. Quoted in *Young Emerson Speaks: Unpublished Discourses on Many Subjects*, ed. Arthur Cushman McGiffert (Boston: Houghton, Mifflin, 1938), p. 2.

18. Michael H. Cowan, *City of the West: Emerson, America, and Urban Metaphor* (New Haven: Yale University Press, 1967), p. 259.

19. Ibid., p. 40.

20. Everett to Thomas Jefferson, 16 April 1826, Everett Papers, Massachusetts Historical Society.

21. Everett to Nathan Hale, 3 March 1837, ibid.

22. Everett to William Jackson, 31 October 1837, ibid.

23. Charles M. Wiltse, ed., *The Papers of Daniel Webster: Correspondence*, vol. 3 (Hanover, N.H.: University Press of New England, 1977), p. 377.

24. For a fuller discussion of the French side of the question see Paul A. Varg, *United States Foreign Relations, 1820–1860* (East Lansing: Michigan State University Press, 1979), pp. 84–92.

25. *Register of Debates in Congress*, 23d Cong., 2d sess., p. 571.

26. Ibid., p. 1577.

27. Ibid., p. 1634.

28. Ibid., p. 1644.

29. Ibid., p. 1622.

30. Everett Diary, 19 December 1834, Everett Papers.

31. P. C. Brooks to Everett, 18 February 1835, ibid.

32. Webster to Everett, 27 January 1836, ibid.

33. Charles Francis Adams noted this in his diary and added: "His career is entirely unexampled in our history. And it is much to be desired that it should never be emulated." Adams Papers.

## Chapter 8

1. Kenneth Bourne, *Britain and the Balance of Power in North America, 1815–1908* (London: Longmans, Green, 1967), pp. 87–102.

2. Ibid., pp. 101–103.

3. *American State Papers: Foreign Relations*, 4:648.

4. Ibid., p. 925.

5. Ibid., pp. 924–25.

6. Henry S. Burrage, *Maine in the Northeastern Boundary Controversy* (Portland, Maine: Marks Printing House, 1919), p. 170.

7. *Congressional Globe*, 25th Cong., 3d sess., p. 209.

8. Ibid., Appendix, pp. 269–72, and Webster to Everett, 23 April 1842, Everett Papers, Massachusetts Historical Society.

9. *Congressional Globe*, 26th Cong., 3d sess., pp. 272–74.

10. Ibid., p. 273.

11. Ibid., p. 274.

12. Everett Diary, 6 May 1838, Everett Papers; *Daily Advertiser*, 11 January 1839.

13. Charles M. Wiltse and Harold D. Moser, eds., *The Papers of Daniel Webster*, vol. 4 (Hanover, N.H.: University Press of New England, 1980), pp. 346–49.

14. Everett Diary, 28 February 1839, Everett Papers.

15. *Daily Advertiser*, 16 January 1839.

16. Ibid., 23 February 1839.

17. Ibid., 22 February 1839.

18. Ibid., 2 August 1839.

19. Ibid., 31 March 1840.

20. *Springfield Republican*, 16 March 1839.

21. *Daily Advertiser*, 11 January 1839.

22. Wiltse and Moser, *Papers of Daniel Webster*, 4:287.

23. *Springfield Republican*, 16 March 1839.

24. Ibid.

25. *Daily Advertiser*, 8 March 1839.

26. Everett to Secretary of War Poinsett, 18 April 1839, Everett Papers.

27. Everett to Buchanan, 4 March 1839, ibid.

28. Everett to Van Buren, 22 March 1839, ibid.

29. Wiltse and Moser, *Papers of Daniel Webster*, 4:346–49.

30. Charles Sumner to Edward Everett, 18 March 1839, Everett Papers.

31. Albert Gallatin, *The Right of the United States of America to the Northeastern Boundary claimed by Them* (first published in 1840) (Freeport, N.Y.: Books for Libraries Press, 1970).

32. George Coffin to Hannibal Hamlin, 9 March 1839, Hamlin Papers, University of Maine.

33. *Daily Advertiser and Patriot*, 31 March 1840.

34. Ibid., 1 April 1840.

35. Ibid., 18 April 1840.

36. "Northeastern Boundary," *North American Review*, April 1841, pp. 424–25.

37. Webster to Everett, 29 January 1842, Everett Papers.

38. Edward L. Pierce, ed., *Memoirs and Letters of Charles Sumner*, 4 vols. (New York: Arno Press, 1969), 2:225.

39. Webster to Everett, 23 April 1842, Everett Papers.

40. Webster to Everett, 25 April 1842, ibid.

41. Webster to Everett, 18 May 1842, ibid.

42. Burrage, *Northeastern Boundary Controversy*, p. 325.

43. Francis O. Smith to Webster, 6 April 1839, Smith Papers, *Maine Historical Society*, Portland.

44. Smith to Webster, 17 June 1841, and Smith to an unnamed correspondent, 12 June 1841, ibid.

45. Ibid.

46. E. Payson, Jr., "A Review of Some of the Doings of the Legislature of Maine During the Session of 1841," Maine Historical Society. See also Frederick Merk, *Fruits of Propaganda in the Tyler Administration* (Cambridge: Harvard University Press, 1971), pp. 64–65. Merk placed emphasis on the overall situation in 1841. The Whig victory that deflated the extremism of some Maine Democrats and the business recession that led people to feel that recovery could only come when good relations were restored with England stimulated a spirit of compromise.

47. The most thorough and careful study of the maps involved is found in the highly useful book by Howard Jones, *To the Webster-Ashburton Treaty* (Chapel Hill: University of North Carolina Press, 1977). Howard Jones concluded that Webster's effective use of the Sparks and Steuben maps was the decisive factor in his success (see page 116). That Webster's use of the maps was important need not be questioned, but a word of caution is in order. As Howard Jones observed in his delightful and valuable account of the maps, no one of the many maps offered conclusive evidence as to the line agreed to by the envoys in 1783. The red-line

maps "contained only proposed boundaries" (see page 112). The success of the Webster-Ashburton negotiations rested on the larger forces operative in British-American relations and the increasing sense of isolation of both Maine and New Brunswick that encouraged a willingness, however reluctant, to accept compromise.

48. Charles Francis Adams, ed., *Memoirs of John Quincy Adams comprising portions of His Diary from 1795 to 1848*, 12 vols. (Philadelphia: J. B. Lippincott, 1874–1878), 9:196.

49. *Congressional Globe*, 37th Cong., 3d sess., Appendix, pp. 53–56.

50. C. H. Van Tyne, ed., *The Letters of Daniel Webster* (N.Y.: Haskell House Publishers, 1969), pp. 286–87.

51. Everett to Webster, 31 August 1842, Everett Papers.

52. Sumner to Everett, 6 April 1839, ibid.

## Chapter 9

1. U.S., Congress, House, Serial Set, no. 386, 26th Cong., 2d sess., House Doc. 122, General Statement of Goods, Wares, and Merchandise of the Growth, Produce, and Manufacture of Foreign Countries, Imported into the United States during the Year Ending 30th September, 1840.

2. Ibid. Of the total tonnage built in 1840, Maine accounted for 38,936 tons and Massachusetts for 17,811 tons.

3. Morison, *Maritime History of Massachusetts*, p. 65; Lagnioppe, "Memo for Mr. Forbes Respecting Canton Affairs . . .", *Business History Review*, Spring 1966, pp. 98–107.

4. Sarah Forbes Hughes, ed., *Letters and Recollections of John Murray Forbes*, (Boston: Houghton, Mifflin, 1899), p. 57.

5. U.S., Congress, House, 26th Cong., 2d sess., House Doc. 119, 26-1.

6. P. W. Snow to Caleb Cushing, 19 April 1839, Caleb Cushing Papers, Library of Congress.

7. U.S., Congress, House, P. W. Snow to secretary of state, 29 August 1839, Serial Set, no. 386, 26th Cong., 2d sess., House Doc. 119.

8. U.S., Congress, House, Commodore George C. Read to the secretary of the navy, 8 July 1839, 26th Cong., 2d sess., House Doc. 119, 26-1.

9. U.S., Congress, House, 26th Cong., 2d sess., House Doc. 40, 26-1.

10. Ibid.

11. *Boston Centinel*, 3 December 1841.

12. Edward V. Gulick, *Peter Parker and the Opening of China* (Cambridge: Harvard University Press, 1973), pp. 98–99.

13. William P. Pierce to Caleb Cushing, 11 February 1843, Cushing Papers.

14. C. W. King to Caleb Cushing, 6 April 1843, ibid.

15. Webster to Cushing, 12 March 1843, ibid.

16. Everett to Cushing, 3 September 1842, and Everett to Cushing, 10 October 1842, ibid.

17. Claude M. Fuess, *The Life of Caleb Cushing* (New York: Harcourt, Brace and Company, 1923), p. 410. Fuess indicates that he believed it to be true.

18. On February 25, 1843 Webster wrote to Everett, "If I knew you would like

our first Oriental mission, I might think possibly, of succeeding you for a year in England." Rumors leaked out in Boston that Webster was about to engage in an atrocious deal and Webster was embarrassed. He was even more dissuaded by happenings in the next few weeks. The British would only negotiate if, in return for a deal on upper California, the United States lowered tariff duties, a step that would have aroused Webster's constituents to anger. In addition President Tyler decided that he would not launch new and important negotiations with England on the Oregon question. As a result, three weeks later Webster gave up his plan to have himself replace Everett in London. He wrote to Everett that he saw no prospect of successful negotiations, and he would take no pleasure in handling mere routine duties. Webster to Everett, 13 March 1843, Everett Papers.

19. Webster to Thomas B. Curtis, 12 March 1843, Cushing Papers.

20. Cushing to Everett, 13 July 1839, published in the *Boston Daily Advertiser* and *Patriot*, ibid.

21. A. H. Bullock to Cushing, 28 October 1842, ibid.

22. Fuess, in his biography of Cushing, presents an able defense of the course pursued by Cushing in loyally defending Tyler time and again in Congress and in his public speeches.

23. Webster to Cushing, 8 May 1843, Department of State, National Archives, Washington, D.C.

24. Tyler Dennett, *Americans in Eastern Asia* (1922; reprint ed., New York: Barnes and Noble, 1941), p. 143.

25. E. C. Bridgman and S. W. Williams, eds., *Chinese Repository*, February 1844, p. 108.

26. Ibid. July 1844, p. 286.

## Chapter 10

1. Speech by Caleb Cushing in House of Representatives, 17 and 22 May 1839, Cushing Papers, Library of Congress.

2. Cushing to Secretary of State John Forsyth, January 9, 1840, ibid.

3. The Cushing papers contain many letters from prospective immigrants, including one from Nathaniel Glover, a resident of Maine who had formed a company made up of farmers and mechanics. Glover was anxious that Congress provide protection for settlers in Oregon. The members, Glover wrote, would be happy to serve as a regiment of "citizen soldiers."

4. Caleb Cushing, "Discovery beyond the Mountains," *North American Review*, January 1840, pp. 75–144.

5. William Heath Davis, *Sixty Years in California: A History of Events and Life in California; Personal, Political and Military, under the Mexican Regime; During the Quasi-Military Government of the United States, and After the Admission of the State into the Union, Being a Compilation by a Witness of the Events Described* (San Francisco: A. J. Leary, 1889), pp. 16, 125.

6. Ibid., p. 637.

7. Adele Ogden, "Boston Hide Droghes along California Shores," *California Historical Society Quarterly*, December 1929, p. 296.

8. Diary of Charles Francis Adams, entry for 3 November 1845, Adams Papers, Massachusetts Historical Society.

9. *Boston Atlas*, 19 October 1842.

10. Diary of Charles Francis Adams, entry for 7 March 1842, Adams Papers.

11. Resolutions were passed in favor of a $350,000 expenditure in both branches of the legislature. The bill passed the House but was defeated in the Senate. Governor Everett supported the bill. Diary of Edward Everett, Everett Papers, Massachusetts Historical Society.

12. Winthrop to Everett, 1 August 1841, Winthrop Papers, Massachusetts Historical Society.

13. Winthrop to J. H. Clifford, 22 January 1842, Winthrop Papers.

14. Howard Jones, *To the Webster-Ashburton Treaty* (Chapel Hill: University of North Carolina Press, 1977), p. 118.

15. Diary of Charles Francis Adams, entry for 4 May 1839, Adams Papers.

16. Diary of Charles Francis Adams, entry for 1 October 1842, ibid.

17. The author is indebted to David Donald whose definitive biography of Sumner is an invaluable source. See David Donald, *Charles Sumner and the Coming of the Civil War* (New York: Alfred A. Knopf, 1965).

18. *The Works of Charles Sumner* (Boston: Lee and Shephard, 1870), vol. 1, p. 7.

19. The most useful books on the Conscience versus Cotton Whigs are Kinley Brauer, *Cotton versus Conscience: Massachusetts Whig Politics and Southwestern Expansion, 1843–1848* (Lexington: University of Kentucky Press, 1967); Martin Duberman, *Charles Francis Adams, 1807–1886* (Boston: Houghton Mifflin, 1961); and Frank Otto Gatell, *John Gorham Palfrey and the New England Conscience* (Cambridge: Harvard University Press, 1963).

20. Hale, in writing a public letter declaring his opposition to the annexation of Texas, went over the heads of the leaders of the Democratic party in New Hampshire, and their wrath knew no bounds. Franklin Pierce, leader of the party, set out to ostracize him. Richard H. Sewell, *John P. Hale and the Politics of Abolition* (Cambridge: Harvard University Press, 1965), pp. 55–57.

21. H. Draper Hunt, *Hannibal Hamlin of Maine: Lincoln's First Vice-President* (Syracuse, N.Y.: Syracuse University Press, 1969), pp. 24–25.

22. *Congressional Globe*, 29th Cong., 1st sess., p. 187.

23. Ibid., p. 62.

24. Ibid., p. 303.

25. Ibid., p. 316.

26. Ibid., p. 189.

27. Diary of Charles Francis Adams, entry for 29 January 1845.

28. Hunt, *Hannibal Hamlin*, pp. 30–31.

29. *Congressional Globe*, 29th Cong., 1st sess., p. 249.

30. Ibid., p. 135.

31. Ibid., p. 56.

32. Ibid., p. 432.

33. *The Oregon Question*, Sturgis Papers, Massachusetts Historical Society.

34. William Sturgis to George Bancroft, 6 August 1845. Bancroft Papers, Massachusetts Historical Society.

35. *Boston Daily Advertiser*, 24 January 1846.

36. Ibid., 2 April 1846.

37. Ibid., 22 April 1846.

38. For a thoughtful analysis on the topic, see David Pletcher, *The Diplomacy of Annexation: Texas, Oregon, and the Mexican War* (Columbia: University of Missouri Press, 1973), pp. 587–92.

Chapter 11

1. *Congressional Globe*, 29th Cong., 1st sess., p. 824.

2. Robert C. Winthrop to J. H. Clifford, 15 May 1846, Winthrop Papers Massachusetts Historical Society.

3. Daniel Webster to Anthony Colby, 20 May 1846, Webster Papers, Dartmouth College Library.

4. Quoted by Jean Matthews, *Rufus Choate: The Law and Civic Virtue* (Philadelphia: Temple University Press, 1980), p. 193.

5. Robert F. Lucid, ed., *The Journal of Richard Henry Dana, Jr.,* (Cambridge: The Belknap Press of Harvard University Press, 1968), p. 161.

6. *The Works of William E. Channing, D.D. with an Introduction to which is added The Perfect Life* (Boston: American Unitarian Association, 1889). See "The Union," pp. 629–42; "Slavery," especially pp. 704–707, 725, 737; "The Abolitionists," pp. 743–50; "The Duty of the Free States," pp. 853–906, especially p. 891.

7. Church denominations, unlike individual antislavery leaders, straddled the question. There was general agreement that slavery was wrong but at the same time an unwillingness to take positive action. The *Christian Examiner*, a major Unitarian journal, published only two articles on slavery in the years 1847 and 1848, and both were written in tones intended to quiet the controversy over slavery. Not once in those two years did the *Christian Examiner* come out in opposition to the Mexican war. When a committee of antislavery advocates presented a set of resolutions condemning slavery and the war at the Unitarian Autumnal Convention held in Salem in October 1847, the resolutions were tabled by a majority vote. See *Christian Examiner*, November 1847, pp. 465–66.

Helpful studies of the clergy and slavery include Daniel Walker Howe, *The Unitarian Conscience: Harvard Moral Philosophy, 1805–1861* (Cambridge: Harvard University Press, 1970); Donald G. Mathews, *Slavery and Methodism: A Chapter in American Morality* (Princeton: Princeton University Press, 1965); Lawrence Lader, *The Bold Brahmins: New England's War Against Slavery, 1831–1863* (New York: E. P. Dutton, 1961); and Ralph A. Keller, "Methodist Newspapers and the Fugitive Slave Law: A New Perspective for the Slavery Crisis in the North," *Church History*, September 1974, pp. 319–39.

8. Hale's public letter was a frank and honest explanation of his position that the state committee sought to counteract but unsuccessfully. Hale's letter and the

response of the state committee are in the Hale Papers in the New Hampshire Historical Society.

9. The report of the meeting in the Hale papers reads: "The meeting was called by those who, like Mr. Hale, had grave doubts about the annexation of Texas. They felt that any direct or indirect advocacy of slavery was wrong and would have evil consequences for the entire civilized world." For a biography of Hale, see Richard H. Sewell, *John P. Hale and the Politics of Abolition* (Cambridge, Mass.: Harvard University Press, 1965). See also Donald B. Cole, *Jacksonian Democracy in New Hampshire, 1800–1851* (Cambridge: Harvard University Press, 1970), pp. 218–29.

10. *Boston Advertiser and Patriot*, 27 June 1846.

11. H. Draper Hunt, *Hannibal Hamlin of Maine: Lincoln's First Vice-President* (Syracuse, N.Y.: Syracuse University Press, 1969), pp. 35–37.

12. For details of the split in the Democratic party in Massachusetts, see the very fine account of Arthur B. Darling, *Political Changes in Massachusetts 1824–1848: A Study of Liberal Movements in Politics* (Cos Cob, Conn.: John E. Edwards, 1925), chap. 8, "The Period of Political Disintegration, 1844–1848."

13. Diary of Charles Francis Adams, entry for 15 July 1845, Adams Papers, Massachusetts Historical Society.

14. Quoted in *Charles Sumner and the Coming of the Civil War*, David Donald (New York: Knopf, 1960), p. 134.

15. Donald, *Charles Sumner*, p. 219.

16. Quoted in ibid., p. 143.

17. Donald, *Charles Sumner*, pp. 144–46.

18. Robert C. Winthrop to John C. Gray, 20 July 1846, Winthrop Papers.

19. William Hayden to Winthrop, 23 July 1846, ibid.

20. "Correspondence between Nathan Appleton and John G. Palfrey, intended as a supplement to Mr. Palfrey's pamphlets on the slave power" (Boston: Eastburn's Press, 1846).

21. Nathan Appleton to Charles Sumner, 20 August 1846, Appleton Papers, Massachusetts Historical Society.

22. Charles Sumner to Nathan Appleton, 22 August 1846, ibid.

23. Nathan Appleton to I. W. Danforth, 2 August 1847, ibid.

24. *Daily Advertiser*, 25 September 1846.

25. Ibid., 23 September 1846.

26. Ibid., 17 October 1846.

27. Ibid., 19 January 1847.

28. Ibid., 20 January 1847.

29. Claude M. Fuess, *The Life of Caleb Cushing* (New York: Harcourt, Brace, 1923), vol. 2, p. 38.

## Chapter 12

1. *The Boston Statesman*, 4 March 1848.

2. Ibid., 26 February 1848.

3. *Boston Daily Times*, 14 May 1846.

4. Ibid., 11 May 1846.
5. *Eastern Argus*, 22 September 1846.
6. Ibid., 19 October 1846.
7. Ibid., 7 December 1846.
8. Ibid., 24 May 1846.
9. *The Age*, 18 May 1847.
10. Ibid., 1 June 1847.
11. *Republican Herald*, 20 May 1846.
12. *Weekly Connecticut Review*, 23 May 1846.
13. *The Hartford Times*, 11 July 1846.
14. *Worcester County Gazette*, 3 June 1846.
15. Ibid., 5 August 1846.
16. *Massachusetts Spy*, 28 May 1845.
17. Ibid., quoted from *Philadelphia North American*, 5 August 1846.
18. *Massachusetts Eagle*, 22 October 1847.
19. *Bellows Falls Gazette*, 1 May 1846.
20. Ibid., 29 May 1846.
21. Ibid., 25 June 1847.
22. *Burlington Free Press*, 1 January 1847.
23. Ibid., 8 January 1847.
24. *Boston Daily Advertiser*, 3 March 1847.
25. Ibid., 18 May 1846.
26. Ibid., 27 June 1846.
27. *Congressional Globe*, 29th Cong., 1st sess., pp. 1089–1107.
28. *Congressional Globe*, 29th Cong., 1st sess., p. 1089.
29. Ibid., p. 1105.
30. Ibid., p. 1153.
31. Ibid., p. 1214.
32. Eric Foner, "The Wilmot Proviso Revisited," *Journal of American History*, September 1969, pp. 276–77. For a highly useful discussion of the divisions in the Democratic party, see Chaplain W. Morrisson, *Democratic Politics and Sectionalism: The Wilmot Proviso Controversy* (Chapel Hill: The University of North Carolina Press, 1967), pp. 7–13.
33. Frederick Merk, *Manifest Destiny and Mission: A Reinterpretation* (Cambridge: Harvard University Press, 1963), pp. 174–75.
34. *Congressional Globe*, 29th Cong., 2d sess., p. 14.
35. Ibid., p. 17.
36. Ibid., p. 48.
37. Ibid., p. 145.
38. *Congressional Globe*, 29th Cong., 2d sess., p. 548.
39. Ibid., p. 419.
40. Ibid., p. 402.
41. Ibid., p. 146.
42. Ibid., p. 531.
43. Ibid., p. 382.

44. Ibid., 30th Cong., 1st sess., p. 122.

45. Ibid., p. 545.

46. Ibid., p. 332.

47. Ibid., p. 534.

48. Ibid., p. 356.

49. Ibid., p. 94.

50. *Congressional Globe*, 30th Cong., 1st sess., pp. 331–33.

51. Ibid., 29th Cong., 1st sess., p. 134. Winthrop's major speech opposing the war, delivered on 8 January 1847, placed the emphasis on what he considered to be Polk's unconstitutional proceedings in bypassing Congress prior to the war, and on the contention that the war was provoked by Polk for the purpose of depriving Mexico of a large part of her territory. That policy, said Winthrop, "dismemberment of Mexico for debts she cannot pay," was unworthy of the United States and "the age in which we live." He condemned "the wild career of national expansion." *Congressional Globe*, ibid., pp. 145–47.

52. Roy Franklin Nichols, *The Stakes of Power, 1845–1847* (New York: Hill and Wang, 1961), p. X.

53. N. Appleton to Charles Sumner, 4 July 1848; Sumner to Appleton, 8 July 1848; Appleton to Sumner, 31 July 1848; Sumner to Appleton, 12 August 1848; Appleton to Sumner, 14 August 1848; Sumner to Appleton, 31 August 1848; Appleton to Sumner, 4 September 1848, Appleton Papers, Massachusetts Historical Society.

54. George Ashmun to Webster, 14 June 1847, Webster Papers, Dartmouth College Library.

55. Webster to Ketchum, 11 June 1848, ibid.

56. Henry Wilson to Webster, 31 May 1848, ibid.

57. E. Rockwood Hoar to Webster, 13 August 1848, ibid.

58. Holman Hamilton, *Zachary Taylor: Soldier in the White House* (Indianapolis: Bobbs-Merrill, 1951), p. 65.

## Chapter 13

1. Charles Dickens, *American Notes* (Gloucester, Mass.: Peter Smith, 1968), p. 73.

2. David Mead, *Yankee Eloquence in the Middle West: The Ohio Lyceum 1850–1870* (East Lansing: Michigan State University Press, 1951), p. 14.

3. *Boston Daily Atlas*, 20 November 1845.

4. Everett to Winthrop, 18 September 1843, Everett Papers, Massachusetts Historical Society.

5. Albert K. Weinberg, *Manifest Destiny: A Study of Nationalist Expansionism in American History* (Gloucester, Mass.: Peter Smith, 1958), p. 143.

# Bibliography

## Unpublished Private Papers

Nathan Appleton Papers. Massachusetts Historical Society, Boston.
George Bancroft Papers. Massachusetts Historical Society, Boston.
Caleb Cushing Papers. Library of Congress, Washington, D.C.
Edward Everett Papers. Massachusetts Historical Society, Boston.
John Fairfield Papers. Maine Historical Society, Portland.
John P. Hale Papers. State Library, Concord, N.H.
Hannibal Hamlin Papers. University of Maine, Orono.
Amos Lawrence Papers. Massachusetts Historical Society, Boston.
George Perkins Marsh Papers. University of Vermont, Burlington.
James Monroe Papers. Library of Congress, Washington, D.C.
Leverett Saltonstall Papers. Massachusetts Historical Society, Boston.
Theodore Sedgwick Papers. Massachusetts Historical Society, Boston.
William Sturgis Papers. Massachusetts Historical Society, Boston.
Daniel Webster Papers. Dartmouth College Library, Hanover, N.H.
Robert C. Winthrop Papers. Massachusetts Historical Society, Boston.
Note: The author examined several of these papers in full, others only insofar as
   they dealt with his subject.

## Newspapers

Connecticut
*New Haven Daily Herald*
*The Hartford Times*
*Weekly Connecticut Review*, Hartford

Maine
*Augusta The Age*
*Portland Daily Eastern Argus*

Massachusetts
*Boston Columbian Centinel*
*Boston Daily Advertiser*
*Boston Daily Chronicle*
*Boston Daily Times*

*Boston Evening Gazette*
*Pittsfield Massachusetts Eagle*
*Salem Essex Register*
*Salem Register*
*Springfield Republican*
*The Boston Atlas*
*The Boston Statesman*
*Worcester County Gazette*
*Worcester Massachusetts Spy*

New Hampshire
*New Hampshire Patriot and State Gazette*, Concord

Rhode Island
*Providence Republican Herald*
*Providence Transcript*

Vermont
*Bellows Falls Gazette*
*Burlington Free Press*

## Books and Periodicals

Adams, Henry, ed. *Documents Relating to New England Federalism.* Boston: Little, Brown, 1877.

Adams, John Quincy. *American Principles: A Review of the Works of Fisher Ames.* Boston: Everett and Munro, 1809.

————. *Memoirs of John Quincy Adams.* Edited by Charles Francis Adams. Philadelphia: J. B. Lippincott, 1874.

————. *The Diary of John Quincy Adams, 1794–1845; American political, social and intellectual life from Washington to Polk.* Edited by Allan Nevins. New York: Longmans, Green, 1928.

————. *The Writings of John Quincy Adams.* Edited by Worthington Chauncey Ford III. New York: The Macmillan Co., 1914.

Aiken, Solomon. *An Address to Federal Clergymen. Early American Imprints.* Published by the minister, 1813.

Ames, Fisher. *Works of Fisher Ames with a Selection from His Speeches.* Edited by Seth Ames. Boston: Little, Brown, 1854.

Ammon, Harry. *James Monroe: The Quest for National Identity.* New York: McGraw-Hill, 1971.

*An Address to Members of the House of Representatives. Early American Imprints.* Boston: Cutler, 1812.

Barton, Titus T. *Fast Sermon in Calvinistic Congregational Church in Fitchburg, July 23, 1812. Early American Imprints.*

Bemis, Samuel Flagg. *John Quincy Adams and the Foundations of American Foreign Policy.* New York: Alfred A. Knopf, 1950.

————. *John Quincy Adams and the Union.* New York: Alfred A. Knopf, 1956.

Bemis, Stephen. *Two Discourses Delivered at Harvard, Mass., August 20, 1813 and May 29, 1813. Early American Imprints.*

Bentley, William. *The Diary of William Bentley.* Salem, Mass.: The Essex Institute, 1907.

Bidwell, Percy Wells. *"Rural Economy in New England at the Beginning of the Nineteenth Century." Transactions of the Connecticut Academy of Arts and Sciences* 20 (1916).

Bigelow, Lewis. *An Oration Pronounced at Templeton, July 5, 1813, in Commemoration of the Thirty Seventh Anniversary of American Independence before the Washington Benevolent Societies in the northern section of the County of Worcester. Early American Imprints.*

Bourne, Kenneth. *Britain and the Balance of Power in North America, 1815–1908.* London: Longmans, Green, 1967.

Brauer, Kinley. *Cotton versus Conscience: Massachusetts Whig Politics and Southwestern Expansion, 1843–1848.* Lexington: University of Kentucky Press, 1967.

Brebner, John Bartlett. *North Atlantic Triangle: The Interplay of Canada, the United States and Great Britain.* New Haven: Yale University Press, 1945.

Bridenbaugh, Carl. "The New England Town: A Way of Life." *Proceedings of the American Antiquarian Society*, April 1946, pp. 19–48.

Brown, Ralph Adams. *The Presidency of John Adams.* Lawrence: University Press of Kansas, 1975.

Burrage, Henry S. *Maine in the Northeastern Boundary Controversy.* Portland, Me.: Marks Printing House, 1919.

Cary, The Reverend Samuel. *Fast Day Sermon in Kings Chapel, September 9, 1813. Early American Imprints.*

Cary, Thomas G. *Memoir of Thomas Handsyd Perkins: Containing Extracts from His Diaries and Letters.* Boston: Little, Brown, 1856.

Clarfield, Gerard H. *Timothy Pickering and the American Republic.* Pittsburgh: University of Pittsburgh Press, 1980.

Clark, Victor S. *History of Manufactures in the United States.* New York: McGraw-Hill, 1929.

*Clergyman's Almanac. Early American Imprints.* Boston: Lincoln and Edwards, 1814.

Cole, Donald B. *Jacksonian Democracy in New Hampshire, 1800–1851.* Cambridge: Harvard University Press, 1970.

Coleman, Peter J. *The Transformation of Rhode Island, 1790–1860.* Providence: Brown University Press, 1963.

Combs, Jerald A. *The Jay Treaty: Political Battleground of the Founding Fathers.* Berkeley: University of California Press, 1970.

Cowan, Michael H. *City of the West: Emerson, America, and Urban Metaphor*. New Haven: Yale University Press, 1967.

Crockett, William Hill. *Vermont: The Green Mountain State*. New York: Century History, 1921.

Current, Richard N. *Daniel Webster and the Rise of National Conservatism*. Boston: Little, Brown, 1955.

Dana, Richard. *An Oration Delivered before the Washington Benevolent Society at Cambridge, July 4, 1814. Early American Imprints*.

Darling, Arthur B. *Political Changes in Massachusetts, 1824–1848: A Study of Liberal Movements in Politics*. Cos Cob, Conn.: John E. Edwards, 1968.

Davis, William Heath. *Sixty Years in California: A History of Events and Life in California; Personal, Political and Military, under the Mexican Regime; During the Quasi-Military Government of the United States, and After the Admission of the State into the Union, Being a Compilation by a Witness of the Events Described.*. San Francisco: A. J. Leary, 1889.

De Conde, Alexander. *Entangling Alliances: Politics and Diplomacy under George Washington*. Durham, N.C.: Duke University Press, 1958.

Dennett, Tyler. *Americans in Eastern Asia*. 1922; reprint ed. New York: Barnes and Noble, 1941.

Donald, David. *Charles Sumner and the Coming of the Civil War*. New York: Alfred A. Knopf, 1965.

Duberman, Martin. *Charles Francis Adams, 1807–1886*. Boston: Houghton Mifflin, 1961.

Dunham, Josiah. *An Oration Delivered at Hanover in the Vicinity of Dartmouth College before the several Washington Benevolent Societies of Hanover, Lebanon, Lime, Norwich, and Hartford on the Twenty Eighth Anniversary of American Independence, and the Commemoration of the Great Events in Europe, which Have Terminated So to the Allied Arms, and So Triumphantly Glorious to the Cause of Humanity. Early American Imprints*. Hanover, 1814.

Dwight, Timothy. *Travels in New England and New York*. Edited by Barbara Miller Solomon. Cambridge: Harvard University Press, 1969.

Emerson, Ralph Waldo. *The Correspondence of Emerson and Carlyle*. Edited by Joseph Slater. New York: Columbia University Press, 1964.

Emmons, Nathaniel. *Sermons on Various Important Subjects of Christian Doctrine and Practice*. Boston: Samuel T. Armstrong, 1812.

Fischer, David Hackett. "The Myth of the Essex Junto." *William and Mary Quarterly*, April 1964, pp. 191–235.

———. *The Revolution of American Conservatism: The Federalist Party in the Era of Jeffersonian Democracy*. New York: Harper & Row, 1965.

Foner, Eric. "The Wilmot Proviso Revisited." *Journal of American History*, September 1969, pp. 262–79.

Foner, Philip S., ed. *The Democratic-Republican Societies, 1790–1800: A Documentary Sourcebook of Constitutions, Addresses, Resolutions, and Tracts*. Westport, Conn.: Greenwood Press, 1976.

Forbes, John Murray. *Letters and Recollections of John Murray Forbes*. Edited by Sarah Forbes Hughes. Boston: Houghton, Mifflin, 1899.

Ford, Worthington Chauncey III. "The Genesis of the Monroe Doctrine." *Massachusetts Historical Society Proceedings*, June 1902, pp. 373–436.

Forman, Samuel E. *The Political Activities of Philip Freneau: Johns Hopkins University Studies in Historical and Political Science*. Baltimore: Johns Hopkins Press, 1902.

Fuess, Claude M. *The Life of Caleb Cushing*. New York: Harcourt, Brace, 1923.

Gallatin, Albert. *The Writings of Gallatin*. Edited by Henry Adams. Philadelphia: J. B. Lippincott, 1879.

————. *The Right of the United States of America to the Northeastern Boundary claimed by Them*. 1840; reprint ed. Freeport, N.Y.: Books for Libraries Press, 1970.

Gatell, Frank Otto. *John Gorham Palfrey and the New England Conscience*. Cambridge: Harvard University Press, 1963.

Gawalt, Gerard W. *The Promise of Power: The Emergence of the Legal Profession in Massachusetts, 1760–1840*. Westport, Conn.: Greenwood Press, 1979.

Gray, Edward. *William Gray of Salem, Merchant*. Boston: Houghton Mifflin, 1914.

Gribbin, William. *The Churches Militant: The War of 1812 and American Religion*. New Haven: Yale University Press, 1973.

Gulick, Edward V. *Peter Parker and the Opening of China*. Cambridge: Harvard University Press, 1973.

Guren, Pamela. "Lost Lynn: The Shoe Industry and Its Architecture, 1750–1810." *Essex Institute Historical Collection*, October 1979.

Hamilton, Alexander. *The Papers of Alexander Hamilton*. Edited by Harold Syrett. New York: Columbia University Press, 1972.

Hamilton, Holman. *Zachary Taylor: Soldier in the White House*. Indianapolis: Bobbs-Merrill, 1951.

Hatch, Nathan O. *The Sacred Cause of Liberty: Republican Thought and the Millennium in Revolutionary New England*. New Haven: Yale University Press, 1977.

Haynes, George Henry, ed. "Letters of Samuel Taggart, Representative in Congress, 1803–1814." *Proceedings of the American Antiquarian Society* 33: 113–226.

Hecht, Marie B. *John Quincy Adams: A Personal History of an Independent Man*. New York: Macmillan, 1972.

Hidy, Ralph. *The House of Baring in American Trade and Finance: English Merchant Bankers at Work, 1763–1861*. Cambridge: Harvard University Press, 1949.

Higginson, Stephen. *Letters of Stephen Higginson*. Edited by J. Franklin Jameson. Annual Report of the American Historical Association, 1896.

Howe, Daniel Walker. *The Unitarian Conscience: Harvard Moral Philosophy, 1805–1861*. Cambridge: Harvard University Press, 1970.

Hunt, H. Draper. *Hannibal Hamlin of Maine: Lincoln's First Vice-President.* Syracuse, N.Y.: Syracuse University Press, 1969.

Jefferson, Thomas. *Letters of Thomas Jefferson.* Edited by Frank Irwin. Tilton, N.H.: Sanbornton Bridge Press, 1975.

————. *Writings of Jefferson.* Edited by Paul Leicester Ford. New York: G. P. Putnam's Sons, 1895.

Jones, Howard. *To the Webster-Ashburton Treaty.* Chapel Hill: University of North Carolina Press, 1977.

Keller, Ralph A. "Methodist Newspapers and the Fugitive Slave Law: A New Perspective for the Slavery Crisis in the North." *Church History*, September 1974.

Lader, Lawrence. *The Bold Brahmins: New England's War Against Slavery: 1831–1863.* New York: E. P. Dutton, 1961.

Lee, Henry. "The Magee Family and the Origins of the China Trade." *Massachusetts Historical Society Proceedings* 7 (1969): 104–119.

Lodge, Henry Cabot. *Life and Letters of George Cabot.* Boston: Little, Brown, 1877.

Luebke, Fred C. "The Origins of Thomas Jefferson's Anti-Clericalism." *Church History*, September 1963, pp. 344–56.

Lyon, E. Wilson. "The Directory and the United States." *American Historical Review*, April 1938, pp. 514–32.

McCarthy, Charles. *The Anti-Masonic Party: A Study of Political Anti-Masonry in the United States, 1827–1840.* Annual Report of the American Historical Association, 1902.

McGiffert, Arthur Cushman, ed. *Young Emerson Speaks: Unpublished Discourses on Many Subjects.* Boston: Houghton, Mifflin, 1938.

Malone, Dumas. *Jefferson and His Time: Jefferson the President*, vol. 4. Boston: Little, Brown, 1970.

Mathews, Donald G. *Slavery and Methodism: A Chapter in American Morality.* Princeton: Princeton University Press, 1965.

Matthews, Jean. *Rufus Choate: The Law and Civic Virtue.* Philadelphia: Temple University Press, 1980.

Mead, C. David. *Yankee Eloquence in the Middle West: The Ohio Lyceum, 1850–1870.* East Lansing: Michigan State University Press, 1951.

Merk, Frederick C. *Manifest Destiny and Mission: A Reinterpretation.* Cambridge: Harvard University Press, 1967.

————. *Fruits of Propaganda in the Tyler Administration.* Cambridge: Harvard University Press, 1971.

*Miscellaneous Remarks on the Police of Boston.* Early American Imprints. Boston, 1814.

Morison, Samuel Eliot. *Maritime History of Massachusetts: 1783–1860.* Boston: Houghton Mifflin, 1921.

Morrison, Chaplain W. *Democratic Politics and Sectionalism: The Wilmot Proviso Controversy.* Chapel Hill: University of North Carolina Press, 1967.

Morse, Jarvis Means. *A Neglected Period of Connecticut's History.* New Haven: Yale University Press, 1933.

Morse, The Reverend Jedidiah. *The Charlestown Association for the Reformation of Morals: A Tract Containing A Discourse Delivered at the Organization of the Association.* Early American Imprints. Boston, 1814.

Nichols, Roy Franklin. *The Stakes of Power, 1845–1847.* New York: Hill and Wang, 1961.

"Northeastern Boundary." *North American Review*, April 1841, pp. 425–52.

*Odes Composed for the 174th Anniversary of the Ancient and Honorable Artillery.* Early American Imprints. Boston: Cutler, 1812.

Ogden, Adele. "Boston Hide Droghes along California Shores." *California Historical Society Quarterly*, December 1929, pp. 289–305.

Osgood, David. *A Solemn Protest Against the Late Declaration of War Delivered on Sunday after the Declaration of War by the Pastor of the Church in Medford.* Early American Imprints. Boston: Hilliard and Metcalf, 1812.

Patterson, M. W. *Sir Francis Burdett and His Times: 1770–1844.* London: Macmillan, 1931.

Pease, William, and Pease, Jane H. "Paternal Dilemmas: Education, Property, and Patrician Persistence in Jacksonian Boston." *New England Quarterly*, June 1980, pp. 147–67.

Perkins, Bradford. *The First Rapprochement: England and the United States 1795–1805.* Berkeley: University of California Press, 1961.

Perkins, Dexter. *The Monroe Doctrine, 1823–1826.* Cambridge: Harvard University Press, 1927.

Pierce, John. "Memoir of President Kirkland." *Massachusetts Historical Society Proceedings*, June 1894, pp. 143–55.

Pitkin, Timothy. *Statistical View of the Commerce of the United States.* New York: August M. Kelley, 1967.

Pletcher, David. *The Diplomacy of Annexation: Texas, Oregon, and the Mexican War.* Columbia: University of Missouri Press, 1973.

Plumer, William. *Address to the Clergy of New England on Their Opposition to the Rulers of the United States.* Early American Imprints. Concord, 1814.

Porter, Kenneth Wiggins. *The Jacksons and the Lees: Two Generations of Massachusetts Merchants.* Cambridge: Harvard University Press, 1937.

Purcell, Richard. *Connecticut in Transition: 1775–1818.* Middletown, Conn.: Wesleyan University Press, 1925.

Robbins, Chandler. "Memoir of Daniel Appleton White." *Massachusetts Historical Society Proceedings*, 1862–1863, pp. 430–69.

Robinson, William Alexander. *The Washington Benevolent Society in New England: A Phase of Politics during the War of 1812. Massachusetts Historical Society Proceedings*, February 1916, pp. 274–86.

Russell, Howard S. *A Long, Deep Furrow: Three Centuries of Farming in New England.* Hanover, N.H.: University Press of New England, 1976.

Schutz, John R., and Adair, Douglas, eds. *The Spur of Fame: Dialogues of John Adams and Benjamin Rush, 1805–1813.* San Marino, Calif.: Huntington Library, 1966.

Seaburg, Carl, and Peterson, Stanley. *Merchant Prince of Boston: Colonel T. H. Perkins, 1764–1854.* Cambridge: Harvard University Press, 1971.

Seager, Robert. *And Tyler too: A Biography of John and Julia Gardiner Tyler.* New York: McGraw Hill, 1963.

Sewell, Richard H. *John P. Hale and the Politics of Abolition.* Cambridge: Harvard University Press, 1965.

Snell, Thomas. *Sermon Preached in North Brookfield July 23, 1812, A Day of Prayer, Recommended by His Excellency the Governor. Early American Imprints.*

Sobel, Robert. *The Entrepreneurs: Explorations within the American Business Tradition.* New York: Weybright and Talley, 1974.

Spivak, Burton. *Jefferson's English Crisis: Commerce, Embargo, and the Republican Revolution.* Charlottesville: University of Virginia Press, 1979.

Stanwood, Edward. *American Tariff Controversies in the Nineteenth Century.* New York: Russell and Russell, 1903.

Story, Ronald. *The Forging of an Aristocracy: Harvard the Boston Upper Class, 1800–1870.* Middletown, Conn.: Wesleyan University Press, 1980.

Sullivan, William. *An Oration Delivered Before the Washington Benevolent Society of Massachusetts April 30, 1812. Early American Imprints.*

Sumner, Charles. *Charles Sumner, Memoirs and Letters of.* Edited by Edward L. Pierce. New York: Arno Press, 1969.

Varg, Paul A. *United States Foreign Relations 1820–1860.* East Lansing: Michigan State University Press, 1979.

Webster, Daniel. *The Letters of Daniel Webster.* Edited by C. H. Van Tyne. New York: Haskell House, 1969.

———. *The Papers of Daniel Webster: Correspondence.* Edited by Charles M. Wiltse. Hanover: University Press of New England, 1977.

"The Principles of the Holy Alliance; Or Notes and Manifestoes of the Allied Powers." *North American Review,* October 1823, pp. 340–75.

Weinberg, Albert K. *Manifest Destiny: A Study of Nationalist Expansion in American History.* Gloucester, Mass.: Peter Smith, 1958.

Wingate, Charles E. L. *Life and Letters of Paine Wingate.* Medford, Mass.: published by author, 1930.

Winthrop, Robert C. "Memoir of Hon. Nathan Appleton." *Massachusetts Historical Society Proceedings,* October 1861, pp. 249–307.

Wolford, Throp Lanier. "Democratic-Republican Reaction in Massachusetts to the Embargo of 1807." *New England Quarterly,* March 1842, pp. 35–61.

# Index